Earth, Wind, and Fire

A "Connections" Book

Earth, Wind, and Fire

Biblical and Theological Perspectives on Creation

Barbara E. Bowe, R.S.C.J.
Joan E. Cook, S.C.
Carol J. Dempsey, O.P.
Mary Ann Donovan, S.C.
Mary Catherine Hilkert, O.P.
Alice L. Laffey
Sheila McGinn
Kathleen M. O'Connor
Mary Margaret Pazdan, O.P.
Barbara E. Reid, O.P.
Judith Schubert, R.S.M.
Tatha Wiley

Carol J. Dempsey, O.P., and Mary Margaret Pazdan, O.P.
Editors

A Michael Glazier Book

LITURGICAL PRESS
Collegeville, Minnesota

www.litpress.org

A Michael Glazier Book published by the Liturgical Press

Cover design by Ann Blattner. Watercolor by Ethel Boyle

1	2	3	4	5	6	7	8

Library of Congress Cataloging-in-Publication Data

Earth, wind, and fire : biblical and theological perspectives on
   creation / Barbara E. Bowe . . . [et al.] ; Carol J. Dempsey and Mary
   Margaret Pazdan, editors.
      p. cm.
   "A Michael Glazier book."
   "A 'connections' book."
   Includes bibliographical references and indexes.
   ISBN 0-8146-5110-0 (alk. paper)
   1. Creation. I. Bowe, Barbara Ellen. II. Dempsey, Carol J.
III. Pazdan, Mary Margaret, 1942– .

BS651.E28 2004
231.7'65—dc22
                                                           2003026976

Contents

Prologue

Carol J. Dempsey, O.P., and Mary Margaret Pazdan, O.P.

*P*ondering the mysteries of the universe, too great to be known fully and too awesome to be comprehended in a gaze, philosophers, mystics, poets, and scientists have tried throughout the centuries to give expression to their experience of the holy, the sacred. For many of them, as for the Hebrew psalmist of old, the heavens did tell of the glory of God, and the firmament did proclaim God's handiwork. Creation did manifest God's presence. It did capture the brilliance of the divine imagination. It did speak of God's heartfelt compassion as described in Psalm 104:1-30, and it was full of the wisdom of God as the wisdom writer teaches in Proverbs 8:22-31.

The philosopher Socrates reminds us that "wisdom begins in wonder."[1] Hildegard of Bingen, like many other great mystics, was able to hold God and creation in a single thought that spilled over into profound reflection. For Hildegard,

> The earth is at the same time
> mother,
> she is mother of all that is natural,
>   mother of all that is human,
> She is the mother of all,
> for contained in her
> are the seeds of all.
>
> The earth of humankind
> contains all moistness,
>   all verdancy
>   all germinating power.

It is in so many ways
fruitful.
All creation comes from it.
Yet it forms not only the basic
raw material for humankind,
but also the substance
of the incarnation
of God's son.[2]

Akin to the spirit of Hildegard, the transcendentalist American poet Ralph Waldo Emerson takes her thought a step further:

When a faithful thinker, resolute to detach every object from personal relations and see it in the light of thought, shall, at the same time, kindle science with the fire of the holiest affections, then will God go forth anew into the creation.[3]

Capturing the wonder about which Socrates spoke, the integrated vision Hildegard possessed, and the poetic insight Emerson put forth, mathematical cosmologist Brian Swimme reflects on the place and role of the human person in the context of the magnificence of the universe. His thought comes as both an affirmation and a challenge:

Our ancestry stretches back through the life-forms and into the stars, back to the beginnings of the primeval fireball. This universe is a single, multiform, energetic unfolding of matter, mind, intelligence and life. All of this is new. None of the great figures of human history were aware of this. Not Plato, not Aristotle, or the Hebrew prophets, or Confucius, or Leibniz, or Newton, or any other world-maker. We are the first generation to live with an empirical view of the origin of the universe. We are the first humans to look into the night sky and see the birth of stars, the birth of galaxies, the birth of the cosmos as a whole. Our future as a species will be forged within this new story of the world.[4]

This volume on creation, written by twelve women biblical scholars and theologians, began as a conversation in the Feminist Hermeneutics Task Force of the Catholic Biblical Association of America. Joining their voices to the philosophers, mystics, poets, and scientists who have gone before them, these women have contemplated with wonder the mysteries of the universe, and have put together a work that celebrates a new vision, one that speaks of the intrinsic goodness of all creation and the presence of God in its midst.

Part of the "Connections Series" begun by Academic Editor Linda Maloney of Liturgical Press, this volume is interdisciplinary in thought and represents an ongoing dialogue between biblical scholars and theologians on a common theme: creation. The book includes twelve chapters, a Prologue and Epilogue, and is representative of multiple interpretative models and foci.

The first chapter, "Creation, Evolution, Revelation, and Redemption: Connections and Intersections," by Carol J. Dempsey, sets the stage for the articles that follow. Given the breakthrough in contemporary science and its research into the mysteries of the universe, Carol points out that one can no longer read the biblical creation story of Genesis 1–2 without acknowledging the interrelatedness of creation and the relational view of God toward and within all creation. She draws on the thought of theologian Denis Edwards, among others, who makes the claim that "the relational view of God is a point of contact with biological science, which understands reality as an independent, relational process."[5] In this chapter Carol offers a rereading of Genesis 1–2 in light of a biological worldview. She suggests that from the biblical account a new theology of creation can be construed, one that celebrates the biblical vision of creation and the scientific theory of evolution as interrelated and not mutually exclusive. Creation, then, becomes the locus for revisioning revelation and redemption from a biblical, theological, and ecological perspective.

Although she was trained in historical criticism, Alice L. Laffey has moved toward a reading of biblical texts in a broader liberation perspective, one that she finds not only egalitarian but also affirming of minorities, those less powerful and, essentially, all creation. Alice acknowledges, however, the major contribution historical critical method has made to the uncovering of patriarchy and hierarchy embedded within the ancient Israelite culture. Thus, for her study entitled "The Priestly Creation Narrative: Goodness and Interdependence," in Chapter 2, she returns to the use of historical critical method in order to try to grapple with the content of Genesis 1–3, and more specifically to discover not only the function of these texts but also why the priestly writer produced a "P-version" of the creation story, and why that writer revised Genesis 2–3. She offers an alternative to the patriarchal and hierarchical interpretation of creation through a focus on the social location of the post-exilic community. Here she discovers a cosmological and independent theology of creation that reverberates today. The questions Alice poses to the Genesis 1–3 text bear much fruit and yield profound theological implications.

With attentiveness to the theme of creation in Genesis 1 and 2 and that of redemption in Exodus and Numbers, Joan E. Cook in Chapter 3, "Everyone Called by My Name: Second Isaiah's Use of the Creation Theme," analyzes five specific passages from Second Isaiah that feature the prophet's juxtaposition of creation and redemption. In particular, she exhorts readers to be attentive to how the message of Second Isaiah can assist in overcoming alienation of any type today.

In Chapter 4, "Wild, Raging Creativity: Job in the Whirlwind," Kathleen M. O'Connor observes that within the book of Job the theme of creation comes to the fore through the text's divine speeches. O'Connor points out that although these speeches are wondrously poetic, they do not prove helpful when viewed through the lens of a feminist/ liberationist hermeneutic. The speeches do not include women, and an inherent sense of violence prevails in their description of the deity. Despite such drawbacks in the text, Kathleen is able to reinterpret the divine speeches of Job as biblical creation accounts by utilizing both Elaine Scarry's theory of aesthetics and her own feminist-liberationist hermeneutic. Her focus on beauty in the content of the speeches makes a new and challenging contribution: it beckons readers to embrace life unabashedly, with a spirit of exuberance, purpose, and strength, and to resist at all cost anything that destroys humankind's beauty and creativity. Kathleen's revisioning of the divine speeches in Job makes clear that justice is to be done on behalf of all creation.

Choosing a scientific and post-modern consciousness of creation in her analysis of several New Testament texts, especially the Johannine writings, Barbara E. Bowe in Chapter 5, "Soundings in the New Testament Understandings of Creation," calls for such a new understanding, one that will be based on love as depicted in the thought of Teilhard de Chardin. Barbara stresses that a new understanding of creation would set the stage for a renewed definition of the relationship between creation and redemption, another point she identifies that needs further development within the biblical and theological traditions. She presents a vision of creation as a reordering of relationships that finds God as its final destiny. Barbara's comments resonate with several points that Carol Dempsey makes in her study, and vice versa.

Barbara E. Reid in Chapter 6, "Sabbath, the Crown of Creation," names overwork, exhaustion, and addictions as anti-creational factors in many cultures today.[6] She proposes a renewed sense of Sabbath through dialogue with the Genesis account of creation, instructions for keeping the Sabbath, and stories of Jesus' healings on the Sabbath. Her contribution offers a vision of harmonious relationships, a liberated sense of time, ability to make wise decisions, and eschatological hope.

With breadth and depth of thought on God's reign, Tatha Wiley in Chapter 7, "Creation Restored: God's *Basileia,* the Social Economy, and the Human Good," identifies "a new creation" as the *basileia,* the reign of God. She locates its characteristics in Jesus' teaching and healing, e.g., social and economic inclusion and freedom from domination and exploitation. She develops a contemporary theology of the human good with economic theory that fosters the values embedded in the symbol of God's *basileia.* Tatha asserts that Jesus announced the good news of a restored creation through his parables, metaphors, and personal encounters and relationships, all of which were characterized by the values of inclusion, equality, and compassion for all life.

Developing the theme of a new creation introduced by Tatha Wiley, Judith Schubert in Chapter 8, "The Samaritan Woman and Martha as Partners with Jesus in Ministry: Re-creation in John 4 and 11," offers a new portrayal of the woman of Samaria (John 4) and Martha of Bethany (John 11). She heralds these women as leaders equal to their male counterparts and holds them up as hopeful models for twenty-first-century women who struggle in the face of little or no ecclesial support. The article celebrates the creativity of women and the receptivity of Jesus to them despite social constraints and obstacles that existed within the early Johannine community. These women who accompanied Jesus effect new life and possibility for others. Though different in focus and emphasis from the other chapters in this book, Judith's article develops the theme of male-female partnership, a theme first heard in the Genesis creation story (Gen 2:18-19, 23; cf. 1:27). The study points out how such a partnership, in the context of gender, community, and Church, can be collaborative, with a potential for mutual support and trust. Judith's contribution invites further consideration and discussion of what it means to be "in right relationship."

Chapter 9, "All Creation Groans in Labor: Paul's Theology of Creation in Romans 8:18-23," by Sheila E. McGinn, offers a detailed analysis of Romans 8:18-23 that shows how Paul has intricately intertwined creation with eschatology. McGinn's analysis yields several conclusions about Pauline theology. For Paul the universe is a creature of God, and as a creature it has both a purpose and a goal. Paul sees creation as a dynamic process, one that continues to unfold with an ever greater striving toward fulfillment. Creation and humanity are intimately connected to one another, though each is distinct in its own way.

For McGinn, Romans 8:18-23 is a challenge to feminist theologians be-cause the passage invites them not only to reconsider the role of escha-tology but also to construct a new and liberating one that unites humanity and all creation as both eagerly await redemption.

Historical theologian Mary Ann Donovan in Chapter 10, "Of New Songs and an Open Window," engages the thought of Joan E. Cook and Sheila E. McGinn as presented in these two biblical scholars' respective chapters. Mary Ann interprets Second Isaiah and Romans 8:18-23, using particular facets of the theology of Irenaeus that weave creation, recapitu-lation, and Eucharist together. In her treatment of the Eucharist, Mary Ann opens a window into time by indicating a convergence between the sacramental principle and liberating eschatology.

In Chapter 11, "Being a New Creation (2 Corinthians 5:17) Is Being the Body of Christ: Paul and Feminist Scholars in Dialogue," Mary Margaret Pazdan develops a new metaphor: being a new creation is being the body of Christ. She explores the Corinthian correspondence in order to describe what the experiences of being the Body of Christ are for the community, especially for its women, and how contemporary feminist theological anthropology enters into the discussion. Mary Margaret sees the body of Christ as the link that connects us all to a common es-chatological future wherein humankind and the cosmos will not only be glorified but also brought to an unfathomable fullness of creation.

Chapter 12, "Creation in the Image of God and Wisdom Christol-ogy," is the final chapter of this collaborative work. Written by system-atic theologian Mary Catherine Hilkert, this chapter reviews the tradition about *imago Dei*, a metaphor for the human person as created in the image of God. Working with the thought of feminist and ecological theologians, Mary Catherine reinterprets the symbol to promote human well-being, including a balance of personal rights and limitations, eco-logical responsibility, and the interrelatedness of all creation. Drawing on the richness of the biblical wisdom tradition of both the Old and New Testaments, Mary Catherine invites the human community to embrace the identity of God's beloved, to grow in communion with God and all creation, and to discover that both human and ecological communities have the capacity to image God. Focusing on the centrality of Christ, she, like Mary Margaret Pazdan, envisions a future bright with hope and promise for all God's creation if only we would all allow our hearts to be transformed so that we could come to recognize our solidarity with crea-tion and thus practice the hospitality *Sophia* extends to all God's beloved creatures.

The volume concludes with a brief Epilogue that not only summarizes the book's main points but also describes several paradigm shifts, all of which have contributed to the richness of this study.

Finally, we the editors and authors of this volume are deeply indebted to Linda Maloney of Liturgical Press for her vision, efforts, patience, words of encouragement, expertise, and wisdom. With Linda's support, this volume has come to fruition. It is our hope that those who read this text will discover the wonder of creation and the collective, transformative vision the volume has to offer to a fragile world so much in need of justice, compassion, healing, and restoration. Would that we hasten the reign of God.

Carol J. Dempsey, O.P.
Mary Margaret Pazdan, O.P.
April 29, 2004
The Feast of Catherine of Siena

NOTES: PROLOGUE

[1] See Michael Reagan, ed., *Inside the Mind of God: Images and Words of Inner Space* (Philadelphia and London: Templeton Foundation Press, 2002) 45 for this quotation from Socrates.

[2] See Elizabeth Roberts and Elias Amidon, eds., *Earth Prayers* (San Francisco: HarperSanFrancisco, 1991) 46, who include in their anthology this quotation from Hildegard of Bingen.

[3] See Michael Reagan, ed., *The Hand of God: Thoughts and Images Reflecting the Spirit of the Universe* (Philadelphia and London: Templeton Foundation Press, 1999) 35 for this quotation selected from Ralph Waldo Emerson's work, "Nature."

[4] Ibid. 156 for this selection from Brian Swimme's work *The Universe Is a Green Dragon: A Cosmic Creation Story* (Rochester, Vt.: Inner Traditions International, 1987).

[5] Denis Edwards, ed., *Earth Revealing, Earth Healing: Ecology and Christian Theology* (Collegeville: The Liturgical Press, 2001) 24.

[6] When we start with contemporary experience and look to the biblical texts for illumination, we engage in a process, i.e., *actualization.* Here the conviction is that the possibilities of a biblical text cannot be exhausted by one culture or one period of history. Actualization occurs when a text is considered in light of a contemporary situation. A community participates in actualization when the group hears the word of God within a concrete situation, identifies aspects of the present situation that it highlights or questions, and realizes insights for the

present situation. See Pontifical Biblical Commission, "Interpretation of the Bible in the Church," IV.A.2. *Origins* 6 (January 1994) 499–524. For identification of principles, methods, and limitations of actualization see Roland E. Murphy, "Reflections on 'Actualization' of the Bible," *BTB* 26 (1966) 79–81.

Foreword

Elizabeth A. Johnson, C.S.J.

*T*he cosmos is an ancient and honorable subject of theology. For centuries the beauty and power of natural phenomena inspired reflection about the Creator of it all. So intrinsic was the cosmos to religious reflection that Augustine could point out that theology was akin to a three-legged stool, being structured by God, humanity, and the natural world. Starting with church fights at the time of the Reformation, however, Christian theology took an intensely anthropocentric turn, focusing mainly on questions of human salvation. How can I find a gracious God? Are we saved by faith alone or do good works have a role? As a result, creation took a back seat in the theology of the church in the West.

In our day, thanks to amazing new scientific discoveries on the one hand and the growing global ecological crisis on the other, the natural world is emerging once again into the center of theological reflection. It is a sign of the times that we feel wonder at news of billions of years of cosmic time, the formation of stars and galaxies, and most marvelously, the evolution of life on Earth even up to *homo sapiens* ourselves. Simultaneously we feel a new kind of anguish at news of the despoiling of our life-supporting systems of water, soil, and air, and the extinction of our fellow species in the community of life. Since this waste is the work of human hands it raises the suspicion that *homo sapiens* may be a most egregious misnomer. Both the wonder and the wasting combine to give the theological value of the natural world a uniquely new urgency.

That this is an issue like no other was brought home to me by a remark a pastor made after a lecture I gave on ecology as a new concern for the Church in the twenty-first century. Next Sunday, he said, we have to take up a collection for the diocesan seminary, and the Sunday after that for the diocesan television station. We'll probably have to start taking up a collection to care for the Earth, too, he continued, thus ranking the natural world as one more issue a busy pastor has to attend to. The vigor of my response startled everyone. This is not one more thing to add to the list of things to care about, I said. If we do not take the Earth more seriously and act in love to protect it, there won't *be* a seminary or television station to support. For human life is profoundly interwoven with the life forces of the natural world. Kill off the latter and you have profoundly compromised the future of the human race. And unlike a seminary or a television station, the cosmos has been valued since early Christian theology as a book of revelation in companionship with the book of Scripture. It is a primordial sacrament of the presence of God.

A number of scientists and ecologists have wondered out loud why people in the churches are not more interested in this matter. Believing as they do that God created the whole developing universe and continues to love it, they should logically be on the front lines of care for Creation. But most are asleep, like the disciples in the Garden of Gethsemane, not making the connection between their own actions and a critical future that is rapidly approaching. Using a homely metaphor, theologian Sallie McFague has urged her fellow scholars in religion to attend to this matter. With their own expertise scholars should piece together a unique square that can be joined to those made by experts in science and economics, government leaders, ordinary citizens, activists of all kinds, even children, to create together a great quilt of planetary care.

Sewing its square with great skill, this timely book, *Earth, Wind, and Fire,* makes a vital contribution to Christian thought about the sacred value of the natural world. It is heartening to see younger and older scholars working together here, and biblical scholars collaborating with historical and systematic theologians. Their expert essays, written accessibly with style and grace, send out a call like the summons heard by Elijah under the broom tree: Wake up! A long journey lies ahead of you.

Delving deeply into the Bible and into relevant Christian doctrines such as creation, redemption, and the image of God, the book offers original insight into key themes that already characterize the budding field of ecological theology. In the literature at large there are two broad lines of discussion. One is foundational, probing how the evolving universe opens up new ideas about the nature of God and, in turn, how the natural world, like a sacrament, makes known the presence of the creating God. The other is ethical, inquiring after right relations and right action between human beings and the earth. In the latter case ecological health has a strong connection with social justice, including economic policies. Like a chorus, the essays sound various notes on these themes, harmonizing in their belief that as God's beloved creation the world has its own intrinsic value and not just instrumental value for human benefit. Taking on critics, testing theses, drawing out the richness in biblical texts, posing and answering new questions, the book makes a genuine contribution to scholarship.

What gives this book a special flavor is that all the authors have also made the connection between the status of women and the plight of the natural world. The dualism that marked traditional philosophy and theology relegated both women and nature to subordinate positions, both being marked by bodiliness that gives life and neither ranking as high as the thinking male in the great chain of being. The ecological view still emerging sees kinship rather than hierarchy as most basic in the community of life and consequently places human beings in interdependence with rather than domination over the natural world. This has far-reaching implications for mutual, liberating relationships within the human community itself in terms of races and classes, and most profoundly for women's equal human dignity with men.

A venerable Hasidic story tells of a rabbi who asked his students how they could tell when night had ended and day begun. One answered, "When I can see the peach tree clearly." No. Another figured, "When I can see three figures walking on the hilltop." Again, no. Night is over, taught the rabbi, when you look into the face of another person and can see there your brother or sister; until you can do that, it is still night. Using the principle of extension articulated by John Paul II, let us gloss this tale in an ecological direction. Writing on New Year's Day 1990, the pope instructed that "Respect for human life and for the dignity of the human person extends to the rest of creation." Until we look at the natural world and see a beloved creation of which we are a part, it is still night. Until we act to cherish its life-systems, condemn ecocide, make an option for nature as the new poor, and love our neighbor species as ourselves, it is still night. Until we understand that God so loves the world that the divine Spirit created it, continually acts to renew its face, and promises it a blessed future, we are dwelling in darkness. Composed by a group of committed earthlings who use all the skills of scholarship at their command, *Earth, Wind, and Fire* contributes to the coming of this critically-needed dawn.

1

Creation, Evolution, Revelation, and Redemption: Connections and Intersections

Carol J. Dempsey, O.P.

Several years ago physicist Charles Townes, the 1964 Nobel Prize winner, made this statement:

> Science wants to know the mechanism of the universe, religion the meaning. The two cannot be separated. Many scientists feel there is no place in research for discussion of anything that sounds mystical. But it is unreasonable to think we already know enough about the natural world to be confident about the totality of forces.[1]

Perhaps no other topic in science and religion has intrigued saints and scholars down through the years as much as creation. Today biblical scholars, theologians, and scientists alike continue to plumb the depths of this topic, only to discover new insights, new ideas, and new ways of seeing and living. The title of this volume, *Earth, Wind, and Fire: Biblical and Theological Perspectives on Creation*, sets the stage for this first chapter, which explores the connections and intersections between creation, evolution, revelation, and redemption. The chapter begins with a discussion of Genesis 1–2, the ancient biblical account of creation, a story that reveals the interrelatedness of all that exists. The creation account is then brought into dialogue with the theological dimensions of evolution.

The next part of the chapter looks at creation as a theme in biblical wisdom literature and focuses on revelation from a biblical and theological perspective. The last section considers creation in relationship to the writings of the prophets and brings to the fore the question of redemption. All these points are then viewed through an ecological lens that offers us startling yet wondrous implications as we continue to contemplate the mysteries of the universe while discovering anew the Creator of all, who calls us to be people of vision and of hope in a defining moment of grace. Will there be new heavens and a new earth, or will history continue to repeat itself into life's extinction?

GENESIS 1–2: AN EVER-ANCIENT, EVER-NEW CREATION NARRATIVE

The creation story found in Genesis 1–2 has traditionally been divided into the Priestly version (Gen 1:1–2:4a) and the Yahwist version (Gen 2:4b-25). Biblical scholars, however, have recently begun to view the two versions as a whole. Bruce Birch, Walter Brueggemann, Terence Fretheim, and David Petersen argue for a newer and more unified reading of Genesis 1–2, one that not only recognizes the texts' inherent differences but also draws upon their points of complementarity:

> Many [readers] of Genesis 1–2 think that these chapters consist of two creation accounts, assigning 1:1–2:4a to the Priestly writer and 2:4b-25 to the Yahwist. Differences in type of literature, structure, vocabulary, style, and center of concern have been noted. Yet, while the two accounts have different origins and transmission histories, they have been brought together in a theologically sophisticated fashion to function *together* as the canonical picture of creation. As such, they reveal key points of complementarity: God as sole creator of a good and purposeful world; the key place of the human among the creatures in a cocreative role; the social character of the human as male-female.[2]

In keeping with this unified canonical picture of creation, Genesis 1–2 presents a beautifully crafted design of interrelated divine, human, and non-human relationships. Before anything comes into existence God's *rûaḥ*, God's "breath," "spirit," "wind" is active, sweeping over the face of the waters (Gen 1:2). With this "wind," this "breath," this "spirit," the creation process begins.

On the first day God creates light, which is then separated from darkness, and both are named accordingly: "day," and "night" (Gen 1:3-5).

These two aspects of creation are distinct from and independent of each other, yet they complement each other and function interdependently.

On the second day a dome is created in the midst of the waters to separate one body of water from another (Gen 1:6-8); though now separated, they were originally one.

On the third day the waters under the sky are gathered together into one place—the sea—so that the dry land, the earth, can appear (Gen 1:9). One aspect of creation gives way to another, and both comprise two central habitats for life on the planet. The waters become home for the sea creatures; the birds fly above the earth across the dome of the sky (1:20-21). Both the sea creatures and the birds receive a divine blessing, enabling them to share in God's creative process. This blessing and its related creative process is also bestowed on human beings (1:20-22, 28).

On the fourth day lights appear in the dome of the sky: the sun, the moon, and the stars. These lights have their respective functions during the day and the night, and they also separate the light from the dark-ness, and day from night (Gen 1:14-19; cf. 1:4-5).

On subsequent days of creation the earth brings forth vegetation (Gen 1:9; cf. 2:9), a food source for human beings, birds, and all other earthly creatures (1:29-30). The vegetation and its growth, however, de-pend on two things: (1) rain, which according to the biblical writer is a phenomenon caused by God, and (2) human cultivation (2:5). Even though a stream rises up to water the face of the ground, the ground does not have the impetus to bring forth the needed vegetation (2:6). Thus in order to be fully "fruitful" the earth needs both God's and hu-mankind's care. Furthermore, the earth brings forth living creatures of every kind; from the earth—out of the ground—God makes cattle, creeping things, and wild animals (1:24; cf. 2:19). Out of the dust of the ground God also forms a human being (2:7). Finally, part of the earth is turned into a garden that God plants (2:8). The garden is entrusted to the human being whom God places in it "to till it and keep it" (2:15). The emerging picture of the creation story thus far is one of interdependent relationships between the divine, human, and non-human worlds.

As the creation account continues to unfold we see that the animals are intended to be helpers as partners for the human being (Gen 2:18-19), and likewise human beings are to be helpers as partners for one an-other as well (2:20). The fact that the first humans created are male and female indicates sexual differentiation; the description that they are to be helpers as partners indicates a sense of mutuality. That the woman is created from human bone suggests equality between male and female genders, an equality the biblical writer celebrates with a vivacious exclamation on the part of the male human being:

> Then the man said,
>   "This at last is bone of my bones
>   and flesh of my flesh;
>   this one shall be called Woman
>   for out of Man this one was taken." (Gen 2:23)[3]

Bone of bone, flesh of flesh, the man and woman become one flesh (2:24), metaphorically symbolized by the language of espousal: "Therefore a man leaves his father and his mother and clings to his wife, and they become one flesh." These human beings are created in God's image, according to God's likeness (2:26-27). They embody the *imago Dei*.

The ancient biblical people understood that to be created in the divine image meant that a person shared in God's creative process and God's work, which was to exercise dominion (Gen 1:28). Birch, Brueggemann, Fretheim, and Petersen make the point that "God is not in heaven alone, but is engaged in a relationship of mutuality and chooses to share the creative process with others. Human beings are thus created . . . in a way that shares power with others, which would be congruent with the command in 1:28."[4] They argue further that

> as image of God, human beings function to mirror God to the world, to be as God would be to the nonhuman, be an extension of God's own dominion. This text democratizes an ancient Near Eastern royal use of image language; all human beings are created in the image of God. That both male and female are so created . . . means that the female images the divine as much as the male. Likeness to God pertains not only to what male and female have in common but also to what remains distinctive to them . . . .[5]

Imago Dei, then, pertains to one's sense of self as well as one's role in creation. Systematic theologian Mary Catherine Hilkert takes the symbol of *imago Dei* a step further and poses this challenge to the present-day Christian community:

> The question facing Christians today is whether the symbol can be interpreted in a way that promotes not only human well-being and rights, but also awareness of human limits, ecological responsibility, and the interrelatedness of all creatures in the larger community of creation.[6]

She asserts that "the symbol can function in the service of life—both human life and the life of God's entire beloved creation."[7] Hence the *imago Dei* is a rich and dynamic symbol that functions on several levels and continues to evoke new interpretations in the context of an evolving biblical and theological tradition.

With respect to "subdue" and "dominion," Birch, Brueggemann, Fretheim, and Petersen offer clarification on the often misconstrued interpretations of these two terms: The command to have dominion (1:28), in which God delegates responsibility for the nonhuman creation in a power-sharing relationship with humans, must be understood in terms of care-giving, not exploitation (see the use of the verb *radah* in Ps 72:8-14; Ezek 34:1-4). The verb for *subdue,* while capable of more negative senses, here has reference to the earth and its cultivation and, more generally, to the becoming of a world that is a dynamic, not a static reality.[8] We have only to look at Psalm 104 to understand the term "dominion" in relationship to God who, as creator, provides bountifully for all creation.

The divine charge to the human being "to till and to care for" the garden follows the same vein of thought as Genesis 1:28. In their report to the 202nd General Assembly, members of Presbyterian Churches USA interpreted this biblical charge through an ecological lens:

. . . "tilling" symbolizes everything we humans do to draw sustenance from nature. It requires individuals to form communities of cooperation and to establish systematic arrangements (economies) for satisfying their needs. Tilling includes not only agriculture but mining and manufacturing and exchanging, all of which depend necessarily on taking and using the stuff of God's creation.[9]

"Keeping" the creation means tilling with care—maintaining the capacity of the creation to provide sustenance, for which tilling is done. This, we have come to understand, means making sure that the world of nature may flourish, with all its intricate, interacting systems upon which life depends.[10]

In retrospect, then, the animals and human beings share a common origin and participate in a wonderful relationship. Created by God from the ground, they are meant to assist one another as helpers, as partners in God's work on the planet and, in the case of the ancient agrarian world, to share in the common work of cultivating the land. Human beings' relationship to the natural world is further enhanced by the divine charge that humanity exercise dominion, a task that goes hand in hand with humankind's being formed in God's image, according to God's likeness. Not only do human beings live by God's breath of life (Gen 2:7), but so does the rest of creation (1:30). At this juncture we see a series of distinctive yet interconnected relationships existing between creator and creation. In sum, Birch, Brueggemann, Fretheim, and Petersen observe that

> Both God and creatures have an important role in the creative enterprise, and their spheres of activity are interrelated. God is not present as powerful and the creatures powerless. In spite of the risks involved, God chooses the way of less than absolute control, for the sake of a relationship of integrity in which power is shared with that which is other than God. In the very act of creating, God gives to others a certain freedom and independence, and catches them up in creativity. . . . Creation is process as well as event. . . . God has established a relationship with human beings such that their decisions about the creation truly count—both for God and the creation.[11]

These interwoven relationships are deepened through divine wonder and freedom, and the process of "naming." God does not name either the animals or the human beings. Rather, God brings the animals to the first human being to see what that person would call them, and whatever names were given, those were to be the names (Gen 2:19-20). The first human being also gives a name to the second human being (2:23). Naming, in the ancient world, was for the purpose of establishing a relationship; it entailed neither control nor subordination.

One last element in the creation story that establishes a sense of order within creation is the element of time. According to the biblical narrative, all of creation takes place in the course of six days; God rests on the seventh. If we view the time element linearly, the creative process leads up to and culminates in the creation of the human being. If it is viewed cyclically—which would be more in keeping with the ancient world's understanding of time in relation to seasons—the human being becomes part of the whole. Sharing in the distinctiveness of each aspect of creation, humankind becomes part of the rich picture of biodiversity presented in the biblical creation story, and helps to form part of the magnificent web of life to which all creation is connected, and God as well.

The seventh day of rest—the Sabbath—is a gift not only enjoyed by God but also extended to people, livestock (Exod 20:10), and the land (cf. Leviticus 25). Like humankind and the animal, the seventh day—the day of rest—is blessed by God. Thus God's blessing implies activity as well as "being."

Finally, each aspect of creation is "good" (Gen 1:4, 10, 12, 18, 21, 25) and all of creation is "very good" (Gen 1:31) not because of any utili-

tarian purpose but simply because it exists. Creation is intrinsically
good. This point retrieved from the biblical creation account is now a
"given" for many theologians developing a theology of creation, one
that flows from the biblical tradition.

If creation is intrinsically good, how is one to understand evil in regard to creation? In a recent work Langdon Gilkey takes up the question
of creation's intrinsic goodness and the existence of evil. He states:

> . . . the Genesis account makes very clear [that] all of creation is "good"
> because it was made by a caring God. Thus there is, and there can be,
> nothing essentially evil, an evil, so to speak, built into things as part of
> their intrinsic nature, and so irremovable and unredeemable, a necessary
> aspect of temporal and worldly existence. On the contrary, each part of
> reality has possibilities for good—even, to Augustine's Hellenistic con-
> sternation, matter and the body, both of which, as he had to admit, God
> had created and, therefore, despite appearances, must be good![12]

In sum, the Genesis 1–2 creation account presents us with a series
of interdependent and interconnected relationships, many of which are
mutual, and all of which comprise the glorious, wondrous, and evolutionary web of life.

CREATION AND EVOLUTION: THE DYNAMISM BETWEEN SCIENCE AND RELIGION, AND THE DEVELOPMENT OF AN EVOLUTIONARY THEOLOGY

Drawing on science as a conversation partner for the biblical-
theological theme of creation, New Testament scholar Barbara E. Bowe argues that "for the modern physicist . . . creation is itself *interrelated* at
every point,"[13] and that "creation . . . viewed through the lens of modern
science is not a single moment in time long ago, nor even a series of evolutionary moments leading to the creation of *homo sapiens,* but it is (at
least in some theories) an infinitely dynamic and open-ended process."[14]
To view creation, then, as an "infinitely dynamic and open-ended process"
is to admit that creation as we know it is not static; it continues to evolve.

One of the most challenging tasks facing biblical scholars and theologians today is not only articulating a new understanding of creation, one
that celebrates its interrelatedness and interdependence, which, in turn, casts
new light on traditional views about revelation and redemption, but also
making the links between science and faith with regard to creation. Here two
competing views come into play: the creationists versus the evolutionists.

On the one hand creationists retain absolute faith in the biblical creation story and maintain that it is scientifically and historically accurate. They dispute and/or disregard any scientific teaching that deals with cosmology, evolutionary biology, astronomy, physics, geology, and they have little or no appreciation for myth and metaphor. On the other hand, some evolutionists have tried to explain away all of creation, leaving nothing to faith and casting doubt on the existence of any divine power, spirit, or presence. Other evolutionists, as theologian John F. Haught notes, "raise questions not only about the Christian God but also about notions of ultimate reality or cosmic meaning as these are understood by many of the world's other religious traditions."[15] Today many biblical scholars and theologians would agree that the Genesis creation account is not to be taken literally or scientifically, and for Christians who are Catholic, creation and evolution are now "in conversation,"[16] with implicit encouragement to develop an evolutionary theology.[17]

The discussion on and development of an evolutionary theology has been the sustained focus and work of John Haught. Haught argues that evolutionary theology provides us with a new way of thinking about God—especially as Creator—and creation. The essential premises of a theology of evolution as outlined by Haught are as follows:

> A theology of evolution does not seek to disclose the divine imprint on human nature. Rather, it tries to show how a new understanding and awareness of cosmic and biological evolution can contribute positively to traditional knowledge about God and God's ways within the context of the world today.

The God of evolutionary theology is not an omnipotent, domineering, controlling God. Instead, the Divine Being is a "persuasive" God who leaves creation free to become all it is meant to be. Thus life's history remains open, undetermined, and graced with free choice by a God who loves and embraces all, who has entered into and remains in relationship with all, and whose Spirit has been poured out upon all creation and thus permeates and pervades all. An evolutionary theology accepts a Trinitarian view of God who suffers and rejoices with all creation, and who embraces the totality of creation's experience—its "travail," "enjoyment," and "creativity."[18] This God of relationship is interested in adventure and novelty and little concerned with preserving the status quo. The source of "order" and new forms of order, the God of evolutionary theology "wills" cosmic beauty to its fullest extent even when instability and disorder—the necessary ingredients for life—become part of the process. In this regard Haught argues that God, an "infinitely lib-erating source of new possibilities and new life,"[19] has a "vision" for the evolving universe instead of a set "plan."

A theology of evolution views the cosmos as an "evolving" one and although creation happened "in the beginning," it is still happening even in the present moment. Creation is a dynamic, ongoing process and not a "once and for all" static event. Following the views of Pierre Teilhard de Chardin, Haught points out that "evolution has allowed theology to acknowledge at last that the notion of an originally and in-stantaneously completed creation is theologically unthinkable. . . ."[20] The point made that creation is "evolving" opens the door to process theology, one branch of theology that has worked with and remains in conversation with evolution.[21] In his discussion of a theology of evolu-tion Haught acknowledges the contributions process theology has made to the discussion.

Furthermore, a theology of evolution celebrates the fact that we live in an "expanding universe," one to which God is intimately related yet one that is distinct from God. All elements of the universe—indeed, all creation—has its own God-given independence, a divine gift. As Haught points out, "only an independent cosmos could dialogue or be truly in-timate with God. From this point of view, therefore, the epic of evolu-tion is the story of the emerging independence and autonomy of the world awakening in the presence of God's grace."[22] Although independ-ent, the entire cosmos has a destiny that, according to a theology of evo-lution, is embraced by God's divine care—a divine care that extends to the entire cosmos itself.

A theology of evolution emphasizes the sacramental aspect of crea-tion and views creation as revelatory of God. Revelation is understood as God's own selfhood communicated to the world. Creation, then, be-comes the locus for divine revelation, and as creation evolves, so does revelation. Here Haught argues that a finite cosmos receives divine in-finity gradually, allowing for the process of self-transcendence and ulti-mately, I would add, transformation into the Divine.

For a theology of evolution, original sin means, as Haught proposes, that "each of us is born into a still unfinished, imperfect universe where there already exist strong pressures . . . for us to acquiesce in an indif-ference to God's creative cosmic aim of maximizing beauty. Original sin consists of all the forces that lead us away from participation in this most essential and vitalizing pursuit."[23] Original sin expresses our "es-trangement from the ideal"—the ideal world being the "enlivening new creation yet to come, not a once perfect world to which we now seek nostalgically to return."[24] Haught proposes further that actual sin is the concrete manifestation of our indifference "to the divinely aroused aesthetic cosmological principle, either by actively destroying that which is good and beautiful, reducing it to disorder and chaos, or by tolerating unnecessary forms or monotony when the creation of deeper beauty is called for."[25]

A theology of evolution influenced by process thought views God's creative and redemptive power cosmologically rather than anthropocentrically, and interprets divine power in the context of an evolving world. Evolutionary theology brings the entire universe into the plan of salvation. Highlighting process theology, Haught points out that

> everything whatsoever that occurs in evolution—all the suffering and tragedy as well as the emergence of new life and intense beauty—is "saved" by being taken eternally into God's own feeling of the world. Even though all events and achievements in evolution are temporal and perishable, they still abide permanently within the everlasting compassion of God. In God's own sensitivity to the world, each event is redeemed from absolute perishing and receives the definitive importance and meaning that religions encourage us to believe in—always without seeing clearly.[26]

Central to evolutionary theology is promise. God is the giver of promises yet to be fulfilled. All creation—indeed, the entire cosmos—exists in a context of divine promise, and thus all that exists has a future, and that future is one of hope. The eschatological hope for final fulfillment is not, therefore, meant for humans alone; it is meant for the entire cosmos. Haught argues that "the entire universe is heir to God's pledge of fidelity. But if the totality of nature and its long evolutionary history are God's creation, and not our own, we can assume that it has levels of meaning and value that we humans may never fully grasp."[27]

Finally, in the context of a theology of evolution Haught argues for an ecological ethic:

> . . . during the present phase of the world's unfolding, at a time when humans are the dominant evolutionary species on earth, we have the responsibility not only of ensuring our own species' survival but also of leaving ample room for the future of other forms of life. We are obliged to adopt styles of living that leave open the possibility of yet more incalculable outcomes as the still unfinished creation of the cosmos continues into the future. Even if these outcomes have little relevance to our own lives and interests at the present moment, a robust creation faith de-

mands that we rejoice in the prospect that other natural beings have a meaning and value to their creator that may be quite hidden from our human powers of discernment.[28]

In sum, a theology of evolution has profound implications for our understanding of God, creation, revelation, redemption, how we view life, and how we understand the ancient biblical symbol of *imago Dei*. A theology of evolution has many of its characteristics embedded in and flowing from the biblical text, particularly those texts that focus on creation. Where creation theology and evolutionary theology intersect, a new understanding of both the biblical text and the text of life emerges, one that is liberating, organic, and grace-filled. This new understanding is deeply rooted in the Jewish and Christian traditions, and it not only enriches ecological theology but also calls us human beings—a single species among millions—to an ever-pressing sense of responsibility. I repeat the question I raised earlier, "Will there be a new heavens and a new earth, or will history continue to repeat itself until life's extinction?"

INTERSECTIONS BETWEEN THE CREATION THEOLOGY OF GENESIS 1–2 AND EVOLUTIONARY THEOLOGY

The earlier examination of the Genesis 1–2 creation account yielded a picture of interconnected, interrelated relationships. While each aspect of creation has its own autonomy, all of creation functions interdependently. Though interconnected and interrelated, each element in creation as represented in Genesis 1–2 is novel and distinct from other elements of creation: light, darkness, a dome, waters, dry land, plants, fruit trees, sun, moon, sea creatures, birds, cattle, creeping things, wild animals, a male human being, a female human being, the heavens, the earth. In scientific terms, Genesis 1–2 is a grand portrait of biodiversity, one that attests to the God of adventure and novelty as heralded by evolutionary theology.

In Genesis 1–2 creation occurs in an orderly fashion. Various elements of human and non-human life come into existence one day at a time, in the course of six consecutive days. Creator God sees that each aspect of creation is "good" and that all of creation is "very good." Creator God, the source of order, "wills" cosmic beauty and has a "vision" instead of a "plan" for creation, as evolutionary theology suggests.

Through the Genesis creation account we also encounter a God who leaves creation free to become all that it is meant to be. The command to humans and nonhumans alike goes forth: "Be fruitful and multiply" (Gen 1:22, 28). The process of life begetting life—of life evolving from life—begins. The God of creation assigns human beings tasks, "to have dominion" (Gen 1:28); "to till . . . to keep" (Gen 2:15), but nowhere in the Genesis creation account do we hear God describing how the tasks are to be carried out. Divine imperatives simply go forth, e.g., let the waters bring forth . . . let the earth bring forth (Gen 1:20, 24), and their non-descriptiveness leaves room for creativity, ingenuity, fecundity, and yes, even chaos, on the part of human and nonhuman life as life thrives in an environment of divine affirmation—"and God saw that it was good," "very good" (Gen 1:4, 10, 18, 21, 25, 31). Furthermore, God, having given names to certain elements of creation, refrains from naming the animals and birds. Instead, God brings the creatures to the first human being "to see" what the human being would call them (Gen 2:19). The biblical text suggests a certain sense of wonder on God's part as well as a certain freedom given by God to the human person to participate in the divine creativity of naming and establishing relationships. Thus the Genesis creation story depicts the God of creation as one who creates and then allows creation to function freely in a series of interconnected relationships that comprise the wondrous web of life. Such is the God of evolutionary theology as well, understood to be non-domineering and non-controlling. This final point is brought home by biblical scholar Norman Habel who, in his analysis of Genesis 1–2, points out that the function of "ruling," with respect to the sun and moon, is not to "dominate" but to "regulate" light for Earth (Gen 1:14).[29] Again, the God of creation, according to Genesis 1–2, is the God of relationship who has entered into relationship with creation and has established creation as a series of relationships meant to function freely, wholly, and interdependently.

Finally, the Genesis creation account opens as follows: "In the beginning when God created the heavens and the earth, and the earth was a formless void and darkness covered the face of the deep, while a wind from God swept over the face of the waters" (Gen 1:1-2). Theology has long accepted three modes of creation: original creation *(creatio originalis)*, continuous creation *(creatio continua)*, and new creation *(creatio nova)*, one that would be considered final. Theology has also acknowledged that creation is ongoing; the universe is still in process of being created and continues to unfold before our eyes. The phrase "in the beginning" signifies original creation and also connotes continuous creation. Creation has begun, and it has not ended. The Genesis 1–2 text hints at its continuation—"be fruitful and multiply"—and the rest of the biblical tradition picks up on this theme, whether the texts talk about the begetting of generations, families, communities, or the development of cities, monarchies, nation states, or even the promise of a new heavens and a new earth to which the prophet Isaiah and the book of Revelation point.[30] Thus, the phrase "in the beginning" starts a process that continues throughout the rest of Genesis 1–2 and the biblical text and world as a whole.

The Hebrew word for "wind" is *rûaḥ*, a feminine noun that can be translated as "breath," "spirit." The Genesis 1–2 creation story makes clear that God's "wind," God's "breath," God's "spirit" was present at the moment when creation commenced. It is God's breath that gives life to all and sustains the life of all (Gen 2:7; Ps 104:29; Job 33:4). This "spirit" of God creates, renews (Pss 33:6; 104:30), inspires, and empowers (Mic 3:8). Wisdom literature tells us that God's spirit is in all things:

> For you love all things that exist,
> and detest none of the things that you have made,
>> for you would not have made anything if you had hated it.
>> How would anything have endured if you had not willed it?
>> Or how would anything not called forth by you have been preserved?
>> You spare all things, for they are yours, O Lord, you who love the living.
>> For your immortal spirit is in all things. (Wis 11:24–12:1)

Similarly, a theology of evolution also maintains that God's spirit has been poured out on all creation, penetrating and pervading all. The biblical creation account, illuminated by the wisdom tradition, offers credence to the God of evolutionary theology, and together the Genesis creation story, along with the other aforementioned biblical texts from the prophetic and wisdom traditions, makes known to us that the God of creation is a divine presence in the midst of all, loving all, in relationship with all, who "wills" not only creation but also the "ongoingness" of creation.[31] The biblical God of creation is a God of compassion who spares all things (cf. Sir 18:13). Thus the biblical portrait of both Creator God and creation converges with evolutionary theology's portrait of God and creation, with the former giving the latter roots in an ancient story and tradition that continues to unfold and evoke new insights from one generation to the next.[32]

TOWARD A RENEWED UNDERSTANDING OF REVELATION:
INTERSECTIONS BETWEEN CREATION, BIBLICAL WISDOM,
AND EVOLUTIONARY THEOLOGY

Both creation theology and a theology of evolution lay claim to the spirit of God that created all and dwells in the midst of all. If God's immortal spirit is in all things as both the biblical writers and evolutionary theologians suggest, how are we to understand revelation in relation to creation? The biblical Wisdom tradition provides us with insights.

For the ancient biblical people, creation was the starting point and locus of revelation. According to the biblical Wisdom tradition the spirit of God that created all (Gen 1:1-2) and dwelt in all (Wis 11:24–12:1) was a spirit of Wisdom (Prov 8:22-31). This spirit of Wisdom—the spirit with which God created—is

> . . . intelligent, holy,
> unique, manifold, subtle, mobile, clear, unpolluted,
> distinct, invulnerable, loving the good, keen, irresistible, beneficent,
> humane, steadfast, sure, free from anxiety, all-powerful, overseeing all,
> and penetrating through all spirits that are intelligent, pure, and
> altogether subtle.
> For wisdom is more mobile than any motion;
> because of her pureness she pervades and penetrates all things.
> For she is a breath of the power of God,
> and a pure emanation of the glory of the Almighty;
> therefore nothing defiled gains entrance into her.
> For she is a reflection of eternal light,
> a spotless mirror of the working of God,
> and an image of [God's] goodness.
> Although she is but one, she can do all things,
> and while remaining in herself, she renews all things;
> in every generation she passes into holy beings
> and makes them friends of God, and prophets;
> for God loves nothing so much as the person who lives with wisdom.
> She is more beautiful than the sun,
> and excels every constellation of the stars.
> Compared with the light she is found to be superior,
> for it is succeeded by the night,
> but against wisdom evil does not prevail.
> She reaches mightily from one end of the earth to the other,
> and she orders all things well. (Wis 7:22–8:1)

Not only does Wisdom give order to all that has been created, but she also has potential for making all "friends of God and prophets," a gift that now needs to be heard cosmologically rather than anthropocentrically. All creation is in relationship with God, and God in relationship with creation. Because creation is full of Wisdom, it is prophetic, forever revealing to us something of the wonder, the mystery, and the beauty of God.[33]

Enriching our biblical understanding of creation and revelation is the thought of systematic theologian Walter Kasper, who adds additional insight into the discussion at hand:

> Since the Spirit is divine love in Person, he is first of all the source of creation, for creation is the overflow of God's love and a participation in God's being. The Holy Spirit is the internal (in God) presupposition of communicability of God outside of himself. But the Spirit is also the source of movement and life in the created world. Whenever something new arises, whenever life is awakened and reality reaches ecstatically beyond itself, in all seeking and striving, in every ferment and birth, and even more in the beauty of creation, something of the being and activity of God's Spirit is manifested.[34]

Denis Edwards comments further:

> The Creator Spirit's role is to enable each creature to be and to become, bringing each into relationship with other creatures in both local and global ecological systems, and in this process of ongoing creation, relating each creature in communion within the life of divine Persons-in-communion.

This means that forests, rivers, insects, and birds exist and have value in their own right. They are not simply there for human use. They have their own integrity. They exist as an interdependent network of relationships in which each creature is sustained and held by triune love. They manifest the presence of the Spirit as the ecstasy and fecundity of divine love. . . .[35]

> The presence of the Spirit cannot be limited by human expectations. . . . The Spirit transcends our humanity and its preoccupations with itself, embracing all creatures. . . . The Spirit transcends our humanity and its preoccupations with itself, embracing God's creatures. . . . The Spirit pervades the whole universe and sees to "the depths of God" (1 Cor 2:10). To be in communion with this Spirit is to be in communion

with the whole of creation. . . . All this is suggesting that Earth reveals. It is the place of encounter with the Holy Spirit.[36]

Hence within the context of the biblical and theological tradition creation is deemed revelatory, and if we accept the biblical idea that God's immortal spirit is in all things, then creation becomes not only revelatory but also sacramental. A theology of evolution emphasizes the sacramental aspect of creation and identifies creation as the locus for divine revelation. Biblical creation theology and evolutionary theology once again converge to offer a deeper, fuller, and renewed understanding of both creation and revelation. Hence Haught is able to argue that:

> Revelation is the ongoing outpouring of God's creative, formative love into the whole world. In this sense it has a "general" character, and it is even constitutive of all things. Thus the idea of revelation in contemporary theology tends to converge with the biblical theme of creation. Creation itself is already the self-revelation of God.[37]

> . . . From the moment of its creation the universe has "felt" the outpouring of God's own being into itself, arousing it to reach out toward ever more intense modes of fulfillment. This divine self-donation is known as "universal" or "general" revelation.[38]

This renewed and fuller understanding of revelation leads Haught a step further where he identifies a major challenge facing Christian theologies today:

> . . . a central question for the theology of revelation today is that of how to reconcile emphasis on the definitiveness of Christ and our acknowledgement of the continual openness to the general revelation of the mystery given universally to our universe, to human existence and especially to religious experience?[39]

Finally, this renewed and broader understanding of creation and revelation offered to us by both creation and evolutionary theologies and the intersections between them has startling implications not only for our present-day escalating environmental crisis but also for the ongoing development of an ecological theology. These points will be taken up at the end of this chapter.

TOWARD A RENEWED UNDERSTANDING OF REDEMPTION:
INTERSECTIONS BETWEEN CREATION, THE PROPHETIC
TRADITION, AND EVOLUTIONARY THEOLOGY

In Chapter 5 of this book, New Testament scholar Barbara E. Bowe writes: ". . . we need today a renewed definition of the relationship between creation and redemption, one that affirms the essential *interrelationship* between the process of becoming of the entire created world and its ultimate destiny."[40]

In past works I have argued that from the writings of the biblical prophets one can retrieve a new vision of redemption, one that is cosmic instead of anthropocentric.[41] Repeatedly in the prophets we see the link between human sinfulness and the devastation of creation on the one hand, and redemption from sin and the restoration of creation on the other. The love of God whose spirit has created and made holy all creation continues to liberate and redeem it from its bondage, which I suggest is caused in part by some human beings' failure to understand the concept of "right relationship" and the biblical mandate that we live in "right relationship" with all creation if we are to participate in the divine work of liberation that leads to the lived experience of God's vision of salvation which, I would argue, is for all creation. This vision, echoed by Paul in Romans 8:18-25, is embraced by many systematic theologians today, among them Francis Schüssler Fiorenza, who offers the following thought:

> Redemption is a central category of Christian theology, for it explicates the Christian proclamation of Jesus as Christ, as our Redeemer and Savior. The English word "redemption" literally means a buying back. . . . The term "redemption" is best understood as a liberation from one state to another: from bondage to liberation. Redemption is the act or process by which the change takes place.[42]

He adds: "Redemption therefore does not simply blot out the punishment of sin, but it frees and liberates humans from the cosmic power of law, sin and death. Although present, redemption is also future and it embraces not only humans, but the whole creation."[43]

A biblical theology of creation and cosmic redemption retrieved from the Old Testament prophets, proclaimed by Paul in the New Testament, and embraced by some systematic theologians coincides with the tenets of evolutionary theology. As Haught has pointed out, evolutionary theology brings the entire universe into the plan of salvation. Furthermore, Haught understands original and actual sin to be humankind's failure to participate in God's creative, re-creative, and redemptive work, to live in right relationship with all creation, and to assume appropriate responsibility for ensuring that the "good" and the "beautiful" are not only sustained but also given the opportunity to thrive.

In sum, the vision of cosmic redemption embedded in the thought and writings of the biblical prophets, together with the voices of various theologians and theological perspectives, offers us hope. Life exists in the midst of divine promise:

> . . . I am about to create a new heavens
>   and a new earth;
> the former things shall not be remembered
>   or come to mind. (Isa 65:17)

Although this divine promise is eschatological, it has already unfolded in our midst through the life, death, and resurrection of Jesus Christ and will continue to unfold as the universe continues to unfold, and as human beings continue to be transformed into Christ who is

> the image of the invisible God, the firstborn of all creation, in whom all things in heaven and on earth were created . . . he who is the beginning, the firstborn from the dead . . . in whom all the fullness of God was pleased to dwell, and through whom God was pleased to reconcile to [God's] self all things, whether on earth or in heaven, by making peace through the blood of his cross. (Col 1:15-20)[44]

Transformation into Christ leads one into the fullness of God. To dwell in that fullness is to live in communion—in right relationship—with all that exists.

Finally, in reflecting on all that has been discussed thus far, I would add that all creation has received God's promise. Because of that promise all creation shares a common destiny. Everything that exists has come from the Source of All Being and continues to evolve in that Source as everything journeys back to the Source, forever evolving deeper and deeper into life. In the end there will be one thing that lives on—Abiding Love—whose compassion will have gathered all of the first heaven and all of the first earth fully into its enduring and forever-transforming embrace. At that moment the new heavens and the new earth about which Isaiah has spoken will have been born. And yes, "on that day, for the second time in the history of the world, we shall have discovered fire"[45] and shall have come to know what John saw and wrote about in Revelation 21:6—"I am the Alpha and the Omega, the beginning and the end"—and what the poets and saints of old understood: "in my beginning is my end, in my end is my beginning."[46]

CREATION THEOLOGY, EVOLUTIONARY THEOLOGY, AND THE ECOLOGICAL CRISIS

Both creation theology and evolutionary theology as outlined in this chapter have provided us with ideas for rethinking and renewing our understanding of God, creation, revelation, and redemption. Because all creation is sacramental, revelatory, evolving, and promised a future, the present-day environmental crisis engulfing the planet becomes ever more tragic. Every time we lose a species we also lose something of the "spirit" and presence of God as Being. The Genesis 1–2 creation account reminds us that humankind is "created in God's image, according to God's likeness," charged with the task of "dominion," of "tilling" and "keeping" the garden. Our vision of the garden must now be expanded to include all creation. Now more than ever, humankind must embody the *imago Dei* symbol that will be recognized as "right relationship" and "our responsibility in relation to the rest of creation" as theologian Mary Catherine Hilkert suggests.[47]

What is needed is not only a change of heart but also a new ethic, one that safeguards and celebrates the intrinsic goodness of all creation, and one that flows from an ever-deepening love that can feel and understand the pain and ecstasy of life in all its interrelatedness. The words of Ephrem of Syria bear repeating:

> An elder was once asked, "What is a compassionate heart?" He replied, "It is a heart on fire for the whole of creation, for humanity, for the birds, for the animals, for demons and for all that exists. At the recollection and at the sight of them such a person's eyes overflow with tears owing to the vehemence of the compassion which grips his [or her] heart; as a result of his [or her] deep mercy his [or her] heart shrinks and cannot bear to hear or look on any injury or the slightest suffering of anything in creation."[48]

Complementing the vision of Ephrem is the thought of theologian Jeffrey G. Sobosan, a former colleague of mine who now enjoys the fullness of the Divine Presence. His words continue to disturb me:

> What is needed is an expansion of our ethical concerns and commitments. While we recognize, for example, that maliciously damaging another

human being is wrong, we must extend this principle (even when at first we think it will be honored more in the breach than in the keeping) to all living things. So too with such generally acknowledged norms as sheltering the homeless, feeding the hungry, caring for the sick. This task is not easy, but it is possible, and we must muffle in our spirits the sweet temptation to give up. With the Buddhist saint we must strive toward that point where we can say, "All that is alive is a part of me, and I am nothing save for them." This is sanctity at a high pitch, beyond the concerns of formal religion, recognizing that nonhuman life includes not just the animals, but God as well. For God too survives in our lives only when we protect and nourish our feelings for the divine.[49]

A SUMMARY REFLECTION

We live in an expanding universe; we are evolving with the earth, with all creation. With the entire planet we are experiencing a dynamic transformation. Everything is moving from a Cenozoic Era to an Ecozoic one. The journey has begun; a defining moment of grace is with us. We humans will need to work hard to reclaim "right relationship" with all that exists, and as difficult and as arduous as the task may be, we must never lose hope. We must find the will to sing with the spheres and the desire to dance with the stars. And we must never forget that before anything came into being, there was an ancient love whose fire and passion will never be extinguished and whose embrace reaches out again and again to heal, to love, to gather, to welcome . . .

> In our beginning is our end . . .
> in our end is our beginning . . . .

NOTES: CHAPTER 1

[1]This quotation from Charles Townes is cited in Michael Reagan, ed., *The Hand of God: Thoughts and Images Reflecting the Spirit of the Universe* (Philadelphia: Templeton Foundation Press, 1999) 36.

[2]Bruce C. Birch, Walter Brueggemann, Terence E. Fretheim, and David L. Petersen, *A Theological Introduction to the Old Testament* (Nashville: Abingdon, 1999) 46.

[3]I am aware of the many interpretations of the creation account, particularly with respect to the creation of man and woman. While I agree that the story is androcentric, anthropocentric, and hierarchical when read through a feminist lens, I am reading the text through a cosmological lens.

[4]Birch, Brueggemann, Fretheim, and Petersen, *Theological Introduction*, 49.

[5]Ibid. 50.

[6]See Mary Catherine Hilkert, "Creation in the Image of God and Wisdom Christology," Chapter 12 below, 148.

[7]Ibid. For further discussion on *imago Dei* see also Ian G. Barbour, *Nature, Human, and God: Theology and the Sciences* (Minneapolis: Fortress) 49–50, 128.

[8]Birch, Brueggemann, Fretheim, and Petersen, *Theological Introduction*, 50.

[9]"Restoring Creation for Ecology and Justice," *A Report Adopted by the 202nd General Assembly* (1990), Presbyterian Church (USA) 7.

[10]Ibid. For further discussion on "to till" and "to keep" see Phyllis Trible, *God and the Rhetoric of Sexuality*. Overtures to Biblical Theology (Philadelphia: Fortress, 1978) 85. Here Trible argues that the exercise of power over the garden means to have reverence for it. Neither "tilling" nor "keeping," according to Trible, implies exploitation. Both words suggest that humankind is to be in service to the garden.

[11]Birch, Brueggemann, Fretheim, and Petersen, *Theological Introduction*, 46.

[12]Langdon Gilkey, *Blue Twilight: Nature, Creationism, and American Religion* (Minneapolis: Fortress, 2001) 66.

[13]See Chapter 5, "Soundings in the New Testament Understandings of Creation," by Barbara E. Bowe in this volume, 58.

[14]Ibid.

[15]John F. Haught, *God After Darwin: A Theology of Evolution* (Boulder, Colo.: Westview Press, 2000) 9.

[16]For further discussion see Pope John Paul II's address, "Message to Pontifical Academy of Sciences on Evolution," in *Origins* 26/2 (Nov. 14, 1996) 350–52.

[17]For an analysis of the Vatican's views on evolution see John F. Haught, *Responses to 101 Questions on God and Evolution* (Mahwah, N.J.: Paulist, 2000) 41–43.

[18]Haught, *God After Darwin: A Theology of Evolution*, 51.

[19]Ibid. 120.

[20]See ibid. 37. See also Pierre Teilhard de Chardin, *Christianity and Evolution,* trans. René Hague (New York: Harcourt Brace & Co., 1969) 239.

[21]For further discussion on process theology see Alfred North Whitehead, *Process and Reality,* corrected ed., David Ray Griffin and Donald W. Sherburne, eds. (New York: Free Press, 1978); John Cobb and David Griffin, *Process Theology: An Introductory Exposition* (Philadelphia: Westminster, 1976), and John Haught, *God After Darwin: A Theology of Evolution,* especially pp. 40–43.

[22]Haught, *Responses to 101 Questions on God and Evolution,* 51.

[23]Haught, *God After Darwin: A Theology of Evolution,* 138.

[24]Ibid. 140. The tradition, doctrine, and Church teaching on original sin have a long history, all of which I acknowledge as integral to any discussion on sin and evil. The view of original and actual sin through an evolutionary theological lens is but one perspective in the mix of a much larger conversation. For a full discussion on original sin see Tatha Wiley, *Original Sin: Origins, Developments, Contemporary Meanings* (Mahwah, N.J.: Paulist, 2002).

[25]Haught, *God After Darwin: A Theology of Evolution,* 138.

[26]Ibid. 43.

[27]Ibid. 159.

[28]Ibid. For a detailed discussion on a theology of evolution see Haught, *God After Darwin: A Theology of Evolution,* especially 36–44, 50–52, 141, 149, 165–66, 189–91, and *Responses to 101 Questions on God and Evolution,* especially 49–51. The discussion on the theology of evolution I have presented here is by no means an exhaustive one. There are many more points to an evolutionary theology. Those selected here relate specifically to the topic and content of this chapter and book.

[29]Norman C. Habel, "Geophany," in Norman C. Habel and Shirley Wurst, eds., *The Earth Story in Genesis* (Sheffield: Sheffield Academic Press, 2000) 44.

[30]See Isaiah 65:17 and Revelation 21:1.

[31]For further discussion of God's relationship to creation see Edward Schillebeeckx, "God the Living One," *New Blackfriars* 62 (1981) 357–70, and "I Believe in God, Creator of Heaven and Earth," in idem, *God Among Us: The Gospel Proclaimed* (New York: Crossroad, 1983) especially 91–102.

[32]Genesis 1–2 enjoys many rich and diverse interpretations. What I have attempted to do here is not to offer an extensive, critical, or new interpretation but rather to suggest links between a theology of creation that emerges from the biblical text and some theological points put forth by a theology of evolution, with the intention of enriching our understanding of creation from a contemporary biblical and theological perspective informed by faith and science.

[33]The understanding of creation as a locus for divine revelation also appears in the thought of Irenaeus (see *Adversus Haereses* IV.6.6, also II.6.1; 27.2, III.25; V.18.3) and Thomas Aquinas (see his *Summa Theologica,* Part One, Questions 1-13).

[34]Walter Kasper, *The God of Jesus Christ* (London: S.C.M., 1983) 227.

[35]Denis Edwards, "For Your Immortal Spirit Is in All Things," in idem, ed., *Earth Revealing, Earth Healing* (Collegeville: The Liturgical Press, 2001) 64.

[36]Ibid. 65.

[37]John Haught, "Revelation," in Joseph A. Komonchak, Mary Collins, and Dermot A. Lane, eds., *The New Dictionary of Theology* (Collegeville: The Liturgical Press, 1987) 884.

[38]Ibid. 887.

[39]Ibid. 894. Theologian Roger Haight offers an excellent discussion on the topic of christology, revelation, and the cosmos in "The Future of Christology: Expanding Horizons, Religious Pluralism, and the Divinity of Jesus," in Anne M. Clifford and Anthony J. Godzieba, eds., *Christology, Memory, Inquiry, Practice*. College Theology Society Annual Volume 48 (Maryknoll, N.Y.: Orbis, 2003) 47–61. See also the lucid discussion on Col 1:15 by Mary Catherine Hilkert in Chapter 12 of this book.

[40]See Barbara E. Bowe, "Soundings in the New Testament Understandings of Creation," Chapter 5 of this volume, 63–64.

[41]For a detailed discussion on redemption, the biblical prophets, and the vision of cosmic redemption see the following: Carol J. Dempsey, "Hope Amidst Crisis: A Prophetic Vision of Cosmic Redemption," in eadem and Russell A. Butkus, eds., *All Creation Is Groaning: An Interdisciplinary Vision for Life in a Sacred Universe* (Collegeville: The Liturgical Press, 1999) 269–84; eadem, *The Prophets: A Liberation Critical Reading* (Minneapolis: Fortress, 2000); and *Hope Amid the Ruins: The Ethics of Israel's Prophets* (St. Louis: Chalice, 2000) especially 119–29.

[42]Francis Schüssler Fiorenza, "Redemption," *The New Dictionary of Theology*, 836.

[43]Ibid. 840.

[44]For additional discussion on this passage from Colossians see Mary Catherine Hilkert, "Creation in the Image of God and Wisdom Christology," below; see also Elizabeth A. Johnson, "God's Beloved Creation," *America* (April 16, 2001) 8–12, especially 9.

[45]Pierre Teilhard de Chardin, *The Divine Milieu* (New York: Harper & Row, 1960) 144; cf. Barbara Bowe's final comments in "Soundings in the New Testament Understandings of Creation," below.

[46]See the writings and poetry of John of the Cross and T. S. Eliot.

[47]See Hilkert, "Creation in the Image of God and Wisdom Christology," 153.

[48]*Hymns of Paradise* (Syriac edition: E. Beck in CSCO, vols. 174–75 [1957]; English translation [with *Commentary on Genesis*, section 2]: trans. S. P. Brock. Crestwood: St. Vladimir, 1990).

[49]Jeffrey G. Sobosan, *Bless the Beasts: A Spirituality of Animal Care* (New York: Crossroad, 1991) 23.

2

The Priestly Creation Narrative: Goodness and Interdependence

Alice L. Laffey

INTRODUCTION

*A*lthough I was trained in the method of historical criticism, my interests in women and ecology have led me to explore other methods of biblical study, especially reader response criticism. Whatever the origin and sources, the received text has been the basis of biblical interpretation in both Church and synagogue for more than two thousand years. Moreover, since historical criticism uncovered the essentially patriarchal character of ancient Israelite culture I have been more attracted to methods that restore the interpretive credibility of the final version of the texts and invite alternative interpretations, insights buried in the texts that, despite themselves, affirm women. Similarly, I have tried to read the texts from a broader liberation perspective, one that is more egalitarian, that affirms the value of minorities, the less powerful and, in fact, all of creation. That having been said, however, in contrast to how the historical methods have revealed the patriarchy and hierarchy of ancient Israelite culture, these same historical methods have also uncovered the interdependent relationship of the ancient Israelites with all other living things. The consciousness of the people of ancient Israel contained an awareness of their own fragility and dependence, an awareness that led them to respect other parts of creation. Thus in this essay I have returned to a historical critical methodology. The goals of this effort are to better understand the historical function of Genesis 1, the Priestly account of creation, and to try to discover why the Priestly source found it helpful to produce its own account. Why did P revise Genesis 2–3, the account of creation produced either by the Yahwist or at least by an earlier source? The essay will suggest that, consistent with other materials authored by P, the account of creation depicted in Genesis 1 affirms the possibility of Jewish restoration, suggests strategies to accomplish it, and posits the goodness of Jewish identity even (or especially) in a post-exilic Israel. Though my questions are historical, they have profound theological significance.

1. HOW DOES GENESIS 1, THE P ACCOUNT OF CREATION, DIFFER FROM GENESIS 2–3, THE J OR EARLIER ACCOUNT?

a. Order

The Priestly source is known for a sense of order (e.g., the numerous genealogies credited to P's authorship), and Genesis 1:1–2:4 presents creation in an orderly six days, with God resting from work on the Sabbath. P may also have written the first chapter to introduce the sources he/they were compiling and editing.

b. God's Creation Is Good

Much has been made, including recently by feminists, of what distinguishes P's creation narrative from the earlier version. Not only does P have creation take place in six days: the account of each day concludes in almost a refrain manner with the assertion that God saw that what God had created was good.

c. Humankind Is Created "In God's Image"

Moreover, the text makes the point that God made humankind (*ʾādām*) "in our image, according to our likeness" with dominion "over the fish of the sea, and over the birds of the air, and over the cattle, and over all the wild animals of the earth, and everything that creeps upon the ground of every kind" (1:26)[1]; God created humankind "in his image, in the image of God he created them;[2] male and female he created them" (1:27). In contrast to the J or earlier account, in which *ʾādām* is created first and then, when no other form of creation is found to be "a suitable helper"[3] for *ʾādām*, God takes from *ʾādām* to form *ʾîš* and *ʾiššāh* (Gen 2:20-23), in the Priestly account the female is created at the same time as the male. P's version on this point is clearly more conducive to a feminist interpretation.

d. Injunction to Procreate, to Subdue, and to Have Dominion

Additional differences between the two accounts include the explicit injunction to male and female *(zākār* and *nĕqēbāh)* to "be fruitful and multiply, and fill the earth," followed by the directives to "subdue it" and to "have dominion over the fish of the sea and over the birds of the air." In this variation, the cattle, wild animals, and creeping things are summarized as "every living thing that moves upon the earth" (1:28). No similar explicit directive occurs in Genesis 2. While other created things were not found to be adequate as "a helper as his partner," *'ādām* is not directed in J's account either to "subdue" or to "have dominion."

e. Freedom to Eat All Seed-Bearing Plants and Every Green Plant

Finally, Genesis 1 varies only slightly from Genesis 2 in its reference to food. Genesis 1:29 provides "every plant yielding seed that is upon the face of all the earth, and every tree with seed in its fruit" to *'ādām* for food, enlarging upon Genesis 2:16, which records that God has allowed *'ādām* to "freely eat of every tree of the garden" except for "the tree of the knowledge of good and evil" (cf. 3:2). Genesis 1 lacks any prohibitions, and thus any literary foreshadowing of evil. In addition, the chapter makes explicit that God gives "every green plant for food" to "every beast of the earth, and to every bird of the air, and to everything that creeps on the earth, everything that has the breath of life" (1:30).

2. WHY ARE THE DIFFERENCES BETWEEN THE J OR EARLIER ACCOUNT AND THE PRIESTLY ACCOUNT SO SIGNIFICANT THAT THEY WARRANTED A SECOND ACCOUNT OF CREATION?

One might posit that the differences are "merely" stylistic, but would mere style warrant a second account? In fact, this second account had been seized upon by many interpreters, long before feminists arrived on the scene, to emphasize that *'ādām* was made in the image of God, according to God's likeness, and to conclude, on the basis of those phrases, along with God's allowing humankind to have dominion, that the biblical author wanted to emphasize that *'ādām* was superior to other parts of God's creation. Yet a cursory reading of the text might lead one to wonder, "If that were the author's motive, why did the Priestly source portray God as bringing forth—on the same day that God created humankind, the sixth day—'living creatures of every kind: cattle and creeping things and wild animals of the earth of every kind' (1:24)?" Surely the Priestly penchant for order would have awarded humankind its own time or "day" of creation? Reflection such as this leads to the next and central question of this historical investigation and reconstruction.

3. WHAT CULTURAL CHANGES BETWEEN THE TENTH CENTURY B.C.E. AND THE EXILIC PERIOD MAY HAVE ACCOUNTED FOR THE SHIFTS EVIDENCED IN P'S CREATION ACCOUNT?

a. Humankind Is Good and Made in the Image of God

Humankind is created on the same day as the other animals but is distinct from the other animals in that *ʾādām* is explicitly and emphatically made/created "in the image of God." When one examines J's account one notes that, shortly after their creation and in the context of the serpent's and Adam's and Eve's wrongdoing, God declares, "*hā ʾādām* has become like one of us, knowing good and evil" (Gen 3:22). Whereas the knowledge that likens humankind to God in Genesis 3 is articulated within the context of humankind's having done evil and having been punished with toil and pain in childbirth, and with patriarchy, P likens humankind to God in the context of good. In Genesis 1, God determines repeatedly that each element of creation is good. Likening humankind to God, affirming that *ʾādām* has been made in the image of God, has nothing to do with evil and the knowledge of evil, a significant divergence from J's account in Genesis 3. Why is this important?

I would like to suggest an exilic/post-exilic context for Genesis 1:27-28. The people had been steeped in sin; they had acted wrongly; they had done evil; they were bad. As the details of the fall of Judah faded, the lasting theological impression—the summary, the bottom line—was that the people of Israel had sinned; their enemies had accomplished their deserved destruction, as well as the destruction and dispossession of all that had been theirs. God reasserts, through Genesis 1, then, that all creation—everything, humankind included, is *good*. The exilic and post-exilic Jews are, from P's perspective, not bad, but good. Whereas the earlier source makes the knowledge of both good and evil liken *ʾādām* to God, the later source emphasizes both humankind's goodness—a characteristic held in common with all elements of creation—and *ʾādām*'s likeness to God. Though dependent on creation, humankind is nonetheless very good; in fact, it is made in the image of God.

The returning exiles needed to have their egos stroked and their self-esteem raised; they needed to hear words of encouragement and empowerment. One can recall Deutero-Isaiah's God "who created you, O Jacob

. . . who formed you, O Israel" (2 Isa 43:1), the exiled people who were "precious" in God's sight and whom God loved (Isa 43:4).[4] Recall also the promises of the prophet Zechariah: (1) that the LORD will dwell in the midst of the people (Zech 2:11), and (2) that the LORD will return to Zion and dwell in Jerusalem (Zech 8:3). Through Jeremiah God has also declared love for the people (Jer 31:3) and promised restoration (Jer 31:4), and some would even attribute to P the omission of David's sin with Bathsheba from Chronicles.[5] The Priestly version of Genesis 1 not only affirms that the people are not bad but good, but also asserts that they have been created "in God's image, according to God's likeness."

Unlike the Genesis 2–3 account in which God declares, after Adam and Eve's eating of the fruit, that "the man has become like one of us, knowing good and evil" (Gen 3:22), P is intent on communicating that ʾādām is good. What an ego-booster to a discouraged and disheartened people! Being made in the image of God, then, is not an assertion of human rationality and/or superiority. Rather, it declares to a disheartened people that they are worthy after all. That is not an easy thing to do—as women who have worked with battered women can attest. The Priestly effort to empower the disempowered spawned the strong and comforting images of exilic and post-exilic prophets and, I suggest, significant variations from Genesis 2–3. Genesis 1:26, 28 are not just part of the Priestly introduction to the Pentateuch; they contain assertions intended to legitimate, with an affirmation of their goodness, human beings who are fully conscious of their potential to do wrong. If the exile were to generate the self-esteem that could lead to restoration, did not the returned exiles need to be convinced of their value? Instead of their being "above" the rest of creation, could not the verses have originally been intended to affirm humankind's value, not in comparison to or in competition with, but simply as the creation of a God who is gracious and will comfort Zion?

b. Male and Female: Fertility

The emphasis on male and female is followed by the injunction to be fruitful and multiply. While God made ʾādām in the image of God, male and female, the following verse adds, "God blessed them, and God said to them, 'Be fruitful and multiply and fill the earth . . .'" (1:28).

Human fertility seems to be affirmed more explicitly in Genesis 1 than in Genesis 2.[6] Is this due to coincidence, or narrative style, or history? Is not a high birth rate every bit as critical to a returning refugee population who seek to reoccupy their land and restore their prosperity as it was to the land's earliest settlers? Had the incentive to produce many children diminished during the exile, especially since many did not have their own land to farm, fewer children were needed, and those who prospered better in Babylon were not those who worked on other people's farms? Could the exile have been a time—like certain Christian centuries—when the affirmation of a comparison to YHWH, a male deity who was not sexually active, implied an absence of sexual activity as a good, though the Hebrew text nowhere explicitly records this? It would thus be important for the Priestly author not only to compare humankind to God but also to liken humankind to the animals. The Priestly author asserts that, like the animals, humankind is created on the sixth day; further, humankind is created male and female. The Priestly author implies, therefore, that humankind is essentially reproductively active. Further, P adds the explicit directive, "Be fruitful and multiply" (Gen 1:28). Humankind was both like YHWH and fertile.

Furthermore, the phrase *zākār ûněqēbāh* (male and female) is found only in Genesis 1:27 with respect to humankind, though it occurs several times with respect to the animals taken into the ark (e.g., Gen 6:18, 19;[7] 7:3, 9,[8] 16). These animals were intended to guarantee that, after the flood, the earth could be fully repopulated. Is the return from exile, then, understood by the Priestly source as a new creation, when repopulating Judah was essential if restoration was to be successful? Humankind as male and female is, then, like "every living thing of all flesh" (Gen 6:19; 7:16), like the birds (Gen 7:3), and even like everything that creeps on the ground (Gen 7:9). If we read the text from the perspective of the late sixth century B.C.E., or even later, a new or, more accurately, a renewed emphasis on reproduction seems appropriate, even necessary.

c. Dominion

Verses 27 and 28 tell humankind to "have dominion over the fish of the sea and over the birds of the air and over every living thing that moves upon the earth." Those whose consciousness is pervaded by their powerlessness as a conquered people do have power, a God-given power to use what they need of creation, a power they have in common with, to the same extent as, their conquerors. They are okay—they are likened to God; they are okay—they share in relationship with creation, similar to their conquerors; they are okay—animals are not their superiors.

What I am suggesting here is that the dominion directed in Genesis 1:26, 28 of human beings over other elements of creation was not originally meant to be interpreted as humans over other living things, but rather as humans being on an equal footing with all of creation. The literary artist chose to liken human beings to God in an effort to convince his audience that they were, in fact, despite their recent history and their current situation, *really* good. With a similar objective the Priestly source here affirms the value of human beings by asserting their positive relationship to other living things.

One may speculate that poor returning and returned exiles, and those who had remained in the land, might have been tempted to value animals and other things more than people. The assertion that human beings could have dominion over other living things, then, may have been an attempt on the part of the Priestly source to assert humankind's value as equal to, not greater than, the value of mules, camels, and other animals. Certain animals might have been considered more valuable than other humans for human survival. Some animals would have been stronger, better able to farm and to provide humans with transportation, and to do other things that human beings could not do. Perhaps animals could even have served as objects for barter. In contrast, human beings might have been considered less powerful, less valuable, even less self-sustaining than some animals, but human beings are here given dominion over them.

Since the earlier creation narrative is quickly followed by Genesis 3 and human beings' unfaithfulness to God, one may wonder whether the Priestly author decided to add the peculiarities of Genesis 1:26, 28 in response not only to Genesis 3 but also to Genesis 6:1-4, where the sons of God *(bĕnê hā ʾĕlōhîm)* take wives for themselves from the daughters of men *(bĕnôt hā ʾādām)*.[9] Although some have interpreted this as part of the evil on account of which God sends the flood, the text does not make an explicit causal connection; verse 3, however, which is inserted between the two references to the sons of God and the daughters of *ʾādām,* asserts that God's "spirit shall not abide in mortals forever, for they are flesh," and concludes by limiting humankind's lifespan to one hundred twenty years. The concluding verses of Genesis 3 record God asserting that "the *ʾādām* has become like one of us, knowing good and evil," and then, immediately following, express God's concern that *ʾādām* "might reach out his hand and take also from the tree of life, and eat, and live forever" (3:22). Genesis 3:22 and 6:3 both suggest that bad behavior results in a limited lifespan. The bad behavior of Genesis 3 results in changed relationships within the cosmos, and the human evil of Genesis 6 results in cosmic destruction. The Priestly creation narrative may intend to shift the emphasis of the earlier author by affirming the potential for new life, omitting any reference to life's ending, and also shifting the negative judgment of Genesis 6:2-4, establishing not a hierarchy but boundaries. God has created both male and female, like the animals of Genesis 7, that will repopulate the earth; ʾādām, both male and female, is created in the image and likeness of God; all this is good. What is not good is the sons of God coming in to the daughters of men. The Priestly version of creation emphasizes good, deliberately omitting any references to evil. Humankind, like God's other gifts of creation, is created good and is likened to God, though the chapter implies by omission that human beings have no knowledge of evil (cf. Gen 3:22). Human sexuality, like the sexuality of other created beings (e.g., Gen 7:3, 16), possesses the potential for reproduction. Though P gives humankind dominion over other living beings and likens them to God, the author does not necessarily intend to imply that humankind, made in the image of God and possessing dominion over other living things, is consequently superior.

d. A Word about Food

In Genesis 1:29 God allows ʾādām to eat "every plant yielding seed that is upon the face of all the earth, and every tree with seed in its fruit." God gives "every green plant" for food "to every beast of the earth, to every bird of the air, and to everything that creeps on the earth, everything that has the breath of life" (1:30). That animals eat, basically, what humankind eats is another expression of what animals have in common with human beings, and vice versa.

Vegetarians sharply contrast these verses not with Genesis 2–3, which allow humankind to eat of the fruit of the trees in the garden (Gen 2:16; 3:2),[10] but with Genesis 9:3,[11] which declares, after the flood, that "every moving thing that lives shall be food for you. . . ." The question arises as to why the Priestly source cites vegetation as the appropriate food for humans in Genesis 1—food similar to that cited in Genesis 2[12]—when Genesis 9:1-17, the Priestly account of the post-flood re-creation, allows humans to eat animals for food as well.

In an attempt to reconstruct the historical situation, I can find the directives of Genesis 1:29-30 that reinforce the content of both Genesis 2:16 and 3:2 helpful in a post-exilic Judah. There are certainly situations when the poor might be better served by keeping the cow or goat or chicken alive as a long-term source of milk and eggs rather than slaughtering them for a much-needed, but perhaps short-sighted meal. The temptation when food is scarce is to slaughter animals, but if the land is to be farmed, the mules and oxen will be needed. An encouragement to eat seeds and fruit and plants is both consistent with the tradition expressed in Genesis 2:16 and conducive to Judah's ultimate restoration.

On the other hand, a very poor people can also succumb to behavior that is not here deemed appropriate, cannibalism. Lamentations suggests that the exile brought with it such famine and hunger that mothers ate their children (Lam 2:20; 4:9-10). Genesis 9 is clear that though animals may be eaten, their blood may not be.[13] What the text emphasizes is that human beings should not be killed, and implicitly, I suggest, not be eaten.[14] Notwithstanding the fact that Genesis 9 allows for the human consumption of animals (v. 3),[15] the Priestly account of creation recorded in Genesis 1 associates vegetation with appropriate human food and accomplishes three goals: it preserves the tradition articulated in Genesis 2; it preserves the animals needed for farming, transportation, and as a consistent source of food; and it outlaws, without mentioning it explicitly, what was perhaps a painful memory of the worst suffering of Judah's destruction, the temptation to cannibalism.[16]

CONCLUSION

My starting point was my conviction that the texts contain potential for interpretation from a cosmological-interdependent perspective. As literature I believe they do; I also believe they do according to the intents of their authors. I have long believed that it is not human beings who are superior to other aspects of creation, but rather it is human beings who are dependent on God's other gifts of creation for our very survival. What I have tried to explore here is why P wrote Genesis 1 as he/they did, with some emphasis on why the Priestly source likened 'ādām to God. This attempt at historical reconstruction nudges me further to the conviction that the earliest writers had no intention of developing a rationale for human superiority, that on the contrary their consciousness was much more aware of the fragility and interdependence of all living things.

The Priestly source made certain significant changes in the earlier version of creation. He/they unqualifiedly affirmed that all creation is good; he/they affirmed that 'ādām, male and female, has been created "in the image, according to the likeness of God." Further, the Priestly author asserted that male and female need to be fruitful and multiply, and that humankind is to have dominion over fish, birds, cattle, wild animals, and every creeping thing. Finally, the Priestly source confirmed that, ideally though not always in fact, fruits and plants are the appropriate foodstuff of all other living things.

Lothar Perlitt's book on covenant,[17] itself ancient history now, makes the insightful point that things begin to be emphasized when a culture no longer takes them for granted. He posits that the Hebrew word *bĕrît* is actually a late term, dating to a time when the sanctity of covenants was called into question. This insight prompted me to question what the Priestly source truly meant when asserting that God created human beings in the image and likeness of God, a phrase that has been used to justify anthropocentrism and hierarchy. His insight supports my conclusion that when the post-exilic community was experiencing its diminished power, the Priestly author affirmed its goodness. Therefore one may legitimately conclude, even from a historical perspective, that no part of the chapter was intended to defend hierarchy and patriarchy, nor should it be so used today.

NOTES: CHAPTER 2

[1]Biblical quotations used in this paper are taken from the New Revised Standard Version unless noted otherwise.

[2]While the NRSV translates "them," the Hebrew pronoun is masculine singular in agreement with its singular masculine antecedent *ʾādām*.

[3]The New International Version translation of *ʿēzer kᵊ negdô*.

[4]Deutero-Isaiah is traditionally dated to the period of Judah's exile.

[5]Historical criticism has traditionally attributed the books of Chronicles to Priestly authorship. Even if this were not the case, the books present an affirmation of Judah consistent with other exilic and post-exilic literature.

[6]While commentators routinely interpret Genesis 2:24 ("Therefore a man leaves his father and his mother and clings to his wife, and they become one flesh") to mean sexual intercourse with the likelihood of children, the verse can include more than a physical relationship.

[7]Also commonly attributed to the Priestly source is Genesis 7:16. See, for example, Lawrence Boadt, *Reading the Old Testament: An Introduction* (Mahwah, NJ: Paulist, 1984) 105, and Frank S. Frick, *A Journey Through the Hebrew Scriptures* (Fort Worth: Harcourt Brace, 1995) 103. My reason for citing introductory texts in the note is to emphasize the common character of the source attribution.

[8]Genesis 7:9 is commonly attributed to the Old Epic (JE) source which is dated earlier than the Priestly source. See, for example, Bernard Anderson, *Understanding the Old Testament* (4th abridged ed. Upper Saddle River, NJ: Prentice Hall, 1998) 44, where he cites both Martin Noth's *Pentateuchal Traditions* and Walter Harrelson's *Interpreting the Old Testament*. What is im-

portant to note is not that the phrase occurs in the earlier source, but that the Priestly source applied the phrase, in Genesis 1, to human beings.

[9] Genesis 6:1-4 is commonly attributed to the Old Epic (JE) source. See Anderson, *Understanding the Old Testament*, 144.

[10] Except, of course, for the forbidden tree of the knowledge of good and evil.

[11] Genesis 9:1-17, the first part of a chapter that details God's unconditional covenant with Noah and through him with all creatures, human and non-human, is commonly attributed to the Priestly source.

[12] The exception, of course, is that in Genesis 1 there is no forbidden plant or tree or seed.

[13] The prohibition against eating blood derives from the belief that one's life somehow resided in one's blood. See, for example, the Priestly Leviticus 3:17; 7:26-27; 17:10-14.

[14] Genesis 9:5-6 reads: "For your own lifeblood I will surely require a reckoning: from every animal I will require it and from human beings, each one for the blood of another. I will require a reckoning for human life. Whoever sheds the blood of a human, by a human shall that person's blood be shed; for in his own image God made humankind."

[15] From a narrative perspective what else was there for food after the flood had destroyed the earth's vegetation? However, the thrust of the chapter affirms the value of animals and humans together. God says, "I will remember my covenant that is between me and you and every living creature of all flesh" (9:15).

[16] The prohibition against shedding human blood is included between the Priestly directive to "be fruitful and multiply, and fill the earth" (9:1) and the repeated directive, "Be fruitful and multiply, abound on the earth and multiply on it" (9:7).

[17] Lothar Perlitt, *Bundestheologie im Alten Testament*. WMANT 36 (Neukirchen-Vluyn: Neukirchener Verlag, 1969).

3

Everyone Called by My Name: Second Isaiah's Use of the Creation Theme

Joan E. Cook, S.C.

INTRODUCTION

S econd Isaiah recapitulates the creation and redemption traditions to offer hope to the community of exiles from Jerusalem living in Babylon during the mid-sixth century B.C.E. In an effort to recognize and draw strength from interconnections, this essay examines not only the development of the two interweaving themes in relation to past, present, and future but also the insights we can glean for our own communities in the midst of profoundly alienating kinds of exile at the beginning of the new millennium.

The study proceeds in the following way: (1) a brief review of two recent collaborative analyses of the creation theme and its relevance for environmental concerns; (2) a summary of the creation theme in Genesis 1 and 2 and the theme of redemption in Exodus and Numbers, with an additional comment on other occurrences of the two themes throughout the Hebrew Bible; (3) an analysis of five passages from Second Isaiah, specifically Isaiah 40:12-31; 41:1-5; 41:17-20; 42:5-9; 43:1-7, all of which provide clear illustrations of Second Isaiah's creative and holistic juxtaposition of the two themes; and finally (4) a comment on the ways in which Second Isaiah's message can energize contemporary communities that struggle to overcome the many forms of alienation in society today.

INTERDISCIPLINARY APPROACHES TO THE THEME OF CREATION

In two recent works that focus on the connectedness of all creatures, various scholars address current concerns for the marginalized within creation. In *All Creation Is Groaning: An Interdisciplinary Vision for Life in A Sacred Universe*[1] contributors highlight human responsibility toward the earth. For example, David Alexander, a microbiologist, acknowledges the divine commission to humans to care for the earth that sustains us.[2] Claude Pomerleau, a political scientist, addresses the necessity brought about by globalization to consider the common good, including that of the environment.[3] Theologian Russell A. Butkus stresses that all creation is fundamentally dependent on the "ongoing sustaining power and presence of God or it will return to its chaotic state."[4] Carol J. Dempsey, biblical scholar, discusses the inherent link between creation and redemption that "leads to a vision of a new creation characterized by a return to harmonious relationships between God, ourselves, and the natural world."[5] Contributors to *The Earth Bible* series work from a list of six ecological principles to address conceptual concerns and analyze specific biblical passages from the perspective of care for the earth.[6] In the series' fourth volume, *The Earth Story in the Psalms and the Prophets,* contributors encourage their audience "to begin relating to Earth as kin rather than commodity, as partner and co-creator rather than property."[7]

CREATION AND REDEMPTION THEMES IN THE HEBREW BIBLE

The two versions of the creation story in Genesis 1–2 (the P narrative, Gen 1:1–2:4a, and the J narrative, Gen 2:4b-25) offer complementary cosmogonies. They also use particular vocabulary words that not only name the divine actions in each story but also portray the dynamic processes the stories describe. The two depictions paint complementary pictures of the Creator as well. Attention to the details of both narratives illustrates these two points.

The story in Genesis 1:1–2:4a depicts a purposeful, orderly calling-into-being of the cosmos over a period of six days. The account names several divine creative acts: speaking, separating, naming, and seeing that it was good. Significant terms that appear in the account are *bārāʾ* ("to create"), the overarching divine act throughout; *rûaḥ* ("wind," "breath," "spirit"), whose persistent stirring over the waters is the story's first action, and the verb *qārāʾ* ("to call"), which designates the process of naming the creatures. God is the Creator whose power speaks all of creation—the heavens and the earth and all that fills them—into existence.

The story that follows in Genesis 2:4b-25 portrays the Creator in a more anthropomorphic way. Here God fashions the universe by performing human acts such as planting, making to grow, and fashioning out of the ground. Various Hebrew words are used to refer to human beings, one of which indicates the relationship the first human being has to the ground. Specifically, *ʾādām*, the first human being, was fashioned from *hā ʾādāmâ* ("the ground"). The second human being, the *iššā* ("woman") was created from the rib of the first human being, was named by *hā ʾādām* (the man), and was said to be a suitable companion to him. The divine acts of creation in the Genesis 2 story are expressed by the verb *yāṣar* ("to form"), a "hands-on word" for the divine creative actions. Human breath, by which the first creature became a living being, is indicated by the noun *nišmat*.

Both Genesis 1:1–2:4a and Genesis 2:4b-25 depict Creator God assigning responsibility to human being. In Genesis 1:26 we hear: "Let them have dominion over the fish of the sea, and over the birds of the air, and over the cattle, and over all the earth, and over every creeping thing that creeps upon the earth." In Genesis 2:15 the first human being is given the task of tilling and keeping the garden.

The books of Exodus and Numbers describe the Israelite experience of deliverance from bondage and oppression at the hands of the Egyptian leaders,[8] and the creation of God's own people Israel, an event that takes shape in the midst of the people's wandering in the wilderness for forty years. Their collective redemption gave them a name and a sense of place. Of particular relevance in Exodus and Numbers is the motif of divine care God has for the people that God accomplishes through their leader Moses. This divine care is seen when God provides food and water throughout the wandering in the wilderness (e.g., Exod 15:22–17:7; Num 11:1-35), when God helps Moses and the people cross the Sea of Reeds as Pharaoh's army pursues them (Exod 14:1–15:21), when God's people encounter and defeat various enemies along the way (e.g., Exod 17:8-16; Num 21:21-35; 31:1–32:42), and when the people cross the Jordan River on their way into the Promised Land (Josh 3:1-17). Throughout the Exodus and journey into the Promised Land, God constantly supports the people, often in spite of their lack of faithfulness, or because of Moses' intercession (e.g., Exod 32:1-35; 33:12-19; Num 14:10b-25).

After the Pentateuch the two themes of creation and redemption usually appear separately in the Hebrew Bible. This is particularly evident in the Psalms, which often treat one or the other theme, but not both. For example, Psalms 8, 104, 146, and 147 focus on creation while Psalms 105, 106, and 114 concentrate on the Exodus. A few, such as Psalm 19 and Psalm 136, combine both themes. The Wisdom corpus highlights creation themes and only sporadically mentions the theme of redemption. For example, Job 38–41 and Proverbs 8:22-31 focus on creation. The book of Sirach, however, does treat both themes. It celebrates initial and ongoing creation in Sirach 42:15-25 and then highlights divine saving actions in its praise of Israel's ancestors in chs. 44–50. Wisdom of Solomon uses both themes in its praise of the works of Wisdom in Wisdom 10:1–11:14.

The prophets tend to treat the theme of redemption apart from creation.[9] For example, Jeremiah is promised divine deliverance (Jer 1:4-8), Hosea remembers the wilderness as a place of deliverance (Hos 2:14-23), and Amos uses redemption themes as part of his proclamation (see, e.g., Amos 2:6-16; 3:1-2). This separation of the two themes, while frequent throughout the Hebrew Bible, does not occur in Second Isaiah. On the contrary, the anonymous prophet of the exile weaves the two themes together to express and celebrate God's ongoing creative redemption of the people.

SECOND ISAIAH AND THE RE-CREATION OF REDEMPTION

Second Isaiah, in Babylon near the end of the exile, reminds the people of their traditions, particularly of creation and redemption, in order to bolster their faith in the God who appears to have deserted them. Throughout chs. 40–55 the prophet tells and retells, reworks, and reweaves the two foundational themes of creation and redemption, and invites the people to find strength for the present by remembering their heritage. The message, however, is not confined to recalling the past. Second Isaiah's message highlights creation and redemption as continuously ongoing divine movements in the life of the people, even during exile in Babylon. Furthermore, Second Isaiah looks beyond the contemporary situation toward a new future and describes it in terms of re-creation and redemption.[10]

Isaiah 40:12-31; 41:1-5; 41:17-20; 42:5-9; 43:1-7 are five passages from Second Isaiah that illustrate the creation-redemption theme with remarkable clarity.[11] Of particular interest in these passages are the descriptions and allusions to the Genesis creation stories, the references to Exodus-redemption events, the depictions of God, the point of view of the passages with regard to issues of human identity, and various perspectives in need of transformation.

Isaiah 40:12-31 is a disputation that can be easily imagined as the response to a question about the power of the gods. It consists of three sections, each of which begins with a question, with additional questions posed within each section. The first, vv. 12-17, begins with "Who?" and repeats the interrogatives "who?" and "whom?" in vv. 13 and 14. The second, vv. 18-26, begins "To whom?" It goes on to ask yes-no questions, and then repeats the questions "who?" and "to whom?" The third section, vv. 27-31, asks "Why?" as well as further yes-no questions.

Each section of the disputation develops a particular topic. Section one alludes to Ancient Near Eastern cosmogony, which highlights the anthropomorphic, immanent aspect of the Creator and earth as the first object of creation. For example, it names such actions as "measured the waters in the hollow of his hand," "marked off the heavens with a span," "enclosed the dust of the earth in a measure," and "weighed the mountains in scales." It asks rhetorically who advised the Creator, asserting by silence that there was no one. The question introduces the term *rûaḥ* YHWH ("Spirit of Yahweh"), using the word from Genesis 1:2. Here *rûaḥ* becomes associated with YHWH as a divine creative agent, bringing "the idea of the divine *rûaḥ* a step closer to God's personhood," a concept that emerged during the period of the exile (see also Isa 34:16).[12] The nations are both vast and infinitesimal: they symbolize the power and influence of large territories, but are "like a drop from a bucket," "dust on the scales," "less than nothing and emptiness."

Section Two declares the incomparability of God by contrasting the Creator with an idol made by human hands and with the short-lived rulers of the earth. It recapitulates the cosmogonic references and highlights divine power over creation. The section describes the ongoing aspect of creation, particularly in v. 24, with an elaboration on the ephemerality of a plant. (One is reminded of the divinely-appointed bush in Jon 4:6-8.)

Section Three acclaims the all-knowing aspect of God by highlighting divine eternity and divine understanding (v. 26b) with adjectives that describe the divine nature rather than divine actions. This kind of depiction is unusual in the Hebrew Bible, which tends to infer the divine attributes from a description of actions such as we find in vv. 12 and 22. Section Three concludes with a mention of the benefit of trusting in the LORD: perseverance is rewarded with strength.

Thus the disputation brings together the themes of cosmogony and the ongoing creation of the cosmos and of humans in one unified defense of the one God whose power made and sustains the universe.

When we consider the point of view of the passage we must acknowledge a discrediting of the nations here. The disputation does not discount all of creation, or even merely all the peoples of the world including the people of Judah, but rather everyone except the inhabitants of Judah. The nations are seen as outside the purview of divine protection. Earth itself is depicted as the first and ongoing object of creation, the clear illustration of divine creative power "to pluck up and to break down, to destroy and to overthrow, to build and to plant" (Jer 1:10).

Isaiah 41:1-5, a trial speech, immediately follows the previous passage. Verse 1 summons three parties: the coastlands, the people, and the LORD. In vv. 2-4 God speaks, taking credit for summoning Cyrus, the "victor from the east," and for making possible his military accomplishments just as God had called the generations from the beginning. The word *qārāʾ*, "to call," in these two instances links Cyrus' military success and the calling of the generations with the divine act of naming in Genesis 1:5, 8, 10 and 2:19. The juxtaposition of cosmogonic and ongoing creation highlights the continuity between the divine creation of the universe and the divine summons to Cyrus. Verse 5 describes the aftermath of the LORD's speech: silence of the other party as well as of the witnesses in the face of what they have just heard.

The speech highlights the divine creative power not only in bringing the cosmos into being but also in continuing to care for the universe by sending Cyrus as divine emissary. Just as in the previous passage the nations created by God were likened to dust, here the action of the victorious Cyrus makes kings "like dust with his sword." Cyrus thus is named the divinely appointed savior who will rescue the people from the Babylonians, just as First Isaiah named Tiglath-Pileser the divinely appointed rescuer of the people from the Assyrians (Isa 10:5-11).

The people are summoned as witnesses to the integrity of creation by symbolic association with the lands they inhabit. Second Isaiah, by using this figure of speech, fuses together the objects of creation: nature and people. The land and its inhabitants serve as plaintiff and witnesses to the divine defense, which is an *apologia* for divine power by reason of the Deity's creating and sustaining the universe.

The point of view of the passage corresponds to the previous one in its assumption that the nations are somehow outside the boundaries of divine concern. At the same time, however, Cyrus, a foreigner, is the divinely appointed savior of the exiles. Thus the position of non-Judahites is complexified here: on the one hand marginalized, but on the other hand recipients of the same divine ongoing concern reserved for the exiles from Judah.

Isaiah 41:17-20 is a proclamation of salvation in which v. 17a alludes to a lament: the poor are thirsty and there is no water. Verses 17b-19 are the announcement of salvation: the LORD will provide water. Verse 20 gives the statement of divine purpose: that all may know that the LORD has done these things.

The proclamation announces in abundant terms that water will spring from dry places, making possible the growth of trees, with the result that the desert will become habitable. The announcement alludes to the creation of the cosmos, specifically the harnessing of water to provide a habitat and to nourish the ground. It also recalls the LORD's caring for the people by providing water during the forty years of wandering in the wilderness. Finally, it foreshadows the return home to Jerusalem in its allusion to Isaiah 40:3-4, which describes the upsetting of the status quo that will mark the end of the exile.

In the statement of purpose the four verbs "see," "know," "consider," and "understand" attest to human ability to grapple with and finally grasp the meaning of the events described. The use of the verb *bārā'* identifies the provision of water as a creative act on the part of God. The statement recapitulates both creation and Exodus themes, asserting that the LORD has provided water in the wilderness. Synonymous parallelism in v. 20b highlights the immanence and transcendence of the LORD by referring to the divine hand and then reiterating the title "Holy One of Israel" that appears frequently in First Isaiah.[13]

Isaiah 42:5-9 is a call narrative within a messenger speech. The messenger identifies the sender (vv. 5-6a, 8) as God who created the cosmos and humans, and who has established a special bond with the one called. He further specifies that God is one, whose name is LORD and who worships no other deity. He announces the commission in vv. 6b-7, linking the prophetic call with the divine acts of creation, naming, and ongoing guidance. The prophet's task is one of redemption: to be a light that will liberate those oppressed by the darkness of blindness and imprisonment, among all the people (in other words, Israel) and the nations (everyone else). The sign of assurance in v. 9 that the divine word is trustworthy is the Deity's ability to name the future about to spring forth.

The links with the Genesis creation stories are numerous. The Creator's actions are described according to Ancient Near Eastern cosmogony, with emphasis on the anthropomorphic aspect of the Creator. This is evident in the verbs "stretch out," "spread forth," and "give breath" (see Gen 2:7). The vocabulary, however, links this call with Genesis 1 as well in the words "create" *(bārā')* and "spirit" *(rûaḥ)*, highlighting the transcendent aspect of God and the gift of divine power and wisdom bestowed on humanity.[14] In addition, the image of bringing light to those in darkness alludes to the divine command, "Let there be light," the first words of creation in Genesis 1:3.

The call also highlights Second Isaiah's belief that God is one, using "I" eight times, six as the subject of a verb. The one God is twice identified by name, YHWH, who cares specially for the people (singular) and sends them (singular) forth with assurances of intimate, nurturing presence. This call to be prophets, given in the singular, highlights the communitarian aspect of the chosen ones.

Further protection can be assured by the divine ability to proclaim the future. Just as God's instructions to Moses regarding how to confront the Pharaoh (Exodus 6–11) included the reassurance that God knew how events would turn out, likewise the prophet can take comfort in the divine knowledge of what would now happen. This juxtaposition of the three themes of creation, monotheism, and redemption illustrates Second Isaiah's insight that the three are interrelated aspects of divine creativity.

The status and role of the nations in this passage is complex. On the one hand they are depicted as needing the redemption the prophet will bring; on the other they are linked with the people Israel as the recipients of redemption. This identification with Israel breaks down the designation of the nations as "other" and creates a unity among all the people in their need for release from bondage. Additionally, the status of earth is that of first object of divine creative activity, source of life to living things, and home to humans.

Isaiah 43:1-7 is an oracle of salvation within a messenger speech. The messenger names God's past action in v. 1b, focusing on the creation of Jacob and Israel—in other words, the people of the covenant. (The two names are synonymously parallel, as God gave Jacob the name "Israel.") The two verbs *bārā'* and *yāṣar* appear in the creation stories in Genesis 1 and 2. This allusion to the creation of the people brings together the themes of cosmogony and the events in the wilderness when God created the people Israel. Moreover, the consonants in the word "precious" are the same as in the imperfect of "form." In addition, the verb "redeem" makes explicit God's rescue of the people.

The customary "Fear not!" introduces the assurance of divine presence and intervention in vv. 1c-2. The assurance goes straight to the heart of the matter: "I have redeemed you; I have called you by name, you are mine." The first assertion identifies God as the one who rescued the people from social ostracism by claiming them as family members. The second part alludes to the giving of names in the creation stories (see Gen 1:5, 8, 10; 2:19, 23) and the divine-creaturely relationship established by that act. The chronology of the two divine acts suggests that the people became God's as a result of redemption rather than creation. Hence they are all God's adopted children. Then the LORD makes promises for the future: the people will not experience harm in trials by water and fire. The parallel statements regarding water recall the crossing of the Reed Sea and the Jordan River at the beginning and end of the Exodus events, alluding by merism to the creation of Israel as God's people. While no specific historical event seems evident in the parallel references to passing unharmed through fire, the words call to mind the bush that was burning but not consumed when God called Moses to lead the people out of Egypt (Exod 3:2). The promise of divine protection in the twin trials of water and fire highlights the divine presence among the people in times of trouble, reminding them of God's constant care throughout the forty years of wandering in the wilderness. (Trial by fire and water appears also in Ps 66:12.) Naming these two extreme conditions also creates a merism that offers assurance of divine presence throughout all of life's difficulties.

The explanation for why God chooses to act (vv. 3-4) reinforces the points made in the assurance of divine presence and intervention, adding the divine appellation favored by First Isaiah: Holy One of Israel. The relational assertion of the previous verses is intensified here with the amazing words "you are precious in my sight, and honored, and I love you." (Note that "you" is singular.) The nations are the items of barter by which God the redeemer buys back the people Israel.

A second assurance follows in vv. 5-7, beginning with the formulaic "Fear not!" This time the LORD promises redemption by means of ingathering of offspring from the four corners of the earth, a possible prediction that the people will be brought back from exile.[15] The strong relational tie between the LORD and the people is highlighted here: v. 5 refers to "your offspring"; then v. 6 calls the same returnees "my sons" and "my daughters."

Throughout the final verse of the passage the relationship broadens to include everyone. This occurs in three steps corresponding to the three clauses of the verse. "Everyone who is called by my name" (v. 7a) identifies Israel by association with the redemptive act of v. 1. The words also envelop the entire passage within the theme of a people called by God, further strengthening the bond with the assertion that the people "called by name" in v. 1 are "called by my name" in v. 7a. In v. 7b the oracle identifies the purpose of their creation: "for my glory." Then in v. 7c God asserts the divine creative role without any qualifiers, using the anthropomorphic verb "form" and the parallel generic verb "make" to describe the divine creative acts. By association with the Genesis creation stories, which assert the creation of all humanity, this final verse includes all people, not only Israel.

The above analysis illustrates Second Isaiah's interweaving of the two creation stories from Genesis 1 and 2 and the Exodus stories from Exodus and Numbers. Both accounts highlight the privileged role of humanity among all created beings.

The reference to "the Spirit of YHWH" in Isaiah 40:13 highlights the particular role of the divine spirit in creation and redemption. Second Isaiah folds the term into the disputation, asserting the divine "supremacy over the idols in his wisdom and power."[16] The same God both brings creatures into being and establishes familial ties with them, both makes them and makes possible for them a life of freedom from various forms of oppression. Isaiah 43:1-7 widens the scope of divine concern for the people by including redemption among the Lord's foundational acts on their behalf. Divine activity takes a further step in commissioning the prophet to continue the task of redemption, extending its reach among the nations throughout the world. This portrayal represents the high point of the Hebrew Bible's depiction of the Deity insofar as its scope encompasses all of creation, and the creative act itself includes creation, adoption, nurturance, and sending forth on a mission of redemption to all the world.[17] From a feminist perspective we may say that the book's point of view respects the integrity of creation to an extent that goes beyond the typical biblical understanding.

For the modern reader, however, the problem remains that the book seems to look on the nations as outside the traditional realm of divine protection. Only by special arrangement does the divine adoption of the nations take place.[18] The difficulty is still more complex because Second Isaiah records the divine commission to Cyrus, who, without knowing that he was God's emissary, released the exiles from their obligations to Babylonia. This complex portrayal of the nations invites and challenges the modern reader to search for a transforming appropriation that can provide meaning for us today.

Furthermore the book, while rich in appreciation for earth as object of divine creative activity, leaves to the contemporary reader's imagination the necessity for humans to care for it as our home and as our fellow creature. (See, however, *inter alia* Isa 51:3, which highlights earth as place and person.)

CONCLUDING COMMENTS

I suggest several possible transformative ways in which we today might read these texts. First, we might focus on the grammatically singular form of "you" in Isaiah 42:5-9 and Isaiah 43:1-7, reading the passages as words to us as individuals. As such they represent not so much a contrast between one people and another as a commission to each one to serve others in creative ways. Second, we might let Isaiah 40:12-31 and Isaiah 42:5-9 energize us with portrayals of the divine spirit that enlightened the Creator, who in turn imbued human beings with its power. That spirit challenges us to overcome the various forms of oppression we encounter and thus transform our world in wisdom. In fact, we hope that the same spirit can enlighten our own scholarly efforts to make the Bible accessible and meaningful for today's readers. Third, we might broaden our interpretation of the book's universal scope to encompass all people, and the earth, as creatures deserving of divine care and of human respect and stewardship. Fourth, we might focus on the desired result of the divine activity throughout Second Isaiah: that all will know the one God. While in Second Isaiah's day the challenge lay in telling "the nations" about the one God, our task today lies in striving to overcome the various forms of oppression we encounter among human beings, nations, and the environment as well as within ourselves. These are a few possibilities. In what additional ways does the creation-redemption theme in Second Isaiah challenge us today?

NOTES: CHAPTER 3

[1]Carol J. Dempsey and Russell A. Butkus, eds., *All Creation Is Groaning: An Interdisciplinary Vision for Life in a Sacred Universe* (Collegeville: The Liturgical Press, 1999).

[2]David Alexander, "Feeding the Hungry and Protecting the Environment," in *All Creation Is Groaning*, 95.

[3]Claude Pomerleau, "Toward an Understanding of International Geopolitics and the Environment," in *All Creation Is Groaning*, 135–36.

[4]Russell A. Butkus, "Sustainability: An Eco-Theological Analysis," in *All Creation Is Groaning*, 156.

[5]Carol J. Dempsey, "Hope Amidst Crisis: A Prophetic Vision of Cosmic Redemption," in *All Creation Is Groaning*, 270.

[6]The Earth Bible Team, "Guiding Ecojustice Principles," in Norman Habel, ed., *Readings from the Perspective of the Earth: The Earth Bible* (Sheffield: Sheffield Academic Press, 2000) 1:38–53.

[7]The Earth Bible Team, "The Voice of Earth: More than Metaphor?" in Norman Habel, ed., *The Earth Story in the Psalms and the Prophets: The Earth Bible* (Sheffield: Sheffield Academic Press, 2001) 4:28.

[8]For discussion of what can be known historically about the Exodus see William G. Dever, "Is There Any Archaeological Evidence for the Exodus?" in Ernest S. Frerichs and Leonard H. Lesko, eds., *Exodus: The Egyptian Evidence* (Winona Lake: Eisenbrauns, 1997) 57–66; and James K. Hoffmeier, *Israel in Egypt: the Evidence for the Authenticity of the Exodus Tradition* (New York: Oxford, 1997) 107–09.

[9]Carol J. Dempsey, however, demonstrates the significance of the two themes in her *Hope Amid the Ruins: The Ethics of Israel's Prophets* (St. Louis: Chalice, 2000).

[10]Richard J. Clifford and John J. Collins, eds., *Creation in the Biblical Traditions*. CBQMS 24 (Washington, D.C.: The Catholic Biblical Association of America, 1992) 8, n. 17.

[11]Carol J. Dempsey discusses this interweaving of themes, particularly of redemption and restoration, throughout the prophetic books in her *Hope Amid the Ruins*, 269–84.

[12]Wonsuk Ma, *Until the Spirit Comes: The Spirit of God in the Book of Isaiah*. JSOTSupp 271 (Sheffield: Sheffield Academic Press, 1999) 81, 109.

[13]Claus Westermann, *Isaiah 40–66: A Commentary*. OTL (Philadelphia: Westminster, 1969) 81.

[14]Ma, *Until the Spirit Comes*, 191.

[15]Westermann, *Isaiah 40–66*, 119.

[16] Ma, *Until the Spirit Comes,* 191.

[17] Genesis 1–11 also encompasses all of creation, depicting divine creative activity in a more concrete and less conceptual way.

[18] See, e.g., Andrew Wilson's explanation in *The Nations in Deutero-Isaiah: A Study on Composition and Structure* (Lewiston, N.Y.: Edwin Mellen, 1986) 325.

4

Wild, Raging Creativity: Job in the Whirlwind[1]

Kathleen M. O'Connor

*T*he divine speeches in the book of Job are creation texts. Among the most exquisite poetry in the Hebrew Bible, they should be numbered among other biblical creation accounts: Genesis 1–3; Proverbs 8; Psalm 104; Wisdom 7–9; and sections of Second Isaiah. Within a feminist/liberationist hermeneutic, however, the divine speeches have hardly seemed helpful. Women do not figure in them, and they appear to inscribe violence and combat in the description of the deity. Much contemporary interpretation has thoroughly desentimentalized the God of Job to reveal *him* to be a patriarchal, overbearing, and dominating deity.[2]

In these approaches, God challenges Job in order to silence, overpower, and shame him. God shows the Divine Self to be the more Macho One who outtalks Job the talker. The issues are predominantly ones of power and knowledge in a kind of intergalactic, pyrotechnical, and zoological rhetoric that falls upon Job like an asteroid from outer space. He is squashed. Splat!

I have some ideas about this. Maybe the point of view I just overstated represents in some cases a not-so-hidden supercessionism. Job needs the kind of revelation found in the New Testament. James G. Williams says, for example, "What Job calls for the Gospels focus on."[3] Or perhaps these interpretations reflect the turn to ethics in theology and the academy wherein power relations of justice and mutuality have become the touchstone of theological adequacy. As a Roman Catholic woman, how can I challenge such a starting point?

But these readings do not foreclose other possible readings. One of the few things about which commentators agree in Joban interpretation is that the divine speeches are beautiful in their literary structures and their imagery. Only rarely, however, does the beauty of the speeches receive critical attention.[4] In this essay I propose that the divine speeches are not about the bullying power of God; they are about the potent beauty of creation, of God, of Job himself.

To make my claims I draw upon form, setting, and the content of the divine speeches, and with the help of Elaine Scarry's theory of aesthetics I reflect on the significance of beauty in those speeches.[5] Then I invent feminist meanings.

1. Forms of the divine speeches. The speeches of God in the storm function as typical Wisdom genre; they give instruction through suggestion, juxtaposition, and indirection. They use the extra-human world to provide knowledge about the human world. The rhetorical questions of the speeches function as a vehicle of divine instruction that invites Job and the reader to come to their own conclusions about events in the storm. The questions are not a mode of intimidation but a "socratic" pedagogical device.

William Brown suggests that the larger genre that underlies the divine speeches is the covenant lawsuit *(rîb)* in which the stars, the mountains, creation itself are called forth as witnesses against humans.[6] God brings all of creation forward, but accusations and guilty verdict do not follow. Instead, the morning stars sing together and the heavenly beings shout for joy. The earth changes like clay under sealing wax and the dawn takes its post. Light disperses, wind scatters, and the water skins of the heavens tilt to water the earth. These aspects of creation are exquisitely beautiful, and they exist independently of Job.

2. The setting of the divine speeches is wild energy. The divine-human encounter takes place in a storm, a whirlwind *(hāsĕʿārāh)*. Layers of meaning associate with the storm. First, there are the obvious references to biblical theophanies. Second and more subtly, the storm evokes Job's own stormy life, whipped about within and without by chaotic forces. But third, if the storm is not only the divine venue for appearance but also an aspect of revelation, the storm itself implies a deity who is wild, beautiful, free, and deeply unsettling.

3. The content of the speeches is creation, its beauty and freedom, what Andrew Walls would call "the Household of Life." The subject of creation was first introduced by the addressee of the speeches, Job himself. In the curse of his birth (ch. 3) Job tries to "uncreate" the world, to turn day into night, light into darkness, life into death.[7] In the divine speeches God replies to Job's *rhetorical destruction* of creation with *rhetorical construction* and re-creation. The divine questions restore the world from the bottom up, from pillars to stars to animals.

Divine questions about creation do reveal that God's power and knowledge is superior to Job's. "Surely you know, for you were born then" (38:21). But Job does not know. No interpretive contest from me here. But what if we shift the hermeneutical emphasis of the questions from their interrogative aspects—"who? where? do you know? have you?" (alleged to be intimidating)—to the content of the questions, the subjects about which Job is ignorant? Such a shift results in a picture of what Dianne Bergant calls "the mind-boggling creativity" of God,[8] and the overflowing beauty of the cosmos and its inhabitants.

God's first speech concerns the habitat and its extra-human inhabitants, the second the specific inhabitants Behemoth and Leviathan. I have time only to sample the speeches' contents.

A. INANIMATE CREATION (38:1-38)

God's questions convey divine pride and delight in the beauty and energy of creation. Who shut in the sea when it burst out of the womb? (38:8). The sea, traditional symbol of chaos, is a newborn baby bursting from the womb, yet penned in and swaddled in clothes of clouds, an infant bursting into life, nurtured and protected.

> Have you commanded the morning . . .
>> and caused the dawn to know its place,
> so that it might take hold of the skirts of the earth,
>> and the wicked be shaken out of it? . . .
> Have you entered into the springs of the sea . . . ?
> Have you comprehended the expanse of the earth?
> Where is the way to the dwelling of light . . . ?
> Who has cut a channel for the torrents of rain,
>> and a way for the thunderbolt . . . ?
> Can you bind the chains of the Pleiades,
>> or loose the cords of Orion?

To all the questions, the answer is "no." Job does not know, cannot understand, cannot bind and loose the constellations because they are unbindable, unloosable. Nor does God claim to do so. The lightning flashes, the rain pours, the constellations are unbound. Creation pulses with beauty and energy. God praises it all by means of these questions. Rather than shaming Job, God glories in the world. The speech conveys divine pride in the cosmos like that of a new homeowner showing off her habitat.

B. ANIMATE CREATION (38:39–40:30)

From the creation of the habitat, the Creator moves to its animal inhabitants. Why these animals? What do they have in common? Why animals at all? Carol Newsom points to Othmar Keel's proposal that these animals derive from royal lists of hunted animals and icons of kings.[9] Keel may provide the source of the list, but wherever they come from, each of the animals is also beautiful and wildly, exuberantly alive. Job, who shares the cosmic habitat with these wild creatures, has nothing to do with their care and feeding. Neither does God. Control is not the issue.

(1) Lions: Can you hunt for their prey? No, nor does God claim to do so. They hunt for themselves, these kings of beasts, these symbols of monarchs, and they flourish.

(2) Do you know how mountain goats give birth? No, but they do give birth, and their young ones grow up and go forth. Job does nothing. God does nothing.

(3) Who let the wild ass go free? It scorns the tumult, ranges the mountain. Can you tie it in the furrow with ropes? No, but neither does God claim to do so.

(4) The horse, do you make it leap, paw, laugh?

Each of these animals is unbounded, fearless, and beautiful. Each follows its own way that Job can neither know nor control. And the only mention of divine control concerns the ostrich, whom God created without giving her wisdom, yet she is wild, fearless, and laughing (39:13-18). When God does claim to act, using "I" language (when I laid the foundations of the earth, I made the clouds for a garment, hail I have reserved for time of trouble: 38:4, 9, 23), the speech accentuates divine creativity more than control. The text celebrates abundant, fecund life that needs no control.[10]

C. THE MONSTERS (40:6[5]–41:34)

Behemoth and Leviathan are central to interpretations that see Job shamed and God as violent controller. Richard Clifford, for example, argues that the Behemoth and the Leviathan are mere playthings in the powerful divine hands.[11] Others find explicit violence in the texts. Tryggve Mettinger sees an "antagonistic theology" in Job.[12] And Jon Levenson writes, "While Behemoth is declared to be a creature of God, Leviathan is not so described in the longer section devoted to him. We hear only of God's heroic capture and conquest of the great sea beast."[13] But do we?

No. Instead, God brags about, celebrates, and praises these beautiful creatures, as if proud, even in awe of them. God's questions neither assert nor imply divine conquest; rather they show God rejoicing in the animal's power, beauty, and independent fearlessness. If the ancient combat myth of creation lurks here, it has been seriously defanged. The text does acknowledge that only God can approach Behemoth with a sword (40:19), but there is no indication that God does, has done, or intends to do so. Instead, both animals become exemplars of divine pride, and as John Gammie proposed, both are mirrors of Job's self, his beauty and fearlessness.[14]

40:15-24: Behemoth

"Look at Behemoth, which I made just as I made you," declares God (40:15). This command invites Job to compare Behemoth to himself.[15] Behemoth, strong, stiff-tailed, iron-boned, "is the first of the great acts of God, only its maker can approach it with the sword" (40:19), but the Creator does not. Instead of engaging in combat, Behemoth, in turn, eats where all the wild animals play, rests under the lotus, finds a place in the shade among the willows, yielding a picture of harmonious contentment. Even if the river is turbulent, it is not frightened. Job has kinship with this fierce beast, and it is his fierce independence that God recognizes and that God further invites in introductions to the speeches. Who is this that darkens counsel? Gird up your loins like a *gêbêr* (38:2-3; 40:7). Have you an arm like God, and can you thunder with a voice like hers? (40:9). "Deck yourself with majesty and dignity . . . then I will acknowledge that your own right hand can save you" (40:14).

41:1-34 Leviathan

The sea monster Leviathan is even more fearsome and resistant to capture. About him God also brags, this time at length, and asks over and over if Job can capture, tame, conquer, or injure this creature. How could he? No one can. Any hope of capturing it will be disappointed, for even the gods are overwhelmed at the sight of it (41:9)! No one is so fierce as to dare to stir it up. Who can stand before, who can confront it and be safe, who under the whole heaven, who? The answer is no one, only God, but God does not. God is not in conflict with the symbol of chaos and terror. God is eloquently proud:[16] "I will not keep quiet concerning its limbs," or its mighty strength, or its splendid frame, its back, its teeth, its breath of fire (41:12-21).

> It makes the deep boil like a pot; . . .
> On earth it has no equal,
>   a creature without fear.
> It surveys everything that is lofty;
> It is king over all that are proud. (41:31-34)

Although both creatures are capable of ferocious battle, this text is not about battle, or conflict, or hostility with God, or Job's inability to conquer them. It is about God's pleasure in their beautiful wildness. God is not a bully in these speeches. Job is not humiliated. Instead he is presented with the beauty and wild freedom of creation and Creator.

D. A FEMINIST HERMENEUTICS OF THE DIVINE SPEECHES: CREATING MEANING

But what significance can an experience of beauty have for Job? Is emphasis on beauty in the speeches not simply another abstraction that ignores Job and his immense suffering? Elaine Scarry's book *On Beauty and Being Just* offers suggestive possibilities to the contrary. Beauty, she asserts, is sacred, unprecedented, life-affirming, life-saving, life-giving.[17] It brings about a transformation at the very roots of the beholder's sensibility. It affirms one's being and becomes an occasion for "unselfing," freeing one to be in the service of something else.

In this light, rather than ignoring Job, the divine speeches greet him, affirm him, bless him. Carol Newsom proposes that Job gains an expanded moral vision of his place in the world during the storm. But if Scarry's theory is correct, something more is taking place. The divine speeches not only expand Job's ethical frame "beyond family and village" to include the cosmos; the heart-stopping beauty revealed in the storm transforms him. The experience of beauty with its intense and involuntary pleasure can have these three effects:

- Beauty focuses one outward, requiring the relinquishment of one's imaginary position at the center of the world.

- Beauty creates a sharpened attentiveness, a "heightened state of alert," necessary also for recognizing injustice and for opening oneself to extend care toward the world.[18]

- Beauty "incites, even requires" creativity in the replication of that which is beautiful.[19] Experience of beauty is, therefore, the source of all creativity.

The beauty of the divine speeches in Job is not an accidental literary feature or merely a pleasant harmonious aesthetics, but revelation itself. The beauty in the storm is fearsome, wild, free. It is attracting power, akin to Rudolph Otto's notions of *mysterium tremendum, mysterium fascinans,* what he calls "the sheer absolute wondrousness that transcends thought."[20] Job's experience of beauty does not explain his suffering, but it transforms him. I have insufficient time to analyze his responses in the storm and the epilogue, but both texts point toward a Job changed by beauty. There is language of sight, "but now my eyes see you," (42:5); there is Job's unselfing, "I put my hand over my mouth, I am of small account," "I repent of, in, or concerning dust and ashes" (42:6). There is evidence that his focus turns outward as he repairs injuries, interceding for his friends and extending extraordinary care to his daughters. Job has received a life-affirming greeting from another world, and however we deal with the many lingering puzzles of this book, its beauty calls to readers were we, in our flattened technological, consumerist world, but open to it.

Within a feminist/liberationist hermeneutic the divine speeches invite us to open ourselves to the amazing beauty divinely loosed in the cosmos, to look for it, to let it whoosh through us, to heed it, and to obey. The speeches invite us to participate in God's wild, raging creativity, to replicate beauty, to create new beauty, to generate harmony and wild freedom in our work, our relationships, to extend our realm of care from our families to the whole cosmos and its denizens, to make a world where creative flourishing is available to all beings. The speeches urge us to be like the animals and the monsters, Behemoth and Leviathan, wild, fearlessly ourselves, exuberantly alive. They call us to pulse with life, to be strong, to yell and shout like Job, to find our place in the world and to take no one else's. They require us to throw off colonized spirits, self-silencing, great fears, endless self-critiques. They demand radical resistance to all forms of silencing, bullying, and denial of and destruction of the beauty and creativity of women, children, men. They call for the disciplined avoidance of such tactics ourselves with students, family, friends, women's groups, colleagues, communities. They invite endless, joyous labor for justice for the earth and all creatures.

NOTES: CHAPTER 4

[1]Earlier versions of this article were presented as a paper at the annual meeting of the Catholic Biblical Association, Feminist Hermeneutics Task Force, August, 1999, and the annual meeting of the Society of Biblical Literature, Feminist Hermeneutics Section, November, 2000. It was previously published in Brent A. Strawn and Nancy R. Bowen, eds., *A God So Near: Essays on Old Testament Theology in Honor of Patrick D. Miller* (Winona Lake, Ind.: Eisenbrauns, 2003) 171–79.

[2]See Edwin Good, *In Turns of Tempest: A Reading of Job with a Translation* (Palo Alto: Stanford University Press, 1990); David Penchansky, *The Betrayal of God: Ideological Conflict in Job.* Literary Currents in Biblical Interpretation (Louisville: Westminster John Knox, 1990); Susan E. Schreiner, *Where Shall Wisdom Be Found? Calvin's Exegesis of Job from Medieval and Modern Perspectives* (Chicago: University of Chicago Press, 1994); and Jon Levenson, *Creation and the Persistence of Evil: The Jewish Drama of Divine Omnipotence* (San Francisco: Harper & Row, 1988). This listing, of course, overlooks other readings, such as Gustavo Gutierrez, *On Job: God-Talk and the Suffering of the Innocent* (Maryknoll, N.Y.: Orbis, 1987) and J. Gerald Janzen, *Job* (Atlanta: John Knox, 1985), but the former views seem to be dominant.

[3]James G. Williams, "Job and the God of Victims," in Leo G. Perdue and W. Clark Gilpin, eds., *The Voice from the Whirlwind: Interpreting the Book of Job* (Nashville: Abingdon, 1992) 226, and see 220 on the "rivalry of God and Job," which leads me to the conclusion that Williams sees the speeches as God's power play.

[4]The few works that do this include Carol Newsom's "The Book of Job," *The New Interpreters Bible* IV, ed. Leander E. Keck (Nashville: Abingdon, 1996) 317–634, and an essay by Corrine L. Patton, "The Beauty of the Beast: Leviathan and Behemoth in Light of Catholic Theology," in Stephen L. Cook, Corrine L. Patton, and James W. Watts, eds., *The Whirlwind: Essays on Job, Hermeneutics and Theology in Memory of Jane Morse.* JSOTSup 336 (Sheffield: Sheffield Academic Press, 2002).

[5]Elaine Scarry, *On Beauty and Being Just* (Princeton: Princeton University Press, 1999).

[6]William P. Brown, *The Ethos of the Cosmos: The Genesis of Moral Imagination* (Grand Rapids: Eerdmans, 1999) 340.

[7]Leo Perdue, "Job's Assault on Creation," *HAR* 10 (1986) 295–315; Kathleen M. O'Connor, "Job Uncreates the World," *TBT* 34 (1996) 4–8.

[8]Dianne Bergant, *Israel's Wisdom Literature: A Liberation Critical Reading* (Minneapolis: Fortress, 1997) 44.

[9]Newsom, "Job," 617.

[10]Brown, *Ethos*, 366.

[11]Richard Clifford, *Creation Accounts in the Ancient Near East and in the Bible.* CBQMS 26 (Washington, D.C.: The Catholic Biblical Association of America, 1994) 196.

[12]Tryggve Mettinger, "The God of Job, Avenger, Tyrant or Victor?" in Perdue and Gilpin, *The Voice*, 39–49, especially 48.

[13]Levenson, *Creation and the Persistence of Evil*, 49; see also René Girard, "Job as Failed Scapegoat," in Leo G. Perdue and W. Clark Gilpin, eds., *Wisdom and Creation: The Theology of the Wisdom Literature* (Nashville: Abingdon, 1994) 192.

[14]John Gammie, "Behemoth and Leviathan: On the Didactic and The-ological Significance of Job 40:15–41:26," in idem, et al., eds., *Israelite Wisdom: Theological and Literary Essays in Honor of Samuel Terrien* (Missoula: Scholars, 1978).

[15]Gammie, "Behemoth," 221.

[16]As Newsom ("Job," 617) observes, there is no hostility between God and these beings.

[17]See Scarry, *On Beauty and Being Just*, 23–28.

[18]Ibid. 58.

[19]Ibid. 5.

[20]Rudolph Otto, *The Idea of the Holy* (Oxford: Oxford University Press, 1924) 81. I am grateful to Walter Brueggemann for this reference and to Christine Yoder for suggestions regarding sight in the text of Job.

5

Soundings in the New Testament Understandings of Creation

Barbara E. Bowe, R.S.C.J.

THE CONTEXT OF THEOLOGY IN AN AGE OF SCIENCE

*A*s theologians and exegetes, we do our exegesis and theology today in the world of quantum physics and in a universe known through the lens of the Hubble telescope. From that vantage point we recognize—today as never before—that *creation*, the whole cosmos, is unfathomably "immense, unfinished, intricately interrelated, and marked on this planet by a uniquely conscious form of life."[1] These four characteristics situate us and provide the context for all our theological inquiry. It is important, therefore, to explore further the meaning of each of these various features of our contemporary, scientific worldview.

First, we claim that creation is *immense* both in its size and in its duration, well beyond even our capacity to conceive or imagine. Some estimate its age between fifteen and twenty billion years. Its size is even more incalculable. We know now that, by some scientific estimates at least, there are literally billions of galaxies in the vast reaches of space, and each galaxy has within it billions of stars. The human mind can hardly conceive of such expansive dimensions. Today we have the capacity to see deep into the farthest reaches of space and to be awed as never before by its beauty, its intricacy, and its ultimate mystery.

In a similar vein, as some scientists remind us, the universe itself is also *unfinished* and continues to grow and expand even as we speak. If the "Big Bang" model of cosmology is correct, then all of creation is the outcome of a primordial moment when the concentration of energy in the universe, perhaps no larger than the head of a pin, exploded outward, forming subatomic particles: protons, neutrons, and electrons. As matter cooled and space continued to expand, atoms formed. This "process of expansion has continued for some fifteen billion years until it has brought forth the cosmos as we now observe it."[2] Creation, therefore, viewed through the lens of modern science, is not a single moment in time long ago, nor even a series of evolutionary moments leading to the creation of *homo sapiens,* but is (at least in some theories) an infinitely dynamic and open-ended process.

For the modern physicist, moreover, creation is itself *interrelated* at every point. Again, Zachary Hayes describes the characteristic well when he comments: "Whether we look down through microscopes or outward through telescopes, we seem to be confronted with systems within systems within yet other systems. That is, we seem not to find a lot of isolated realities, but [rather] realities that seem to be remarkably interrelated at a variety of levels."[3] Or, as Diarmuid O'Murchu suggests, "In modern physics, the image of the universe as a machine has been transcended by the alternative perception of an indivisible, dynamic whole whose parts are essentially interrelated and can be understood only as patterns of a cosmic process."[4]

A fourth aspect of the cosmos is *the uniqueness of Planet Earth,* which has produced a rich variety of living organisms, from the simple to the most complex, culminating in "the particular form of life that is *intelligent, conscious life* in the form of human beings."[5] This planet is the jewel-like sphere the Apollo astronauts saw from space. Scientists recognize that planet Earth's relatively paper-thin atmospheric covering preserves a precarious and mysterious balance of particles and chemicals whose precise mathematical relationships converge to support life. This apparent "fine tuning" of the universe toward the support of conscious life forms prompted the scientific theory of the "anthropic principle" that claims that the very laws and structures of the universe appear to be critically adjusted somehow to make human life possible.

> . . . the conditions operative at the beginning of cosmic history were remarkably congenial to bring forth intelligent life. . . . only where these particular conditions prevail will we find a universe that is able to bring forth beings capable of being observers of the universe. These conditions have to do, above all, with the strength of gravity and the speed of expansion in the expanding universe, as well as with the forces that bind

neutrons and protons in the nucleus of the atom. If these were even minimally different, the universe would not be able to bring forth intelligent life, as we know it. The properties of matter, then, at the broader cosmic level and at the smallest scale of atomic structure seem to be uniquely suited to the origin of intelligent life.[6]

Nonetheless, although we know more about the cosmos, many contemporary scientists stand silent and dumbfounded before the fundamental and age-old question, "Why creation at all? What is it all for?"[7] Or, as the psalmist asked centuries ago about such wondrous immensity, "Who are *we* that you are mindful of us?" (Ps 8:4). This new, scientific, and post-modern consciousness of the character of creation and matter itself is the place from which we should explore biblical perspectives on creation and examine the biblical tradition as a "revelatory text."

CREATION THEMES IN THE NEW TESTAMENT

In the New Testament the belief in a Creator God (and, we might add, in the original goodness of all creation) "does not stand in the foreground of Christian reflection, but recedes behind the idea of God's saving acts in Christ."[8] The only direct reference to Genesis 1–2 in the New Testament is found in Mark 10:6 (*par.* Matt 19:4). Echoes of and allusions to the Genesis myth, however, are much more frequent, for example, in 1 Corinthians 11:8-9 and 1 Timothy 2:13-14. In addition, notions of new creation and the ultimate destruction of "this world" undergird the whole apocalyptic schema of Hellenistic Jewish and early Christian thought. The related ideas of an inaugurated and/or future reign of God (*basileia tou theou*) that would establish a new order of things, a renewal and re-creation or reversal of the present order, belong to the general landscape of our discussion of creation themes in their biblical contexts. The words and deeds of Jesus in the gospels, moreover, point to a new covenantal relationship with the God who is the source of all life. Healings, exorcisms, new liberating teaching with authority characterize the re-creative acts of God mediated through Jesus. In particular, belief in Jesus' resurrection, his ultimate vindication by God in a life beyond the grave, confirms the hope in an ultimate newness, a re-creation beyond death for those who are in Christ. New Testament notions of "creation," therefore, ought to be seen in this wider context of ideas and beliefs.

The most fruitful New Testament resources for our reflection, however, reside in the Pauline and post-Pauline traditions as well as the

Johannine writings. In Paul we encounter the most numerous occurrences of the specific terminology related to the creation theme *per se* in the *ktizō* word group. The principal meaning of these terms is clear. They point implicitly to God as Creator or to the entire work of God's creation. The ordinary meaning of the verb *ktizō* (establish, found) conveys the *intentional* dimension of the founder's creative act. In the Roman period it was the emperor, especially, who was hailed as the *ktistēs* (founder) of cities. This is the verb preferred in the New Testament for speaking of God's creative activity, rather than the term *dēmiourgeō* (engage in construction of something) that was preferred in non-Christian sources. Just as in Genesis 1, *ktisis* (creation) in the New Testament involves God's intentional activity and implies the powers of "order" gaining sway over "chaos." Joseph E. Fontenrose states: "Faith in the Creator God is thus faith in the reliability of the course of things," that is, faith in God's continuing presence and care for all of creation, "and trust in the future . . . dependence on powers beyond human control."[9]

Another term related to creation motifs in the New Testament is the term *kosmos.* While it occurs 186 times in the New Testament, including 37 occurrences in the Pauline writings, it is most prominent in the Johannine corpus (78x). The basic meaning of *kosmos* points to the "arrangement" and "order" of our "world/universe." The immediate origin of the term is probably Hellenistic Judaism, notably Wisdom 7:17; 9:3; 4 Maccabees 16:18; and Philo, *Spec. Leg.* I.81. Here the whole world was created by God "out of formless matter" (Wis 11:17; 2 Macc 7:28). The *kosmos* is the "earth" that humankind inhabits (Wis 2:24; 4 Macc 16:18), or humankind itself (Wis 6:24; 4 Macc 17:14). Two different but related referents for the term appear: where *kosmos* is "the totality of everything created by God, thus including all that is created and transitory," and where it refers "to the world as the dwelling place of humankind or as the totality of humanity or of human relationships."[10]

"This world" *(ho kosmos houtos)* refers to creation especially as the place of the transitory and sin, characterized by the absence of salvation and knowledge of God (John 8:23; 9:39; 12:25, 31; 14:30; 1 Cor 3:19; 5:10; 7:31, etc.). Nonetheless, it is the place of God's activity through Jesus the One Sent (John) and through the Spirit (especially in Paul). Above all, the created world is the locus of revelation and the object of God's abundant love.

It is clear from this review of vocabulary about creation themes that any discussion of the New Testament needs to be grounded in something much broader than mere references to the stories in Genesis 1 and

2 or to the occurrences of isolated vocabulary. New Testament ideas and beliefs about creation are more often implicitly present in symbolism and metaphor, not in explicit discussion of the Genesis stories. Tatha Wiley, for example, discusses Jesus' teaching on creation by examining his preaching about "the reign of God" as the symbol *par excellence* for the created order desired by God.[11] I prefer to explore Johannine language and symbols related to the diverse creation themes as a neglected resource for our contemporary understanding.

SYMBOL, METAPHOR, AND MYTH OF THE NEW CREATION: JOHANNINE INSIGHTS

Technical terminology like *kainē ktisis* (new creation) is not the only New Testament resource for new ways of thinking about creation in a feminist mode. The symbolic ways in which the author of John speaks about God's creative activity as mediated by the life and death of Jesus are particularly rich and fruitful. Josephine Massyngbaerde Ford has opened new ground as she has explored these symbolic, metaphoric, and mythic dimensions of the imagery of new creation in the Gospel of John.[12] A few examples will suffice to point out the significance of this perspective. First of all, the whole of the Fourth Gospel presents the story of Jesus as a "new act of creation." Beginning with the echo of Genesis 1:1 in John 1:1, "in the beginning" *(en archē),* readers are alerted to understand the whole story of Jesus' life, death, and resurrection in cosmic dimensions. The very structure of the prologue, moreover, alternates between the celestial-divine/terrestrial-human realms. By doing so it claims that the *logos* of God who, like Wisdom, has "pitched a tent" (John 1:14) with us, has fused forever the realms of the divine and the human. The created world mirrors the divine since its very fabric has been charged with the divine creativity: "all things came into being through [the Logos], and without him not one thing came into being" (John 1:3). This fusion of worlds, with Jesus as the creative agent and the "ladder" on whom the angels of God ascend and descend (John 1:51), is the creative, life-giving principle animating the whole Gospel. In this divinely infused world "light shines into darkness and darkness has not overcome it" (John 1:5), and rebirth in the Spirit (John 3:6) is the creative, regenerating energy of the life of the world. Ford comments: "Through the begotten, the life of the deity overflows into the human realm and becomes light for humanity. . . . This light flows into the world, that is, it is the *ekstasis* of the deity."[13]

John 1 and 2 continue this creation motif by means of the literary and structural division of "days": 1:29, 35, 43, and 2:1—*tē epaurion*; *kai tē hēmera tē tritē*—to suggest the inauguration of the Jesus story as a new "week of creation." Here the new creation effected by the Word made flesh draws its fundamental meaning from its connection with and evocation of God's new, life-giving activity long ago at Sinai. Just as Moses had told the people to ready themselves in preparation for God's coming "in a thick cloud" (Exod 19:9) *on the third day,* so Jesus' revelation of God's glory begins *on the third day* (John 2:1) at Cana.[14] The marriage context for the Cana story adds the unmistakable connection with biblical traditions of the messianic banquet as the crown and summit of the created world. Grandiose hyperbole marks the detail of the amount of wine created by Jesus' powerful action, i.e., between 120 and 160 gallons of wine. The messianic image from 2 Baruch comes immediately to mind:

> The earth will also yield fruits ten thousand fold. And on one vine will be a thousand branches, and one branch will produce a thousand clusters, and one cluster will produce a thousand grapes, and one grape will produce a cor[15] of wine. And those who are hungry will enjoy themselves and they will, moreover, see marvels every day. . . . And it will happen at that time that the treasury of manna will come down again from on high, and they will eat of it in those years because these are they who will have arrived at the consummation of time. (2 Bar 29:5-8)

This same text colors our interpretation of John 6 and the bread of life discourse, where the bread that Jesus gives is himself, the Word made flesh "for the life of the world" (v. 51). As a sign of the fullness of time when creation's destiny is finally made known, this bread is creative nourishment, and the person "who eats this bread will live forever" (v. 58).

Another Johannine text that is rarely cited as a resource for creation motifs is the scene of Jesus' death on the cross. Ford's reading of John 19 is particularly rich and insightful. She draws from the writings of the Syriac tradition (Ephraem and Jacob of Serugh in the sixth century) and interprets the lance thrust with the opening of Adam's side. For the Fourth Evangelist, therefore, the death of Jesus—redemption/new creation itself—is portrayed as a new act of giving birth, with vivid details of water and blood. The allusion to Adam's side further links the acts of creation and redemption as new creation. Ford concludes: "I suggest that Jesus goes to his passion and death not as a victim, nor as a scapegoat, nor as a bloody sacrifice, nor to appease a deity, nor to trap or pay a debt to the devil, but as a woman to give birth to her child through blood and water."[16]

Ford also analyzes the giving of the spirit in the gospel (19:30 and 20:22) and names it as "an act of creation or procreation and resurrection." She argues, and I agree, that one must "read the text against the background of the creation of Adam [Gen 2:7] and the resuscitation of Israel in the famous vision of the valley strewn with dead bones [Ezekiel 37]. . . . Jesus breathes upon the disciples to bring them the life and Paraclete he had promised. It may also be possible that the insufflation reflects the action of the midwife helping the newly born child to breathe."[17]

Along the same lines, could we not view the scene in the garden with Mary Magdalene as a new creation as well? Among the gospels only John points out that the new tomb where Jesus was laid was in a garden (*kēpos,* 19:41). Though John's Greek term differs from the "paradise garden" *(paradeisos)* of Genesis 2–3, the allusion to the Genesis account may still lie in the background. Mary's encounter with Jesus in that garden (John 20:11-18), in fact, fulfills and completes the promise of new "birth" announced in the Prologue (John 1:12). "But to all who received him, who believed in his name, he gave power to become children of God." This promise of new birth, new creation as God's children is now fulfilled in John 20:17, as Jesus says to Mary: "Stop holding on. . . . Go to my *adelphous* and say to them: I am ascending to my Father and your Father, to my God and your God." Mary, the *apostola apostolorum,* becomes the herald, the midwife of the new creation in the family of God. These few examples of the rich symbolism of the Gospel of John provide a new resource for considering the ongoing work of creation and redemption.

THEOLOGICAL IMPLICATIONS AND THE CONTEMPORARY FEMINIST AGENDA

Finally, what theological implications and questions emerge from this brief review of these diverse New Testament traditions and creation motifs? These traditions speak both explicitly, with technical vocabulary of creation *(ktizō, ktisis),* as well as implicitly, with a host of varied images and symbolic language. They convey both the nature and the purpose or ultimate destiny of God's creative activity in the world.

Creation and Redemption/Transformation/Reconciliation

First, it is clear from the foregoing survey that we need today a renewed definition of the relationship between creation and redemption, one that reaffirms the essential *interrelationship* between the process of becoming of the entire created world and its ultimate destiny. This comment raises again the question of Stephen Hawking: "Why creation at all? What is it all for?"[18] According to Ford, creation must be seen as "the result of that dynamic action of the triune God that brings to humankind, animals, and the whole creation the fullness of their being, the totality of their potential."[19]

Creation and Eco-feminism: Ethics of Creation as Interconnectedness/ Mutuality

Paul's emphasis in Romans 8 on the "whole of creation groaning" toward its ultimate goal should point the way for us, calling us to abandon our myopic androcentrism and to relinquish all our dualistic categories so abhorrent to feminist critics, namely, "binary opposition," inherited in part from a Platonic worldview of "good/bad, ideal/real, male/female, divinity/humanity, heaven/earth, spirit/body, slavery/freedom"[20] and in their place to embrace a new reverence for all forms of life.

Furthermore, we are invited to affirm a vision of the new creation, established by the one Spirit that lives and moves among us, that enlivens both our bodies and our minds, and that fuses us together as one fabric with all created life. Voices from the "new science" referred to in the beginning of this paper echo a similar chord. Margaret Wheatley, another contemporary voice, states:

> The results we observe speak to a level of quantum inter-connectedness, of a deep order that we are only beginning to sense. There is a constant weaving of relationships, of energies that merge and change, of constant ripples that occur within a seamless fabric. There is so much order that our attempts to separate out discrete moments create the appearance of disorder."[21]

Creation: Reordering of Relationships

Another insight and challenge for contemporary reflection on creation is the realization that creation's fulfillment lies not so much in an apocalyptic new order radically different from the present, but in a gradual *process* of regeneration and growth. Pierre Teilhard de Chardin is the outstanding contemporary defender of this view. In his *The Divine Milieu* (1957)[22] Teilhard championed the conviction that the cosmos was in the process of becoming, and that this process was marked simultaneously by increasing convergence and complexification of cosmic elements. Hayes declares, "Teilhard sees the cosmos to be thoroughly drenched with an almost magnetic energy that takes the form of a universal attraction to unite."[23]

Reordering, realignment, and re-creation of the cosmos are happening at every moment. "Chaos theory," in the new physics, posits the "complementarity of the principles of order and chaos—not their opposition."[24] A correlate notion is the theory of "strange attractors," whereby the "most chaotic of systems never goes beyond certain boundaries; it stays contained within a shape that we can recognize as the system's strange attractor."[25] At precisely this juncture chaos theory and process theology intersect. The process theologian recognizes that God wields power, "but it is exactly the power of attraction. God can be seen as the 'lure for creative advance into novelty.'"[26] This is the image of creation, and creation's destiny, as the seed growing secretly (Mark 4:27), or the leaven in the dough (Matt 13:33; Luke 13:20-21) that affirms the salvific/re-creative principle within the very structure of creation itself.

Creation as the Gradual Triumph of Love

Finally, this new understanding of creation will be based on love. Again Teilhard blends his scientific and mystical insights to affirm a process of the world's transformation effected through the power of love: "The image of fire stands for the warmth and radiance of love and light as well as the fusion and the transformation of the elements."[27] Teilhard's mystical vision of creation is a vision of love, similar to Paul's in Romans 8. "The day will come when after we have mastered the winds, the waves, the tides and gravity, we shall harness for God the energies of love. Then for the second time in the history of the world, [humankind] will have discovered fire."[28]

NOTES: CHAPTER 5

[1] Zachary Hayes, "New Cosmology for a New Millennium," *NTR* 12/3 (1999) 29–39.

[2] Zachary Hayes, *The Gift of Being: A Theology of Creation* (Collegeville: The Liturgical Press, 2001) 55.

[3] Hayes, "New Cosmology," 33.

[4] Diarmuid O'Murchu, *Quantum Theology: Spiritual Implications of the New Physics* (New York: Crossroad, 1997).

[5] Hayes, "New Cosmology," 34.

[6] Hayes, *The Gift of Being,* 84.

[7] Stephen Hawking, *A Brief History of Time* (New York: Bantam, 1988) 174.

[8]Gerd Petzke, art. *ktizō,* EDNT 2:325.

[9]Ibid.

[10]Ibid. 2:311.

[11]Tatha Wiley, "Jesus' 'Theology of Creation,' Economic Vulnerability, and the Human Good," unpublished paper presented at the Catholic Biblical Association meeting, August 8, 1999.

[12]Josephine Massyngbaerde Ford, *Redeemer, Friend and Mother: Salvation in Antiquity and in the Gospel of John* (Minneapolis: Fortress, 1997).

[13]Ford, *Redeemer, Friend and Mother,* 148–49.

[14]Francis J. Moloney, *The Gospel of John.* SP 4 (Collegeville: The Liturgical Press, 1998) 66.

[15]A cor measured approximately 35.4–60.738 gallons. See "Weights and Measures," *IDB* 4:834.

[16]Ford, *Redeemer, Friend and Mother,* 198.

[17]Ibid. 200.

[18]Hawking, *A Brief History of Time,* 174.

[19]Ford, *Redeemer, Friend and Mother,* 7.

[20]See Elizabeth Castelli, "Romans," in Elisabeth Schüssler Fiorenza, ed., *Searching the Scriptures: A Feminist Commentary* (New York: Crossroad, 1994) 285.

[21]Margaret Wheatley, *Leadership and the New Science. Learning about Organization from an Orderly Universe* (San Francisco: Berrett-Koehler, 1992) 20.

[22]Pierre Teilhard de Chardin, *The Divine Milieu* (New York: Harper & Row, 1960).

[23]Hayes, *A Gift of Being,* 109.

[24]Wheatley, *Leadership and the New Science,* 19.

[25]Ibid. 21.

[26]Ford, *Redeemer, Friend and Mother,* 76.

[27]Hayes, *A Theology of Creation,* 110.

[28]Teilhard de Chardin, *The Divine Milieu,* 144.

6

Sabbath, the Crown of Creation

Barbara E. Reid, O.P.

INTRODUCTION

*I*n the past, the formula 24-7-365 might have been mistaken for a telephone number or a lock combination. Today it is universally recognized as the shorthand way in which the culture in many first-world countries can be characterized: available twenty-four hours a day, seven days a week, 365 days a year. The speed of the Internet and the demands of a global marketplace now require that work continues around the clock, not only for providers of emergency services, but also for many businesses. Customer services, grocery stores, and video rental stores are open twenty-four hours a day. Seventy-hour work weeks and accessibility by beeper, cell phone, or e-mail after one has left the office are expected. Sleep deprivation, exacerbated by the lack of extended vacation time, has become a major health concern, and ironically contributes to decrease in productivity. In industrialized countries this scenario increasingly applies to upwardly mobile women as well as men.

For the poor, when work is available, the reality is that women often hold multiple jobs, working long hours seven days a week in order to try to make ends meet to feed their families. In remote regions of the Andean mountains of Ecuador, for example, extreme poverty, rapid population growth, and the degradation of the environment hold indigenous women in a vice-like grip. Men are often obliged to migrate to cities in search of employment. They leave the women behind to take responsibility for both the fields and households.[1] Overwork is taking a brutal toll on women at both ends of the economic spectrum. Moreover, huge inequities exist regarding work hours and economic prosperity. The United Nations Commission on the Status of Women reports that women's work comprises two-thirds of the world's work hours, for which they receive only one-tenth of the world's income. They own only one one-hundredth of the world's property. In the United States women make up two-thirds of all minimum-wage earners. The pay gap between men and women still yawns, with women of color most adversely affected. Women average 76 cents for every dollar earned by men. At the managerial level, white women earned 74 cents for every dollar earned by men; Asian-American women earned 67 cents, African-American women earned 58 cents, and Hispanic women earned 48 cents.[2]

Sabbath gives a vision for a world in which such inequities and imbalances are set aright, where all creation enjoys God's abundance and freedom, and where all is in harmonious relation for the praise of God and the well-being of all. It is women who are most adversely affected by the imbalances of our world, and it is women who are most adept at taking the lead toward renewing practices of Sabbath for the life of the planet. In this essay we will look at the Sabbath healing of a woman who was bent double for eighteen years (Luke 13:10-17) as a paradigm for new creation, liberation, and celebration that Sabbath embodies. Before examining this text, however, we need first to understand the importance of Sabbath from a biblical perspective that would have been part of the value system of Jesus and other Jews of his day.

IMPORTANCE OF THE SABBATH[3]

One of the most startling aspects of Jesus' ministry is the number of healings he performed on Sabbath days. The gospels tell of persons who are healed on the Sabbath: a man with an unclean spirit (Mark 1:21-28// Luke 4:31-37), a man with a withered hand (Mark 3:1-6//Matt 12:9-14// Luke 6:6-11), a woman crippled for eighteen years (Luke 13:10-17), a man with dropsy (Luke 14:1-6), a man lame for thirty-eight years at the pool of Bethesda (John 5:1-18), and a man born blind (John 9:13-17). Except for the first story, in each case a controversy ensues with other Jewish leaders about the breaking of the Sabbath. In addition, the synoptic gospels recount an episode in which Jesus and his disciples pluck grain on a Sabbath, which likewise provokes other Jewish leaders (Mark 2:23-28//Matt 12:1-8//Luke 6:1-5). The questions with which Jesus' followers are faced are: Why does an observant Jew break the Sabbath? And what are the implications of this for his disciples?

To begin, it is important to emphasize that Jesus was an observant Jew, and that he did not advocate doing away with Sabbath practices. Luke depicts Jesus going to the synagogue on the Sabbath "as was his custom" (Luke 4:16; similarly Mark 6:1-6), where he read and preached from the prophet Isaiah and inaugurated his public ministry. Jesus' followers are portrayed as Sabbath-observant, e.g., when the women disciples wait until the Sabbath is over before they come to the tomb to anoint his body (Matt 28:1; Mark 15:42; 16:1; Luke 23:54-56; John 19:31). Likewise, Paul throughout the Acts of the Apostles continues to pray and teach in the synagogue on the Sabbath (13:14, 27, 42, 44; 16:13; 17:2; 18:4). The reason for Jesus doing healing work on the Sabbath is not simply to highlight the importance of compassion over legalism. Rather, these healings were deliberately provocative acts that demonstrated the very purpose of Sabbath as found in the commandments in Exodus 20:8-11 and Deuteronomy 5:12-15.[4] The two biblical injunctions are very similar in their articulation of who is to observe Sabbath, what is to be done, and what is forbidden. They differ, however, in the reasons given about why Sabbath must be observed. We turn now to an examination of each of these texts.

Exodus 20:8-11

> Remember the sabbath day, and keep it holy. Six days you shall labor and do all your work. But the seventh day is a sabbath to the LORD your God; you shall not do any work—you, your son or your daughter, your male or female slave, your livestock, or the alien resident in your towns. For in six days the LORD made heaven and earth, the sea, and all that is in them, but rested the seventh day; therefore the LORD blessed the sabbath day and consecrated it. (Exod 20:8-11)[5]

In this text the reason why Israel is to observe the Sabbath is that God rested at the culmination of creation. The command begins with the admonition to "remember the Sabbath," which, in biblical parlance, does not refer merely to intellectual recall, but means "to make present again." Sabbath is to be kept "holy," *qodesh,* that is, "separated, set apart," from the other six days. As Abraham Joshua Heschel points out, this is holiness in time. With Sabbath, God does not give Israel an object or a place that is to be set apart and consecrated, but a day in which God's people can become attuned to holiness in time.[6]

Sabbath rest is patterned on God's rest at the completion of creation (Gen 1:1–2:4); it is the very crown of creation. Out of the uncontrollable chaos *(tōhû wābōhû)* God created order and well-being, making day and night, the skies, the waters, and dry land, the heavenly lights to mark the days and nights and seasons, the animals of the sky, water, and land, and finally, human beings. The crowning glory of it all is Sabbath that completes God's life-giving work and provides ultimate coherence for the cosmos. What is underscored in the Genesis account is not that God stopped working for a day in order to gather up energy to continue to work again. Rather, God rested when the divine work of ordering creation was completed in order to celebrate and take delight in the creation. In other words, simply being present to creation and taking joy in it on the Sabbath is the very purpose for which God's creative work has been done. Everything that exists has been created for God's delight. Creation is the divine love affair with the created world and beings. Sabbath is the space God creates to enjoy and celebrate this love.[7]

Moreover, with Sabbath God sets creation free to flourish. "In creation, God went out of God's self. In God's rest, God returns to God's self. In creation, God engaged God's creatures. In God's rest, God gives them space."[8] The Creator is not indifferent to creation and creatures, but God does not intrude; God sets them free to become what they will become in God's love.

The command to Israel, then, is not to observe Sabbath rest so that they can gather up their energies for work for the other six days, but it is to refrain from work so as to participate in this love affair of God. The purpose of Sabbath is to experience, with God, joy in the peace and harmony of rightly ordered creation, exclaiming with God, "How very good!" (Gen 1:31). This is different from the Babylonian creation myth, in which human beings were invented as a labor-saving device for the gods. They do the tasks that might otherwise fall to the lesser gods. After finding this way to secure their own leisure, the gods then celebrate with a drinking party. In the Hebrew Scriptures, however, human beings are not created as slaves of God, but to share in God's very image and likeness (Gen 1:26-28), and so participate in the same rhythm of creative activity and re-creative rest.

Deuteronomy 5:12-19[9]

> Observe the sabbath day and keep it holy, as the LORD your God commanded you. Six days you shall labor and do all your work. But the sev-

enth day is a sabbath to the LORD your God; you shall not do any work—you, or your son or your daughter, or your male or female slave, or your ox or your donkey, or any of your livestock, or the resident alien in your towns, so that your male and female slave may rest as well as you. Remember that you were a slave in the land of Egypt, and the LORD your God brought you out from there with a mighty hand and an outstretched arm; therefore the LORD your God commanded you to keep the sabbath day. (Deut 5:12-15)

In this second version of the Decalogue the command is basically the same, but the motive is different. In the text from Exodus 20 the reason for keeping Sabbath is grounded in creation; here it is framed in terms of remembering the creation of God's own people as God liberated Israel from servitude to Egypt. Sabbath is a practice that sets Israel apart from other nations, identifying a people uniquely God's own. The purpose of Sabbath is to create a holy people, free from bondage, free from want, free from all exploitation and oppression, free to praise God.

Closely linked to this freedom is the trust needed on the part of Israel that God will always provide for their needs. The story of God providing daily manna for Israel during the wilderness wandering illustrates this truth (Exod 16:17-30). The Israelites were to gather only as much as each needed, some more, some less, and not leave any over for the next day, for God provided what was needed on each day. Any who tried to hold over manna for the following day would find it rotten in the morning. The exception was on the sixth day, when they were to collect a double portion so that they could observe Sabbath rest. Some, however, who mistrusted, went out to collect manna on the Sabbath, and found none.

Sabbath itself is a means of liberation. In both versions of the commandment all, from the least to the greatest, were to keep the day of rest: householders and all their family, their servants, and even their foreign guests, as well as their beasts. Sabbath is the great equalizer, as all enjoy the same freedom together as God's holy people. Even the land was to rest every fiftieth year. During the jubilee year not only were Israelite slaves to be freed, but all land was to be left fallow and returned to its ancestral owners (Lev 25:8-17, 23-55; 27:16-25; Num 36:4).

Another dimension of the freedom Sabbath provides can be seen in prophetic texts, e.g., Amos 8:4-6. There the prophet rails against those who make a mockery of the Sabbath. They trample upon the needy, impatient for the end of the Sabbath so they may resume cheating the poor. Sabbath allows for one day of hiatus from exploitation of the poor.

A MATTER OF LIFE AND DEATH

So serious is the commandment to observe the Sabbath that it is the most oft-repeated injunction in the Hebrew Bible. Not only that, but Exodus 31:14 asserts that whoever profanes the Sabbath "shall be put to death; whoever does any work on it shall be cut off from among the people." That Sabbath violators were ever actually executed is highly questionable, but the rhetoric makes clear the seriousness of the offense. The other side of the life and freedom Sabbath brings is the threat of death if it is not practiced.[10] It is against this background that we should understand the seriousness of the accusations against Jesus about breaking the Sabbath. Now we turn to a story in Luke.

Release for Glory[11]

> Now [Jesus] was teaching in one of the synagogues on the sabbath. And just then there appeared a woman with a spirit that had crippled her for eighteen years. She was bent over and was quite unable to stand up straight. When Jesus saw her, he called her over and said, "Woman, you are set free from your ailment." When he laid his hands on her, immediately she stood up straight and began praising God. But the leader of the synagogue, indignant because Jesus had cured on the sabbath, kept saying to the crowd, "There are six days on which work ought to be done; come on those days and be cured, and not on the sabbath day." But the Lord answered him and said, "You hypocrites! Does not each of you on the sabbath untie his ox or his donkey from the manger, and lead it away to give it water? And ought not this woman, a daughter of Abraham whom Satan bound for eighteen long years, be set free from this bondage on the sabbath day?" When he said this, all his opponents were put to shame; and the entire crowd was rejoicing at all the wonderful things that he was doing. (Luke 13:10-17)

Incapable of Standing Upright

The narrative opens when Jesus is teaching in the synagogue on the Sabbath and a woman who has been bent over for eighteen years enters the scene. Her bondage recalls two lengthy periods of servitude in Israel's history: eighteen years of bondage to Moab (Judg 3:14) and the same number of years of affliction from the Philistines and the Ammonites (Judg 10:8). The gravity of her illness is emphasized both by the description of her extreme disability—she is completely incapable of standing upright (v. 11)—and by the attribution of it to satanic forces (v. 16). Whatever the medical diagnosis of this woman,[12] it is still not at all uncommon to see women's bodies showing the effects of overwork and undernourishment. Osteoporosis, far more common in women than in men, is a weakening of the bones that can lead to a stooped posture. It sometimes occurs as a direct result of women subordinating their nutritional needs to those of their husbands and children.

Glorifying God

Seeing the woman bent over, Jesus interrupts his teaching, calls to her, affirms that she has been set free, and lays his hands on her. Her response is immediate: she stands upright and continues glorifying God. Although weighed down with her disability, the woman has come to the synagogue on a Sabbath, presumably to offer praise to God,[13] and continues to do so.[14] Jesus' words to her, "you have been freed" *(apolelysai)*, are expressed in the perfect passive form of the verb. That is, her freedom has already been accomplished by God before Jesus' intervention.[15] As daughter of Abraham and Sarah (v. 16) she is part of the people freed from Egypt and created for God's delight. Sabbath, created for the praise of God and the liberation of God's people, is not broken, but more visibly fulfilled when this woman is freed from her infirmity and is enabled to praise God more fully.

Controversial Timing

In the second part of the narrative (vv. 14-17) the focus shifts away from the healing and it now becomes a controversy story. The reaction of the synagogue official stands in stark contrast to the woman's praise (v. 13) and the crowd's acclamation (v. 17). A play on the word *dei,* "it is necessary," (vv. 14, 16) underscores the conflict. The synagogue official argues from the necessity of working on the six other days (v. 14). Jesus, however, insists on the necessity of God's saving plan being realized (v. 16). Jesus criticizes the hypocrisy of his opponents, and argues from the lesser to the greater. If an animal, who is bound only a few hours, can be loosed on the Sabbath, how much more this daughter of Abraham and Sarah, fettered for eighteen years? Another word play strengthens the ironic contrast. One loosens *(luein)* an ox or ass (v. 15); so must the woman be loosed *(luein,* v. 16). Moreover, Jesus' work on the Sabbath is identified with the freeing action of God (v. 12). This is underscored by the use of the term *endoxois,* "mighty deeds" (v. 17), the same word used for what God had done for Israel (Deut 10:21; Exod 34:10).[16]

While the synagogue official objects to the timing, Jesus' action reveals the necessity for all to be freed from their oppression for observance of holy time. The question is not so much one of compassion taking precedence over legalism as it is the urgency that *now* is the time of salvation offered by Jesus. After eighteen years, the woman could have endured her disability one more day, but in Lukan theology *now* is the time to accept God's liberation (e.g., 4:21; 19:9; 23:43). The ability of the whole people of God to be holy and to glorify God on the Sabbath is at stake. No less urgent is the liberation of women from all forms of oppression in today's world; the well-being of the whole created world depends on it. The controversy in the gospel episode strikes a realistic chord, reminding those who struggle for liberation that, in the eyes of persons with power, "now" is never the right time for freeing those they oppress.

SABBATH AND CREATION TODAY

As people today struggle with burnout and exhaustion, addictive overworking, unbridled production, and consumerism, accumulation of more things with less time to enjoy them, all the while searching for meaning in their lives, part of the solution lies in developing a renewed sense of Sabbath. Harmonious relations within all of creation are not achieved without the proper rhythms of creativity and rest, liberation and delight. Sabbath carves out a space in which the work that consumes us can be set aside to enable the quietness of heart needed to be at one with the Creator and all creation. It is not empty time, but sacred time in which praise of God takes center stage. Nor is it free time to pursue individualistic interests; rather it is liberated time for the creation of community—a people who together are holy and free. It opens up space for those with resources to attend to those in need. It stops us from our daily cycles, opening up those who are privileged to attend to the cries of those oppressed. It shuts down for a day sweatshops and exploitative employs, giving a glimpse of equal dignity for all God's beloved.

This hiatus in reliance on our own work increases our trust in providence and restores our awe at God's design of the universe. It energizes us for the work of justice that ensures that all God's people have dignified work with just recompense and rightful rest. As we participate in this way in God's love affair with creation we grow in the ability to perceive the beauty and fragility of the earth and its ecosystems—indeed, the whole of the cosmos. We are enabled to make choices in the way we live that show reverence for earth's resources, ensuring their sustainability and just distribution. It becomes increasingly clear that

Sabbath is not simply a nice option if you have the time, but is a matter of life and death for the planet and all its creatures.

A FORETASTE OF THE FUTURE

It is perhaps women who are best able to lead the way in this endeavor to restore our sense of Sabbath. Women's sensitivity to bodily rhythms and their proper balance and timing is an aid to helping all become better attuned to the right rhythms of creation and Sabbath. Moreover, women are the majority of those exploited by injustice in the workplace and thus have the most to gain by Sabbath liberation from 24-7-365. Women's gifts for celebration and for creation of community, like those of the woman who found her lost coin (Luke 15:8-10), are needed to lead communities of believers into delight with God. Additionally, the practice of our Jewish brothers and sisters in which women preside over the Sabbath meal provides us with an icon for Christian women leading eucharistic celebrations.

Finally, the joy of right relation that the Sabbath brings is a foretaste of its eschatological completion. The author of Hebrews speaks of a Sabbath rest that still remains for the people of God, exhorting Christians to make every effort to enter that rest (4:1-11). Thus, when we pray "eternal rest grant unto him/her" it is not comatose sleep for all eternity for which we pray, but the culmination of this love affair of God with all creation.

NOTES: CHAPTER 6

[1] See stories of the work of women who try to break the downward cycles of poverty, for example at http://www.workofwomen.org/index.htm.

[2] These statistics are from 1998 and Hilary M. Lips cites them in her keynote address "Women, Education, and Economic Participation." It is available at http://www.runet.edu/~gstudies/sources/nz/keyecon.htm.

[3] The origin of Israel's Sabbath observance is still unknown. Scholars have looked to Babylonian, Kenite, Arabic, and Ugaritic influences, as well as to various sociological contexts to try to explain the origin of Sabbath. Nonetheless, there is no scholarly consensus. See Gerhard F. Hasel, "Sabbath," *Anchor Bible Dictionary,* ed. David Noel Freedman. 5 vols. (Garden City, N.Y.: Doubleday, 1992) 5:849–56 for more details about the various hypotheses. That the Israelites kept one day per week as a day of rest is attested in the Hebrew Scriptures. Christian practice, in turn, is rooted in and distinct from Jewish tradition.

[4]Marcus Borg, *Conflict, Holiness, and Politics in the Teachings of Jesus* (rev. ed. Harrisburg, Penn.: Trinity Press International, 1998) 160, 167.

[5]Biblical citations are taken from the *NRSV.*

[6]Abraham Joshua Heschel, *The Sabbath: Its Meaning for Modern Man* (New York: Farrar, Strauss and Giroux, 1951) 9–10.

[7]Jürgen Moltmann, "Sabbath: Finishing and Beginning," *The Living Pulpit* 7/2 (April–June 1998) 4.

[8]Ibid.

[9]Ellen Davis, "Sabbath: The Culmination of Creation," *The Living Pulpit* 7/2 (April–June 1998) 6–7.

[10]Ibid.

[11]Portions of the following appeared previously in my book *Choosing the Better Part? Women in the Gospel of Luke* (Collegeville: The Liturgical Press, 1996) 163–68.

[12]Commentators such as J. Wilkinson ("The Case of the Bent Woman in Lk 13:10-17," *EvQ* 49 [1979] 195–205) speculate on the woman's condition and suggest she may have suffered from *spondylitis ankylopietica,* a deformation resulting from fusion of the spinal joints.

[13]This episode belies the common assumption that women were not allowed in the synagogue with men. See also the work of Bernadette Brooten (*Women Leaders in the Ancient Synagogue: Inscriptional Evidence and Background Issues.* Brown Judaic Studies 36 [Chico: Scholars, 1982]). She shows from inscriptional evidence not only the presence of women in the ancient synagogue, but also their various leadership positions.

[14]The verb *edoxasen* in the imperfect tense in v. 13 carries the connotation of continued action, not an action that is just begun, contrary to the translation of the *NRSV.*

[15]Elisabeth Schüssler Fiorenza, *But She Said: Feminist Practices of Biblical Interpretation* (Boston: Beacon, 1992) 199. The formulation is similar to Luke 5:20 and 7:47, where forgiveness on the lips of Jesus is spoken in the perfect passive tense. The effect in these instances is the assertion that it is God who frees one.

[16]Dennis Hamm, "The Freeing of the Bent Woman and the Restoration of Israel: Luke 13:10-17 as Narrative Theology," *JSNT* 31 (1987) 27.

7

Creation Restored: God's Basileia, the Social Economy, and the Human Good

Tatha Wiley

THE EXPERIENCE OF *BASILEIA*

*T*hat Jesus is the Word of God is a methodological imperative embedded in the Christian proclamation. What was central for Jesus should be central for us.[1] Discovering what motivated Jesus' preaching and life is as important theologically as it is historically. Biblical scholars concur that the focus of Jesus' message, both spoken and lived, was the announcement of the inbreaking and presence of God's *basileia*.

Although the Greek term *basileia* is commonly translated *kingdom*, *reign*, or *rule*, it is rendered more accurately by *empire*. In Israel's political context of foreign occupation the Roman *basileia* was the empire of everyday experience. The symbol of *basileia* spontaneously evoked a contrast for Jesus' listeners. To appeal to an empire as *God* would rule it was a not-so-subtle critique of the empire as *Rome* actually ruled it.[2] Today the subtlety of this contrast is lost. In preaching, reference to "the reign of God" may not be connected even to the social order. However, the same question can be asked of a modern democracy as Jesus did of an ancient empire: What would the social order be like if God were running things? In his own time Jesus appropriated the symbol of *basileia* as means of social critique.

By envisioning God's *basileia* by way of parables and sayings, Jesus embodied it in his compassionate response to the exploited and marginalized. This symbol enabled Jesus to identify both the sinful distortion of creation and its restoration. Easily overlooked is that both the distortion and the restoration are *economic* realities.

The economy is a central concern in the Hebrew Bible.[3] The "creation faith" of the biblical writers joins praise of the Creator with attention to creation as well as to the absence or presence of human well-being.[4] The Hebrew prophets spoke powerfully against a political economy that created unjust social structures.[5] Jesus' sharp challenge to "sell all that you own and distribute the money to the poor" clearly demonstrates an economic dimension to his message (Luke 18:22).[6] Luke shows Jesus beginning his ministry by proclaiming release to captives, referring to those imprisoned for debt (Luke 4:16-30).[7] His Gospel is good news for the poor. Good news for the poor—women as well as men—is economic: food, clothing, shelter, ongoing work. Jesus' group of disciples models the primary value of inclusion in God's *basileia* (cf. Mark 15:40-41).

To bring into focus the economic dimension of Jesus' vision of the restoration of creation, I will develop a twofold thesis: (1) that Jesus envisioned God's *basileia* as a participatory economy, and (2) that a contemporary theology of the human good should include economic theory that fosters the values embedded in the symbol of God's *basileia*. Jesus' deliberate egalitarian attitude and relations with women point to gender equality as intrinsic to God's *basileia*. Women, too, are invited to the table. Human sinfulness that is at the core of the distortion of creation is the absence of gender equality and the exclusion of women from the table. Equality and inclusion are not only personal values but also key economic considerations in an analysis of the human good.

GOD'S *BASILEIA*

The New Testament gospels are confessional sources for our knowledge of the historical Jesus. Although disinterested documentation was scarcely the gospel writers' aim, historical memories of Jesus' words and deeds that are embedded especially in the synoptic gospels do allow for judgments about the focus of Jesus' preaching and the nature of his activity.[8] Most evident is that Jesus drew from Jewish eschatological expectations and hopes (Matt 6:10). He shared the hope of fellow Jews for God's action on behalf of Israel. The eschatological symbol of *basileia* was familiar from prayer and liturgy, Scripture, and apocalyptic traditions. Like the *Kiddush,* a first-century Jewish synagogue prayer, Jesus' prayer expressed his desire for God's kingdom to come.[9] The symbol of *basileia* expressed hopes for national liberation as well as the transformation of the whole creation by God's intervention. The political meaning of *basileia* lay in this interrelationship of creation and salvation. In contrast to Roman imperial domination, Elisabeth Schüssler Fiorenza writes, the *basileia* of God

> envisioned an alternative world free of hunger, poverty, and domination. This "envisioned" world was already present in the inclusive table community, in healing and liberating practices, and in the domination-free kinship community of the Jesus movement, which found many followers among the poor, the despised, the ill and possessed, the outcast, the prostitutes, and the "sinners"—women and men.[10]

Jesus' designation of John the Baptizer and himself as Sophia's prophets highlights the particular significance of the Wisdom tradition in shaping his religious world.[11] What the biblical writers had said of Sophia would later be said of Jesus himself. The Palestinian Jesus movement understood "the ministry and mission of Jesus as that of the prophet and child of Sophia sent to announce that God is the God of the poor and heavy laden, of the outcasts and those who suffer injustice."[12] Paul preached Christ crucified, the wisdom of God (1 Cor 1:23-24). Elizabeth A. Johnson states that the early Christians "tapped deeply into the tradition of personified Wisdom to articulate the saving goodness they experienced in Christ."[13]

The *basileia* includes all creation. For the biblical writers the whole created order, including the social order, is the fruit of divine freedom, creativity, and decision. God deems that it is good through a divine *value* judgment. Jesus' vision of God's *basileia* frames his own "theology" of creation. It is symbolic and metaphorical, mediated by parables, challenges, and performative actions. It is a *theology* because it articulates Jesus' apprehension of God's desires for the human world. It is a theology of *creation* because Jesus affirms the basic tenet of biblical creation faith: "the earth is God's" (Ps 24:1). The earth is God's possession, not the possession of the elite who exploit it for debt and control it as absentee landlords. God's *basileia* is the social order as it *could* and *should be.*[14] It restores well-being to the subordinated and dispossessed.

Among the marginalized were women. They experienced wholeness through his healing power (Mark 5:25-34) and by Jesus' inclusion of them in his group of disciples (Mark 15:40).

The transformation from *what is* to *what ought to be* requires a reversal of values. Primarily this reversal entails a withdrawal from the false values that generate social, political, economic, and religious inequities.[15] The values of compassion, help for those in need, inclusion, and equality offset injustice.[16] Unjust economic orders restrict the benefits of society to a few.[17] Just economic orders generate political and economic strategies in which social benefits can be extended to all. The values underlying the Roman *basileia* generate one kind of social order whereas the values of God's *basileia* generate another type.

Jesus' acute consciousness of the disparity between what is desired by God and the existing imperial order informed his whole ministry. His sensitivity was shaped not only by the biblical creation faith that furnishes themes in Torah, Prophets, and Wisdom writings, but also by Jesus' experience of the compassionate presence of divine mystery.[18] Jesus' followers experienced in his words and deeds a disclosure of what God desires for human living. For women especially, this disclosure was one of acceptance of them as persons, not as the property of men, subjects existing to serve them.[19]

SUBMERGING THE SYMBOL

Proclamation of the risen Jesus in the post-resurrection messianic movement gradually overshadowed the centrality of Jesus' *basileia* preaching. The Fourth Gospel, not the synoptics, provided the dominant images for the doctrinal development extending over three centuries and ending with the credal affirmations of the Councils of Nicaea (325 C.E.) and Chalcedon (451 C.E.).[20] *Logos,* a masculine noun that defines "reason," became *the* christological title, thereby relegating to a place of insignificance *Sophia of God,* the primitive designation.[21] The object of Jesus' preaching in the Gospel of John is his own transcendent origin and identity, not the sinful consequences of elite and male privilege.

This development neither carried Jesus' critique of economic injustice nor retained the historical import of his *basileia* preaching. For Jesus the pressing issue had been the redemptive transformation of the imperial *basileia* into what God desired. For the patristic writers the question was how to maintain Hebrew monotheism and the Christian confession of the risen Jesus as Lord.[22] The Deutero-Pauline letters indicate that some Christians failed to see patriarchal privilege as a problem by the end of the first century or in the early second century.[23] Now, in the name of Jesus, slaveholding and the subjugation of women were legitimized as part of the natural order.

The social and political referent of the *basileia* symbol and the significance of Jesus' actions as performative enactments of the symbol were gradually submerged.[24] The focus on an otherworldly salvation was less able to appreciate history as the locus of God's engagement with humankind and redemption as a transformation of history. Woman's redemption now became linked to acquiescence in her reproductive function, not to her personal commitment to Jesus as Sophia's prophet.[25] Once original sin became an unquestioned theological postulate, the meaning of other theological doctrines was grounded by it and related to it as solutions to a problem. In a theology of redemption, Jesus' vision of the restoration of creation by a radical reversal of values was overshadowed by a concept of redemption as Christ's forgiveness of original sin mediated through the institutional church.[26] The basic human problem for Augustine, for example, was not economic exploitation (as in Jesus' preaching) or even the "world" (as in Paul's letters), but the remaining effect of an original disobedient act, *concupiscence.*

THE SYMBOL RE-CENTERED

A remarkable contribution of New Testament scholars today is recovery of the social and political referent of Jesus' preaching. Walter Wink writes: "The gospel is not a message of personal salvation from the world, but a message of a world transfigured, right down to its basic structures."[27] We are challenged to reappropriate the meaning of Christian doctrines in relation to history and social transformation.[28] For women, the news that redemption has to do with the reversal of their status in the human community as non-persons is good news indeed. Paul evokes this theme in making this appeal to the Galatians who followed Jesus: "For freedom Christ has set us free. Stand firm, therefore, and do not submit again to a yoke of slavery" (Gal 5:1).

The New Testament data for Jesus' vision of God's *basileia* extend beyond specific use of the term. The *basileia* symbol is explicitly mentioned or evoked in: *basileia* parables[29] and similitudes;[30] parables suggesting the transformation of human relations and values;[31] references to God's *basileia* as here, not-yet, in our midst, yet to be found, as inner and as outer[32] eschatological reversal sayings[33] and beatitudes subverting conventional values;[34] Jesus' healings and exorcisms integrating persons back into the community;[35] Jesus' open tableship with sinners, the shamed, outsiders, and expendables;[36] Jesus' rejection of the patriarchal household[37] and formation of a community of disciples as equals;[38] the prayer of Jesus, and Jesus himself in his relationships, actions, and words.[39]

Jesus signaled the nature of the redemptive restoration of creation by what he did *not* do as much as by what he did do. It is significant that Jesus did not privilege men, diminish women, advance elite privilege, promote an ethics of purity that rendered some non-persons, equate holiness with ethnicity, class, or gender, bless the patriarchal family as divinely willed. What Jesus held up as *redemptive* inversely revealed *sin*. His compassionate acceptance of a prostitute rebuked her dehumanization and economic exploitation by others.[40] His formation of the group of disciples as a new family rejected the subordination of human beings in the patriarchal household to commodity status.[41]

Jesus' vision of God's *basileia* evoked images of social and economic changes for those kept powerless by imperial rule. Norman Gottwald notes that many Christians think of Jesus' preaching as simply ethical and spiritual, having little to do with social and economic conditions. It is an entirely mistaken notion. Jesus' ministry indicates that he is

> in opposition to the native tributary power represented by the Sadducees and the Jewish elite in Jerusalem and ultimately to the foreign tributary power of Rome. The strategy of Jesus and his movement seems to have been to aim at the Jewish elite and the temple economy rather than to target Rome directly. It was this Jewish elite and temple economy that imposed native tributary servitude on the people, while it simultaneously served Roman interests.[42]

Walter Wink describes a domination system such as the Roman empire of Jesus' day as characterized by "unjust economic relations, oppressive political relations, biased race relations, patriarchal gender relations, hierarchical power relations, and the use of violence to maintain them all."[43] Jesus' appeal to God's *basileia* was directed specifically against such an unjust reign. His relationships with women and actions toward them reveal that the gospel is also good news about gender. Male privilege is a distortion of creation, not its intended order. The power of the *basileia* symbol lay in its capacity to evoke an alternative to the present social order of domination.

A system of domination generates an economic configuration in which the flow of wealth moves directly upward to upper-stratum groups. It is a sinful system because it meets the needs of only a few people, and leaves the needs of most people unmet. Jesus marked this economic reality as sin. His beatitudes honoring the poor, the hungry, and the sorrowing address desperate economic situations. To say that "theirs is the kingdom of God" evokes an image of God intervening on their behalf so that their fortunes might change for the better.[44] In contrast to Rome's *basileia,* Jesus characterized God's *basileia* as one of partnership, interdependence, equality, and mutual respect between men and women.[45] These values would generate a political economy unlike the one driven by elite interests. Restoration of creation requires economic changes because its distortion is enmeshed in economic realities.[46]

THE ECONOMICS OF EXCLUSION

Social, political, economic, and religious inequities are endemic to imperial rule and to a tributary mode of production. This type of economic system generates wealth for a small number of upper-stratum groups.[47] For the masses, economic despair is a permanent feature of life. In Jesus' day, poverty-stricken peasants lost their land to wealthy absentee landlords because of a double and triple taxation system that often enslaved them to their creditors.[48] Religious purity systems contributed to social stratification by linking sickness and despised occupations with sin.

Jesus saw this economic despair through the critical and communal lens of the prophets.[49] Peasant debt and loss of land were contrary to the biblical call for a Sabbath day every seventh day, a Sabbath year every seventh year in which the land was to lie fallow, and a Jubilee year every fiftieth year, in which the legal codes called for slaves to be set free, property to be returned to its original owners, the land to lie fallow, and debts to be totally remitted.[50] Jesus envisioned God's *basileia* as a redemptive economic correction to a system in which economic privilege perpetuated economic vulnerability.[51] To the powerless, he announced surprisingly good news: *God is for us.*[52]

Jesus' parables and stories unveil a world in which the disenfranchised and powerless become participants in the social order. In his brief ministry, Elizabeth Johnson proposes,

> Jesus appears as the prophet and child of Sophia sent to announce that God is the God of all-inclusive love who wills the wholeness and humanity of everyone, especially the poor and heavy burdened. He is sent to gather the entire outcast under the wings of their gracious Sophia-God

and bring them to *shalom.* This envoy of Sophia walks her paths of justice and peace and invites others to do likewise. . . . Scandalous though it may appear, his inclusive table fellowship widens the circle of the friends of God to include the most disvalued people, even tax collectors, sinners, prostitutes. In all of this, his compassionate, liberating words and deeds are the works of Sophia reestablishing the right order of creation: Wisdom is justified by her deeds (Matt 11:19).[53]

Jesus' table fellowship and evocation of the inclusive banquet are a rebuke to a tributary economic system. The demonic powers of imperial violence and exploitation that the poor experienced cannot develop human well-being. Human misery is produced by a particular type of system in which a politics of oppression, an economics of exploitation, and religion of legitimation militate against the well-being of nearly all.[54] Jesus did not design an alternative system. Nonetheless, he did hold up the values that would reorient the existing system back to its primary created function of sustaining human well-being.

REDEMPTIVE INCLUSION

At a minimum, human well-being is contingent upon participation in the social economy.[55] There is no way to meet basic familial needs and desires outside the existing economy. A tributary system divides persons into the few whose interests the system serves and the many that exist to serve them. The needs and interests of the many are disregarded. That they are expendable is taken for granted. Jesus' image of such persons who have a place at the table reflects an underlying insight not only that a social order is a created reality that can be distorted but also that it exists for human well-being. Those whose worth the existing *basileia* denies will have their value as persons acknowledged in the *basileia* of God. Like Mary and Martha, women will be acknowledged as persons and have a place at the table (Luke 10:38-42). To bring God's *basileia* into being entails a radical reordering of human priorities. It was this reordering Jesus envisioned.

A tributary economic system reflects the development of an already hierarchical and stratified social order. The baptismal proclamation of the early Jesus followers explicitly counters hierarchy: "There is no longer Jew or Greek, there is no longer slave or free, there is no longer male and female; for all of you are one in Christ Jesus" (Gal 3:28).[56] If there is no longer Jew and Greek, then there is no religious privilege. There is no restriction on the inclusive covenantal relation of God with humanity.[57] Salvation is belonging. If there are no longer masters and slaves, then there is no economic exploitation that reduces persons to expendable chattel. Salvation is freedom. If there is no longer male rule and female subjugation, then there are no separate and unequal gender spheres for women and men. Salvation is mutuality. In God's *basileia* human beings are persons, not property.[58] Jesus' preaching and the early followers' baptismal proclamation point to redemptive reality, i.e., an inclusive social order in which needs are met, desires are balanced, and the economics of well-being is allowed to flourish.

Jesus' listeners would have heard his stories of inclusion as pointing to the social order God desires. It is one that is very different from the social order elites have created. His stories were not intended to pacify, but to energize according to the tradition of the outspoken prophets.[59] Jesus evoked a world in which social reality changes for persons who need change the most. If the beggar is invited to the table only to share in the privileges of another, the *basileia* has not changed. In God's *basileia* the beggar does not leave the table to return to begging, but becomes a participant in the social economy. The beggar is no longer reduced by systemic inequities to a former, dehumanizing status.

Through the symbol of God's *basileia* Jesus evoked the image of a political and economic order that has undergone real change. It has transformed its oppressive politics, corrected its exploitative economics, and abandoned its religious legitimation of elite interests. He knew it did not exist, yet it *could* exist. Different values would generate new political strategies, economic policies, and religious worldviews. The symbol of God's *basileia* denotes not only eschatological hope but also economic hope. *Being at the table* points to an economic system in which degrees of desperation for the *penētes,* the "relatively poor" and the *ptōchoi,* the "absolutely poor" no longer have to be named.[60]

THE LOSS OF *BASILEIA* VALUES

In its later otherworldly turn, Christian theology located freedom and equality for the disenfranchised in the beatific vision. The redemptive transformation of history was overshadowed by the focus on redemption as after history. As the Deutero-Pauline texts insist, women remain subordinate to male rule and slaves stay obedient to their master's will in this world. The existing culture provided the norm for the structure of the *ekklēsia.* The charismatic, inclusive, and egalitarian communities of the Pauline letters gave way to the household of God as declaimed in 1 Timothy.[61] The sinfulness of privilege that is eschewed in Gal 3:28 was restored. Sin became *opposing* hierarchical relations rather than the relations of domination and subordination themselves.[62] In the household codes and otherworldly focus a new language of religious legitimation covered over the radical invitation to freedom embedded in Jesus' vision of the restoration of creation.

Patriarchal cultures create women's economic dependency. Jesus' raising the widow's only son implicitly addresses the economic vulnerability of women (Luke 7:11-17). Without husbands or sons, women's economic options could often be reduced to prostitution.[63] Luke's story of the widow may be read with the son at the center as a story of the son's resurrection.[64] Alternatively, Jesus may be put at the center. The story then becomes a proof-text for Jesus' divine power. To see the real significance of Jesus' action requires bringing the woman into the center of the story. The widow, already without her husband, a person crucial to her survival, now has lost her only son. He is her sole means of economic survival. She faces a bleak economic future, perhaps even death. In raising her son, Jesus restores her prospect for economic, even physical survival. With her son, and through him, the widow remains a participant in the social economy.

That prostitution was often the only option for women's personal survival in patriarchal societies reveals its origins in economic destitution. Generally, the social evil of prostitution is blamed on prostitutes and their promiscuity: women become prostitutes because they enjoy having sex. This notion of prostitution as women's choice is an androcentric illusion. Through political, religious, and legal means, patriarchal societies close off avenues of self-sufficiency for women.[65] The lack of independent access to the social economy points to the economic origins of prostitution in female poverty.

In both the ancient and modern worlds prostituting vulnerable persons is a lucrative business. Individuals, organized crime, even governments who sell others' bodies benefit economically.[66] Like slavery and the slave trade, the business of selling and using sexual labor can generate immense profits. Destitute people expand the labor pool and become expendable.[67] Women and children are forced into prostitution by dire poverty, by the social dislocation created by war, and by parents or husbands.[68] Mercenary prostitution, the selling of women's sexual labor, has its origins in ancient Greece as the government's way of raising money for warfare.[69] Jesus' teaching on divorce should be seen in this economic context:

Jesus also attempts to change a major structural cause of prostitution: the ease with which a man could divorce a woman. The severity of his pronouncement—he allows *no* cause for divorce, not even adultery—is intended to prevent the wholesale dumping of ex-wives onto the streets.[70]

Jesus' bold statement that "Tax collectors and prostitutes go into the reign of God before you" (Matt 21:31//Luke 7:36-50) announces the reign of God as a different social order. We need to hear its radical and particular implications. God's *basileia* is good news for the prostitute because her economic situation is no longer dictated by the gender inequities of a patriarchal culture (cf. 1 Tim 1:15). In a social order in which human worth and inclusion are primary values, she is no longer an exploited body but a person.

THE ECONOMICS OF REDEMPTION

Social inclusion is a value. It carries economic meaning. Genuine inclusion demands access to participation in the social economy, not exclusion or exploitation. Jesus' vision of God's reign implies transformation of economic vulnerability. Stephen Patterson portrays how Jesus called sinners to follow him:

> Jesus . . . recognized the structural nature of expendability in his social world and the illegitimacy of labeling expendables as "sinners" in need of repentance. A tax collector does not need to repent; he just needs land, or a better job. A prostitute does not need better morals; she just needs a legitimate, respectful place to be in the world.[71]

In a sinful order that is distorted by ideologies of privilege, designating some human beings as non-persons renders them economically exploitable as cheap or free labor. It generates income for those whose first privilege is personal status. Categories such as "clean" and "unclean" create social divisions that economically benefit some and penalize others. Jesus' inclusive perception of the created order that was grounded in the great commandment of biblical creation faith to love God and neighbor carries direct economic implications. His rejection of the values of a system of domination eliminated economic privilege as the order of creation to be promoted and enjoyed. If God's reign is to become actual, it will become so through the creation of a participatory economy. To "seek God's empire" means to order life in such a way that the Empire of God becomes a reality. If one does this, or rather if a *community* does this, the necessities of life will fall into place . . . . Jesus' words speak about ordering human relationships in such a way that no one is expendable and all have unbrokered access to the means for life.[72]

UNRESTRICTED GOOD

In the ancient world only limited good was available. The common perception was that all goods existed in finite, limited supply, and were already distributed. Just as land was finite, to be divided and subdivided but never increased, so also with all goods in life. This included not only material goods, but honor, friendship, love, power, security, and status as well. Literally everything in life was a limited good.[73]

No doubt the oppressive politics and exploitative economics of imperial rule made this perception axiomatic. Imperial rule restricted meaningful participation in the social order and, by default, restricted virtually all the goods of human life. Its tributary economy sustained two unequal spheres, one of power and wealth and another of powerlessness and intractable poverty.[74] Only a few had the goods of basic necessities, land, food, and a stable family life. Some could hope for them. For most, however, the human good remained a remote possibility.

In fact, the human good is not a limited entity from which everyone takes a piece or misses out on it. The human good is unrestricted in its possibility.[75] Nonetheless, it does have conditions for its realization. A complex web of forces in a domination system militates against this possibility. These forces generate the exclusion of some from the social economy that results in the social injustice denounced by the prophets. Exclusion deprives the powerless of the economic means of meeting the basic necessities of life. The human good is not just a remote possibility for most, but an impossibility.

Jesus appealed to the eschatological symbol of God's *basileia* to extend hope to the economically vulnerable and judgment to the economically privileged. In contrast to the limited-good imperial *basileia* experienced in day-to-day existence, Jesus portrayed the unrestricted character of the human good in God's *basileia*. The primary value that motivates the imperial *basileia* is exclusion of most from the basic necessities of life. The value that generates God's *basileia* is inclusion in the social economy, "having a place at the table."[76] Just as exclusionary practices of the privileged distort and restrict the human good, so, too, inclusionary practices are an intrinsic dimension of the redemptive restoration of creation.[77] Matthew brings his narrative of Jesus' life to an end with the parable of the sheep and the goats (Matt 25:31-46). By identifying Jesus with those who lack basic necessities of life, Matthew places the transformation of human need at the heart of redemption. The parable does not say "Jesus is this one hungry person," but identifies Jesus with all those who suffer deprivation. To meet someone's need of food once is a charitable act. To meet needs of hunger or homelessness on a recurring basis is to engage in a redemptive social and economic process.[78]

SHAPING ECONOMIC PROCESS

The *basileia* of God has an inextricable economic dimension. It contests imperial economics and envisions a participatory economy that affirms human worth, addresses human vulnerability, and seeks the human good. How can we understand its relevance to the complex and diverse economic, political, and social configurations today? We can begin by identifying, through our questions, the source of both the human good and the economy.

The search for the origin of the human good is an individual and social process of raising and answering questions for deliberation: "What should we do?" "What is worthwhile?" "What is responsible?" "What is of genuine value?" "What will meet the needs of this situation?"[79] Personal lives and the particular features of communities and nations are shaped by the answers we give. Questions that evoke moral deliberation are also economic. The social and political economy originates in individual operations of thinking, deciding, and doing, and in the social process of group cooperation and collaboration. Complex and cumulative, economic processes are not fully under the control of individuals or even groups, yet they are not outside the realm of human control and change either. The kind of economy that exists in a particular social context reflects insights into the common good as well as competing biases advancing self- and group interests.

The moral dimension of economic activity resides in the authenticity of economic actors. Human beings bring about the good in concrete situations by being attentive, intelligent, reasonable, and responsible. Cumulative instances of the good over long periods of time result in historical progress. Nevertheless, each instance of the good requires that persons grasp what is genuinely responsible and actually do it. This is no small matter. In each instance persons have to transcend the pull of immediate satisfactions, vested interests, and myriad blind spots to which they are subject. The common good and historical progress cannot be separated from authentic subjectivity.[80]

The intelligent and moral process required for the human good is thwarted by the pull of self- and group interests, by the blind spots of hatred and disdain created by ideologies of superiority, and by sheer laziness, habitual rationalization, and intractable ignorance. To grasp what is worthwhile, determine a responsible course of action, summon the willingness to act upon it, and actually carry it out takes concerted moral effort. History offers ample evidence that the easier and less responsible course of action often appears the more attractive.

If human beings were pure intellects, the dynamic process that ends concretely in this or that good would be a straight course. Instead, rather than cultivating insights that grasp situations correctly and responsible decisions that meet the needs of these situations, we settle for incomplete insights and inadequate responses as "good enough." Further, the social situation itself is a combination of rationality and irrationality. The defense of irrationality as rational makes things worse. The objective situation is all fact. However, Bernard Lonergan defines it as "partly . . . the product of intelligence and reasonableness and partly . . . the product of aberration from them."[81] It is a false fact, the existence of what should not be. The basic form of ideology is this justification of oversights and bias. From this basic form, Lonergan declares, "all others can be derived. For the basic forms corrupt the social good. As self-transcendence promotes progress, so the refusal of self-transcendence turns progress into cumulative decline."[82]

The institutions of human living—family, government, law, economy, religion—reflect these cumulative decisions in social cooperation and collaboration. As ongoing schemes, they meet human needs and desires on a regular and recurring basis. As historical realities, they are more or less good. The social institutions of family, legal and economic systems, politics and religion are blends of insights into the human good and blind spots fostered by vested interests. Their authenticity or inauthenticity as social institutions is a matter of which one has come to dominate, the insights or the oversights.

The elements of imperial economy, the patriarchal family, kingship, and a tributary economy are not fixed entities.[83] They developed historically. They can be vigorously justified and presented as givens in creation and fixed in nature. They can also be challenged by a new apprehension of value. What has been promoted as the order of creation—slavery, the subordination of women, and kingship as divinely willed—can be recognized as the elements of an unjust property system that they are. The economic interests that drive the privileged to accord themselves status as persons while designating others as non-persons available for their sexual or manual labor can be exposed as an arbitrary system of exploitation. The flow of economic benefits to a few can be unmasked as the maneuvering of human wills, not a transcendent will with a preferential option for the elite. What was thought unchangeable—male headship of the family, the divine right of kings, the prohibition of females from public and sacred space—can be abandoned completely. New insights are the means for shaping new structures, including those needed for an economy that functions in relation to the common good and not against it. These insights will not only be practical, grasping what will work, but moral. To answer the question, "What are the economic conditions for the human good?" requires moral insight and evaluation as a dimension of economic analysis.

THE MORAL IMPERATIVE OF ECONOMIC THEORY

Unlike those who see economics, ethics, and theology as entirely unconnected, Bernard Lonergan gives attention to economic theory as a moral and theological imperative. The human good is intimately bound to the social economy.[84] Development of intelligent and effective economic policies is a moral task. Such policies are the means for ensuring that basic human needs are met and an adequate standard of living is a realistic possibility. In theological terms, responsible economic policies are an intrinsic dimension of the human collaboration with God in the creation of the world. Economic policies that have the common good of the social order as their goal require a theoretical grasp of the variables of the economy. What generates economic growth? How does an economy expand? What brings us into recessions and out of economic depressions? Historical progress and decline are intimately related to the insights or oversights present in the answers given to these and many other questions.[85]

Social economies are always subject to judgment. A tributary economy, for example, never has the common good as its goal because as a set of intentional policies it exploits the resources of the social order as a benefit for a few. A tributary economy contributes directly to historical decline since it lacks internal moral critique and authentic religious insight. The gap between rich and poor inevitably widens. Whole groups and institutions—soldiers, tax-collectors, debtor prisons—are devoted to its daily maintenance. The economic system requires violence to sustain it. As people become more desperate, violence is incited against those who receive its benefits. While it is different from ancient empires, the modern global economy is equally in need of moral and theological critique and contribution.

In Lonergan's view, economic failure to realize the human good is often due more to ignorance than greed. Like Reinhold Niebuhr, Lonergan does not dismiss the influence of vested interests in economic policies and the damage to the social economy that group bias effects. He focuses attention on the relationship between economic decisions and economic processes. Some decisions appear intelligent but initiate a short cycle of recession. Policies that are replete with incomplete insights turn recessions into full-scale depressions. Decisions that privilege the wealthy contribute to widespread human suffering. The human good depends on increasing economic insights and exposing economic oversights.

Economies are a compound of human authenticity and inauthenticity. Ideologies rather than insights often drive policies.[86] As Dorothee Soelle points out, poverty in industrialized countries is continually rationalized away, e.g., "the poor are poor through their own fault." "Tax cuts for the rich help the economy." "In actuality, though," she writes, "tax cuts for the rich increase their wealth, and the gap between the rich and the poor grows wider."[87] Moral evaluation of economic decisions and policies is a necessary part of economic analysis. Is economic growth an unqualified good to be protected at all costs? On purely economic grounds, some might argue "yes." If the sexual exploitation of women and children in the sex tourism industry is fueling economic growth, such growth cannot be considered a good under any circumstances.[88] Lonergan argues that a moral and theological perspective calls for a "radical criticism of the market economy itself."[89] Concretely, the market economy is not just the exchange of money, but the buying and selling of human beings.

APPROPRIATING THE SYMBOL

The principle that was articulated earlier, namely, that what was central for Jesus must be theologically central for us, links contemporary theology to the historical Jesus. His insights into God's *basileia* reflect a symbolic apprehension of the human good. The appropriation of the symbol does not stay at this level, but it draws out theoretical implications in moral and theological reflection. Since the symbol places before us the human good as the chief aim of redemption, reflection must also include economic theory. A theoretical grasp of the variables of economic process contributes to the development of social policies that can further the common good. Intelligent economic theories and policies offset the initial interference of human oversights and biases in the social economy and the enduring distortion of creation created by the rationalization of stupidity and vested interests as intelligent and responsible.

Moral critique of the modern market economy takes into account an often overlooked fact. The most vulnerable members of society—single mothers, children, racial-ethnic minorities—are the first to be hurt by economic failures and the last to be lifted up by economic recoveries. Beverly Harrison describes the principle of theological and ethical interpretation she employs in economic analysis as a socialist-feminist liberation hermeneutic that adopts a hermeneutic of suspicion. Her aim is to illuminate "the concrete suffering of those victimized by the social orders we human beings have constructed." This hermeneutic "accepts accountability for the 'poorest of the poor'—women and men of marginalized racial, ethnic, and religious cultures excluded from full social empowerment and participation by barriers of class, gender, or sexual orientation and preference."[90]

Jesus' preaching concerned those who were excluded from full social empowerment. The symbol of God's *basileia* evokes the world Jesus imagined would embody God's values. From the perspective of a biblical creation faith the world exists as the fruit of a dynamic and creative process that is immanent in divine subjectivity. Its historical development reflects the tension in human subjectivity between intelligent and responsible collaboration with God in the ongoing creation of the world and irresponsible distortion of creation and sinful alienation from God. Redemption transforms this distortion by an ongoing reversal of sinful personal relations and social structures.[91]

Through parable and metaphor, in personal encounters and relationships, Jesus announced the contours of a restored creation. For those to whom he spoke, Rome's *basileia* kept the human good a virtual impossibility. In contrast, God's *basileia* opens up the good as unrestricted and as a realistic possibility. Integrated into economic decisions and policies, the values Jesus marked as God's—inclusion, equality, compassion—increase the probability that the goal of social and economic policies will be the human good. It decreases the potentiality for self-destruction embedded in a social order that restricts the good of human well-being to a few.

NOTES: CHAPTER 7

[1] Roger Haight emphasizes this point in *Jesus: Symbol of God* (Maryknoll, N.Y.: Orbis, 1999) 55–87. "The fact that the reign of God was so central to Jesus' life and teaching makes it normative for the Christian theologian: Christologies that neglect it are inadequate, and, positively, Christians must find some meaning for the reign of God in their theological understanding of the world" (p. 80).

[2] On translating *basileia* see Stephen Patterson, *The God of Jesus: The Historical Jesus and the Search for Meaning* (Harrisburg: Trinity Press International, 1998) 60. Gerd Theissen and Annette Merz note the scholarly agreement regarding the object of Jesus' preaching in *The Historical Jesus: A Comprehensive Guide* (Minneapolis: Fortress, 1998) 240.

[3] The English term *economy* comes from the Greek *oikos* (household) and *nomos* (rules, law), meaning household rules. M. Douglas Meeks underscores the centrality of economics for the Bible in *God the Economist: The Doctrine of God and Political Economy* (Minneapolis: Fortress, 1989). See also Rob van Drimmeien, *Faith in a Global Economy: A Primer for Christians* (Geneva: WCC Publications, 1998).

[4] On "biblical creation faith" see Anne M. Clifford, "Creation," in Francis Schüssler Fiorenza and John P. Galvin, eds., *Systematic Theology: Roman Catholic Perspectives* (Minneapolis: Fortress, 1991) 2:193–248.

[5] The prophet Amos denounces those who trample on the needy and bring to ruin the poor of the land, "buying the poor for silver and the needy for a pair of sandals" (Amos 8:4-6).

[6] The man who asks Jesus how he is to inherit eternal life is a member of an upper-stratum group. Jesus' demand to "sell all" urges the man to sell the possessions most fundamental to him as an ancient Mediterranean person, the family home and land. See Bruce J. Malina and Richard L. Rohrbaugh, *Social-Science Commentary on the Synoptic Gospels* (Minneapolis: Fortress, 1992) 384; 323–24.

[7] Ibid. 309.

[8] The Johannine Jesus talks about himself, not about the reign of God. For a comparison of the Gospel of John with the synoptic gospels see Mark Allan Powell, *Fortress Introduction to the Gospels* (Minneapolis: Fortress, 1998) 112–22.

[9] Among important works in this recovery is E. P. Sanders, *Jesus and Judaism* (Philadelphia: Fortress, 1985). Theissen and Merz discuss *basileia* as an eschatological symbol pointing to the future but also referring to past and present. See *The Historical Jesus,* 240, 252, 261–65. In *Jesus: Miriam's Child, Sophia's*

Prophet: Critical Issues in Feminist Christology (New York: Continuum, 1995) Elisabeth Schüssler Fiorenza points to its centrality: "The central symbol of this movement, the *basileia tou theou,* expresses a Jewish religious-political vision common to all the movements in first-century Israel. This central vision spells freedom from domination" (p. 92).

[10] Elisabeth Schüssler Fiorenza, *Jesus,* 93. For an elaboration see pp. 131–62.

[11] Cf. Proverbs 1:20-33; 3:13-18; 8:1–9:12; Sirach 1, 4; Wisdom 6:12–11:1.

[12] Elisabeth Schüssler Fiorenza, *In Memory of Her: A Feminist Theological Reconstruction of Christian Origins* (New York: Crossroad, 1984) 135.

[13] Elizabeth A. Johnson, "Redeeming the Name of Christ," in Catherine Mowry LaCugna, ed., *Freeing Theology: The Essentials of Theology in Feminist Perspective* (San Francisco: HarperSanFrancisco, 1993) 121. On early Sophia christology see pp. 120–27.

[14] In citing the landlord and tenants parable as his example (Mark 12:1-9), Stephen Patterson *(The God of Jesus)* writes "that not all of Jesus' parables were designed to reveal Jesus' vision of how life would be if only it were lived consistently with God's rule. Some of his parables do not reveal the Empire of God at all. Rather they reveal the world as it really is" (p. 140).

[15] Cf. Mark 10:35-44: "whoever wishes to become great among you must be your servant, and whoever wishes to be first among you must be slave of all."

[16] Galatians 3:28 captures this redemptive reversal: "There is no longer Jew or Greek, there is no longer slave or free, there is no longer male and female; for all of you are one in Christ Jesus." Cf. Jesus' miracle activity. Healings and exorcisms do not simply effect physical or psychic changes but reintegrate the person into the community. In the context of a purity system the healing reverses the outsider status imposed by the impurity of disease or demonic possession to the insider status of community participant. On purity see L. William Countryman, *Dirt, Greed, and Sex: Sexual Ethics in the New Testament* (Philadelphia: Fortress, 1988) 11–65. Marcus Borg contrasts Jesus' advocacy of a "politics of compassion" with the "politics of purity," in *Conflict, Holiness, and Politics* (Harrisburg: Trinity Press International, 1998).

[17] In his book *The Prophetic Imagination* (2nd ed. Minneapolis: Fortress, 2001), Walter Brueggemann's description of Solomonic affluence holds true generally for imperial rule: "The Solomonic achievement was in part made possible by oppressive social policy" (p. 27). Forced labor was fundamental. An economics of affluence and politics of oppression received religious sanctification by "the establishment of a controlled, static religion . . . in which the sovereignty of God is fully subordinated to the purposes of the king" (p. 28).

[18] Marcus Borg draws out the significance of Jesus' religious experience in *Jesus: A New Vision* (San Francisco: HarperSanFrancisco, 1987) 39–56.

[19]Cf. the stories of the woman anointing Jesus (Luke 7:36-50) and Mary and Martha (Luke 10:38-42).

[20]See John P. Galvin, "Jesus Christ," in Schüssler Fiorenza and Galvin, eds., *Systematic Theology: Roman Catholic Perspectives*, 1:249–324.

[21]On Sophialogy as the earliest histological reflection see Elisabeth Schüssler Fiorenza, *Jesus*, 139ff.

[22]Cf. Larry W. Hurtado, *One God, One Lord: Early Christian Devotion and Ancient Jewish Monotheism* (Philadelphia: Fortress, 1988).

[23]E.g., Ephesians 6:5-8; Colossians 3:22-25; 1 Timothy 6:1-2; 1 Peter 2:18-21.

[24]Cf. Elisabeth Schüssler Fiorenza, *In Memory of Her*, 92.

[25]Cf. 1 Timothy 2:15 with Galatians 3:2, 26 and the active participation and leadership of women reflected in Romans 16. Appeal to household codes (Eph 6:5-8; Col 3:22-25; 1 Tim 6:1-2) inverted the redemptive liberation that Galatians 3:28 affirms.

[26]This is the case for contemporary theology, too. Gerard S. Sloyan (*The Crucifixion of Jesus: History, Myth, Faith* [Minneapolis: Fortress, 1995]) notes that "If Protestant and Catholic theologians may be said to be at present still largely absorbed with redemption by the cross as God's response to human sin, chiefly Adam's sin in the manner of Paul and Augustine, it should be said that there is a growing concern in all the churches with redemption as the liberation of the poor and of the oppressed. Among the oppressed are peoples of color and women everywhere on the globe" (p. 162).

[27]Walter Wink, *Engaging the Powers: Discernment and Resistance in a World of Domination* (Minneapolis: Fortress, 1992) 51. Here he discusses three important New Testament terms and their meaning: (1) *kosmos,* "the human sociological realm that exists in estrangement from God" (p. 51): Jesus says that he is "not of this world," meaning he is not part of the *domination system* around him; (2) *aion,* usually translated "world," better translated *domination epoch,* the time in which oppression and injustice endure; and (3) *sarx,* commonly translated "living by the flesh," better *dominated existence,* i.e., life under the rule of the domination system, a world of little freedom in which some are subordinated to the rule of others, the pursuit of personal satisfactions, and securing one's life through one's own power.

[28]An example is Roger Haight's transposition of neoscholastic categories in "Sin and Grace," in Schüssler Fiorenza and Galvin, eds., *Systematic Theology: Roman Catholic Perspectives*, 2:75–142. In contrast to the tradition's individualism, Haight unfolds the meaning of human freedom and divine grace in social terms by emphasizing the structural features of redemption. Again, he highlights the meaning of *basileia* for history: "The kingdom of God is an eschatological symbol. . . . The kingdom of God, then, as God's will, God's values, God's intention for historical existence, also applies to history" (p. 133).

[29]E.g., Matthew 20:1-16, the vineyard; Matthew 22:1-14, the wedding banquet.

[30]Matthew 13:31-33, the mustard seed, the woman and leaven. The parables of the treasure, the pearl, and the net follow (Matt 13:44-49).

[31]Cf. Matthew 25:1-46.

[32]Cf. Luke's opening of Jesus' ministry (Luke 4:14-21).

[33]E.g., Mark 8:35; 9:35; 10:43-55.

[34]Luke 6:17-26.

[35]E.g., Mark 1:23-26, 34.

[36]Cf. Mark 6:53-56; 1:21-28.

[37]Mark 3:31-35. See Joanna Dewey, "The Gospel of Mark," in Elisabeth Schüssler Fiorenza, ed., *Searching the Scriptures: A Feminist Commentary* (New York: Crossroad Publishing Co., 1994) 470–509. For women, Jesus' replacement of the blood kinship group with a new, fictive group open to those who do the will of God is especially significant. The new group "is open to women independently of their embeddedness in the social unit of the family, where they owe obedience to father or husband" (p. 478).

[38]The term belongs to Elisabeth Schüssler Fiorenza. See *In Memory of Her,* 107.

[39]Matthew 6:9-13//Luke 11:2-4.

[40]Luke 7:36-50.

[41]Mark 3:31-35. Like slaveholding, the chattel status of women is part of a patriarchal economy.

[42]Norman K. Gottwald, "From Tribal Existence to Empire: The Socio-Historical Content for the Rise of the Hebrew Prophets," in J. Mark Thomas and Vernon Visick, eds., *God and Capitalism: A Prophetic Critique of Market Economy* (Madison, Wisc.: A-R Editions, 1990) 11–29, at 18.

[43]Walter Wink, *The Powers That Be* (New York: Doubleday, 1998) 39.

[44]Luke 6:20ff.//Matthew 5:3ff. Cf. Theissen and Metz, *The Historical Jesus,* 253–54.

[45]The values are cited by Walter Wink. See *Engaging the Powers,* 107.

[46]The Bible does not proffer a specific economic model. However, it does offer something more valuable, Gottwald argues: "A perspective and criteria for evaluating political economies and a framework and ground for accepting personal responsibility for one's economic views and actions. The 'communitarian' yardstick is a significant one for assessing any political economy: Does the mode of production, and the power relations governing it, build up the whole community, providing it basic services and creating opportunities to realize the

life possibilities of the greatest number of people?" Gottwald, "From Tribal Existence to Empire," 25–26.

[47]On the economics of imperial rule see K. C. Hanson and Douglas E. Oakman, *Palestine in the Time of Jesus* (Minneapolis: Fortress, 1998) 99–129. On lower- and upper-stratum groups see Ekkehard W. Stegemann and Wolfgang Stegemann, *The Jesus Movement: A Social History of Its First Century*, trans. O. C. Dean, Jr. (Minneapolis: Fortress, 1999) 68–95.

[48]Hanson and Oakman discuss peasant indebtedness and land in *Palestine*, 112–20. On debtor slavery and causes for debt see Stegemann and Stegemann, *The Jesus Movement*. Children as well as adults were sold into slavery to satisfy indebtedness (idem. 86). Providing for the Roman military—calculated to be around 300,000 soldiers with need for about 100,000 tons of grain per year— put a great burden on the local population, as did a variety of compulsory levies, duties, taxes, and forced labor of the native population for building projects and obligations to the military (idem. 47–49). The authors note that the "vast majority of the rural populace in antiquity lived on the fine line between hunger and the assurance of subsistence" (idem. 51). The reasons for their miserable living conditions were numerous: fields too small to produce adequately, catastrophic consequences of crop failures, and overtaxation of small farmers. A majority of the urban population was also poor, but their needs for food were met by magistrates in order to forestall social unrest (idem. 51–52).

[49]In "From Tribal Existence to Empire" Norman Gottwald writes that the "prophetic movement is a long-sustained exploration and criticism of how the tributary mode of production permeates and distorts Israelite (and later Jewish) culture and religion" (pp. 18–19). Prophets evaluate society from the perspective of the communitarian mode of production and its values, an economy well defined in the time of the judges and still existing in villages throughout Palestine. Jesus' preaching was in line with these communitarian values and practices of rural Galilee (p. 18).

[50]Exodus 23:11; Leviticus 25:1-13. See Dorothee Soelle, "God's Economy and Ours: The Year of the Jubilee," in Thomas and Visick, eds., *God and Capitalism*, 87–103; see also Meeks, *God the Economist*, 83–92. In Luke, Jesus' ministry opens with the proclamation of "the year of the Lord's favor" (Luke 4:19), a reference to the Jubilee year, a year-long Sabbath. Cf. Malina and Rohrbaugh, *Synoptic Gospels*, 309.

[51]Wink (*Engaging the Powers*, 113–14) states: "The gospel of Jesus champions economic equality, because economic inequalities are the basis of domination. Ranking, domination hierarchies, and classism are all built on accumulated power provided by excess wealth. In a peasant society, those in power see to it, by taxation, expropriation, debt, and monopolistic control of prices, that the poor are never able to rise above their station. . . . Breaking with domination means ending the economic exploitation of the many by the few."

[52] Brueggemann, *The Prophetic Imagination,* 16.

[53] Johnson, "Redeeming Christ," 123.

[54] Cf. Brueggemann, *The Prophetic Imagination,* 26–31.

[55] Cf. Meeks (*God the Economist,* 95) who specifies that the invitation of the Gospel is "the right to be included in God's own economy, which is the source of life."

[56] The form-critical judgment is that this text is a pre-Pauline baptismal fragment. See Hans-Dieter Betz, *Galatians.* Hermeneia (Philadelphia: Fortress, 1979) 181–85.

[57] The history of Christian Anti-Semitism reflects a tragic conception of the opening of God's covenant to Gentiles. John T. Pawlikowski traces the origin and development of Christian theological Anti-Semitism in "Christology, Anti-Semitism, and Christian-Jewish Bonding," in Rebecca S. Chopp and Mark Lewis Taylor, eds., *Reconstructing Christian Theology* (Minneapolis: Fortress, 1994) 245–68.

[58] For a history of the fate of this proclamation for women see Rosemary Radford Ruether, *Women and Redemption: A Theological History* (Minneapolis: Fortress, 1998).

[59] Cf. Brueggemann, *The Prophetic Imagination,* 59–79.

[60] Stegemann and Stegemann (*The Jesus Movement,* 91–92) state that the "relatively poor" are those who could meet their basic needs but with little or nothing left over. The "absolutely poor" are those who did not have enough even to live.

[61] 1 Timothy 3:15. M. Douglas Meek's *God the Economist* is a masterful and insightful recovery of the liberating meaning of the economy of the "household of God" *(oikos tou theou).* In this context, however, I emphasize the fact that its introduction as a description of the *ekklēsia* is dramatically at odds with the self-understanding embedded in the choice of the term *ekklēsia.* The *ekklēsia* is no longer imagined as an assembly of free persons, but one in which persons "have their place." The place of women and slaves is the same in the household of God as in the patriarchal household. Subordination to authorities now becomes a Christian obligation.

[62] Cf. 1 Timothy 6:1-2: "Let all who are under the yoke of slavery regard their masters as worthy of all honor, so that the name of God and the teaching may not be blasphemed. Those who have believing masters must not be disrespectful to them on the ground that they are members of the church; rather they must serve them all the more, since those who benefit by their service are believers and beloved."

[63] Stegemann and Stegemann, *The Jesus Movement,* 91. On women and social stratification see 65–67 and 364–77.

[64]Malina and Rohrbaugh note: "Since no family connection remained, such a woman's life expectancy was extremely short" (*Synoptic Gospels,* 329). A woman's son was her closest emotional support; he was the blood relation on whom she could depend (p. 287).

[65] Ibid. 102.

[66] Rita Nakashima Brock and Susan Brooks Thistlethwaite, *Casting Stones: Prostitution and Liberation in Asia and the U.S.* (Minneapolis: Fortress, 1996) especially 5–6, 104, 114.

[67] Ibid. 121–22: "In labor intensive industries [those that cannot be mechanized], slavery is enormously profitable because wages paid to the large number of workers constitute by far the greatest part of the overhead. Workers are not trained, and so little money is wasted if they are worked literally to death; there must, however, be a large and continuous supply of workers. The large profits that the sex industry generates are related to low overhead."

[68] Schüssler Fiorenza (*In Memory of Her*) indicates: "Prostitutes usually were slaves, daughters who had been sold or rented out by their parents, wives who were rented out by their husbands, poor women, exposed girls, the divorced and widowed, single mothers, captives of war or piracy, women bought for soldiers . . ." (p. 128).

[69] In *A Herstory of Prostitution,* Jesse Wells writes: "Mercenary prostitution— the selling of sexual intercourse—originated in ancient Athens in approximately 594 B.C.E. as a government-run enterprise to finance the building of the Greek military. The first Athenian brothel was staffed by Asian slaves, prisoners of war, and women cast out by their families who were kidnapped or bought from slave traders." (Quoted in Brock and Thistlethwaite, *Casting Stones,* 111.)

[70] Wink, *Engaging the Powers,* 132.

[71] Patterson, *The God of Jesus,* 82.

[72] Ibid. 105–06.

[73] Malina and Rohrbaugh, *The Synoptic Gospels,* 251.

[74] The two spheres are dramatically illustrated in Jesus' story of the rich man and Lazarus (Luke 16:19-31). Poverty-stricken, landless, outcast, Lazarus sits with Abraham at the eschatological table. See Meeks's discussion of this text and the just use of property in *God the Economist,* 121–22.

[75] Bernard J. F. Lonergan, S.J., *Method in Theology* (New York: Herder and Herder, 1972): "What is good, always is concrete. But definitions are abstract" (p. 27). To define the good requires analysis of the components that enter into it. A systematic theology of the human good transposes Jesus' symbolic apprehension of God's *basileia* into a theoretical apprehension of concrete realities.

[76] Cf. Luke 14:7-24, the eschatological banquet. Not only are the non-elite invited, but the lowest of the non-elite—those outside the city walls (beggars, prostitutes)—are invited. See Malina and Rohrbaugh, *The Synoptic Gospels,* 364–69.

[77]Cf. Matthew 20:16, Jesus' parable of the laborers. Day laborers were among the poorest, usually landless peasants who had lost their ancestral lands through debt. Loss of land usually meant loss of family (Malina and Rohbaugh, *The Synoptic Gospels,* 124–25).

[78]See Matthew 25:31-46. The parable promotes human participation in the redemptive restoration of creation by meeting basic human needs (food, clean water, clothing, shelter). On basic necessities as human rights see Meeks, *God the Economist,* 90–91.

[79]My consideration of the human good draws from Bernard Lonergan's *Method in Theology,* especially 27–55, and idem, *Insight: A Study of Human Understanding* (London: Darton, Longman and Todd, 1957), especially 595–633. Lonergan's economics work, *An Essay in Circulation Analysis,* is described as a "pure economic analysis of the exchange process." For a brief overview see Bernard J. F. Lonergan, "Moral Theology and the Human Sciences," in *Method: Journal of Lonergan Studies* 15 (1997) 5–18. Helpful secondary sources are William Mathews, s.j., "Lonergan's Economics," *Method: Journal of Lonergan Studies* 3 (March 1985) 9–30; Eileen O'Brien de Neeve, "Suspicion and Recovery: Ethical Approaches to Economics," *Method: Journal of Lonergan Studies* 15 (1997) 29–49; and Patrick Byrne, "Economic Transformations: The Role of Conversions and Culture in the Transformation of Economics," in Timothy P. Fallon, s.j., and Philip Boo Riley, eds., *Religion and Culture: Essays in Honor of Bernard Lonergan, s.j.* (Albany: State University of New York Press, 1987) 327–48.

[80]On the principles of progress and decline see Lonergan, *Method in Theology,* 53–55. Decline is initiated and sustained by the various forms of bias (e.g., individual egoism, group egoism) that interfere with understanding correctly, deciding responsibly, and acting accordingly. In *Insight* see pp. 627–30.

[81]Lonergan, *Insight,* 630.

[82]Lonergan, *Method in Theology,* 55.

[83]"The family, the state, the law, the economy are not fixed and immutable entities . . . they can be reconceived in the light of new ideas. . . . But all such change involves change of meaning—a change of idea or concept, a change of judgment or evaluation, a change of the order or request" (Lonergan, *Method,* 78). For a theological example of reconceiving the family see Lisa Sowle Cahill, *Family: A Christian Social Perspective* (Minneapolis: Fortress, 2000).

[84]This is a theme developed at the Second Vatican Council in *Gaudium et Spes (Pastoral Constitution on the Church in the Modern World),* Walter M. Abbot, s.j., ed., *The Documents of Vatican II* (New York: Guild Press, 1966) especially 271–82.

[85]Cf. Lonergan, "Healing and Creating in History." The reversal of decline has two requirements: "From economic theorists we have to demand, along with as many other types of analysis as they please, a new and specific type that reveals

how moral precepts have both a basis in economic process and so an effective application to it. From moral theorists we have to demand, along with their other various forms of wisdom and prudence, specifically economic precepts that arise out of economic process itself and promote its proper functioning" (p. 108).

[86]Cf. Lonergan, "Moral Theology and the Human Sciences." "Its three principal variants, all operative to some extent, are the traditional market economy, the Marxist-inspired socialist economy, and the new transactional economy constituted by the giant corporations which are not socialist and are not controlled by the market. In all three the influence of ideology is discernible and what, I believe, is needed in the first place is a pure economic analysis of the exchange process untainted by any ideology" (p. 17).

[87]Soelle, "God's Economy and Ours," 95.

[88]Ibid. 96. The Nehemiah reference to the indebtedness of farmers and the consequent selling of children into slavery and exposure of their daughters to the lust of the rich (5:5) has its modern counterpart in countries where peasant girls are sold as slaves to the sex tourism of the rich.

[89]Lonergan, "Moral Theology and the Human Sciences," 16.

[90]Beverly Harrison, "The Fate of the Middle 'Class' in Late Capitalism," in Thomas and Visick, eds., *God and Capitalism,* 53–71, at 55.

[91]*Gaudium et Spes* develops this theme in its reflection on the interdependence of humankind (Abbot, ed., *The Documents of Vatican II,* 222–31). Affirming the centrality of the common good and acknowledging that in the matter of justice the social order requires constant improvement (p. 225), the writers link this process with divine presence: "God's Spirit, who with a marvelous providence directs the unfolding of time and renews the face of the earth, is not absent from this development" (p. 226).

8

The Samaritan Woman and Martha as Partners with Jesus in Ministry: Re-Creation in John 4 and 11

Judith Schubert, R.S.M.

INTRODUCTION

*T*he Gospel of John presents women who effect a creative reversal in the lives of others. It also describes women who encourage Jesus to produce a change in others, thereby assisting in re-creation. Each relevant pericope results in a change of heart in the characters because of the fortitude and heroism of a particular woman.

Throughout the Fourth Gospel certain narratives promote women as partners in ministry with Jesus, e.g., the mother of Jesus (John 2:1-12), Mary of Bethany (John 11:1-44, 12:1-8), and Mary of Magdala (John 20:1, 2, 11-18). In this limited study I focus on John 4 and 11 and two important women within these chapters, namely, the Samaritan woman (John 4:4-42) and Martha of Bethany (John 11:1-44).[1] These two women freely interact with Jesus. Both develop a close friendship with him as Jesus also responds openly and positively to them. He even shares with these women some of his deepest thoughts.

The biblical texts I present identify these two courageous women as influential leaders whose inner strength inspires Jesus to act on their requests or to entrust them with the proclamation of the "good news." In these narratives others benefit from the fearless strength of the women. Their actions effect a re-creation in other people that changes lives for the good. Jesus offers new life through the mediation of these women.

Furthermore, the texts promote the advancement of women leaders and their relationship with Jesus, the protagonist in the gospel. In both narratives I emphasize the role of a particular woman rather than analyzing the entire narrative. Throughout the study each pericope is prefaced by background material that includes the context of the narrative, literary and cultural features, and other pertinent information. Whether or not the woman or narrative represents historical moments of Jesus' ministry is not discussed because in either case she functions as an instrumental model of imitation. Both figures symbolize the initiative of a woman who collaborates with Jesus in his mission to others. The study seeks to uncover in each chosen pericope the prominent role of the woman as a ministerial partner of Jesus and as one who offers re-creation to others.

To accomplish a feminist critical reading of each character I employ various methodological approaches. At different points my inquiry utilizes historical-literary criticism as well as cultural, social, and theological analysis so as to uncover the creative ministry of the particular woman within the pericope. To obtain a critical feminist interpretation it is necessary to study these women figures in the Johannine texts with an acknowledgment that they are products of a biased patriarchal system, where women are viewed as inferior. Consequently, the stories about the women must be viewed with suspicion. At times it is necessary to rethink the role of the woman by means of historical reconstruction and/or in light of cultural mores. In certain instances I include a discussion of androcentric biases in previous interpretations when these undercut the creative leadership role of the woman within the text.

THE SAMARITAN WOMAN LEADS AND INITIATES RE-CREATION (JOHN 4:4-42)

Background

The energized exchange between Jesus and the Samaritan woman at the well takes place amid unusual circumstances within the culture and religion of first-century Palestine. First, a man appears alone with an unknown woman at the well at a peculiar time.[2] Second, a man addresses this unknown woman. Third, the man, a Jew, dialogues with the woman, a Samaritan. The history between Jews and Samaritans over the topics of cultic worship and purity was marked by hostility. In this powerful Johannine drama, however, both Jesus and the unnamed woman cross social, geographic, gender, religious, and ethnic boundaries. In doing so they redefine the boundaries of "in group/out group" as well as public and private space that separate women and men.[3] Jesus initiates the breakthrough in his request for a drink of water (4:7). As he speaks to this unknown foreigner he anticipates shared drinking utensils. In both instances he transgresses Jewish ritual purity laws. The woman's immediate response also breaks barriers because she speaks in a public space to an unknown Jewish man (4:8).

Contextually, the story comes early in the Gospel of John amid other accounts that highlight relationships between Jesus and other people. For example, Jesus calls Andrew and Simon, Philip and Nathaniel in John 1:35-51, dialogues with Nicodemus in John 3:1-21, and meets other Galileans in John 4:43-45. The characters in these other stories frame that of the Samaritan woman in John 4:4-42. Yet these others need more assurance than Jesus' words to sustain a relationship with him. Their anxiety cannot be alleviated without some type of sign (John 2:11; 4:45). The woman at the well needs no signs, has no doubts, and demonstrates no fear of Jesus. She comes to believe in him solely on his word.[4]

Of all the episodes in John 1–4, Jesus' encounter with the Pharisee, Nicodemus (John 3:1-21), offers the most striking contrast to his dialogue with the Samaritan woman (John 4:4-42). Both conversations employ the technique of question, answer, and misunderstanding as a way to allow Jesus to expand on the topic and as a means to deepen the faith of the person to whom Jesus speaks. Nicodemus' questions, however, do not lead to a deepened faith. On the contrary, Jesus becomes so frustrated with his inability to listen and to grow that he complains, "Are you a teacher of Israel, and yet you do not understand these things?" (John 3:10). Furthermore, the respected leader comes to Jesus only in the dark hours of the night when his colleagues cannot see him.

Although the Samaritan woman receives no respect from her peers, she acts much more courageously than Nicodemus. Throughout the narrative she continually listens to what Jesus discloses to her. Her initial misconception leads to insight because the woman opens herself to Jesus and thereby comes to believe in him. Unlike Nicodemus, she speaks and listens to Jesus in an atmosphere of enlightenment, suggested by their meeting at high noon, which represents the brightest light of day. Moreover, her heightened identity with Jesus leads the Samaritan woman to invite the villagers to a new level of creation.

A Developing Discipleship

The Samaritan woman arrives at the well at noon, a rare time of day to draw water because of the intensity of the heat. In addition, water would have been needed for household duties long before that time. While the gospel presents no explanation for her arrival at this late hour, her marital status might have caused her neighbors to banish her from drawing water with others (4:16).

Whatever the reason, the narrative implies that the neighbors ostracize the woman. Thus she represents the marginalized in three ways: society scorns her gender, Judaism rejects her religion, and the townspeople disdain her person. In effect the Samaritan woman at the well receives no honor or concern. With this context in mind, the dramatic crescendo of the dialogue between the woman and Jesus, the woman's increasing faith in him, and her unselfish invitation to the villagers astonish the reader. Certain motifs and texts within the story highlight the development of the woman's belief and leadership skills.

The narrative begins with the arrival of Jesus and his disciples at the village of Sychar in Samaria. Jesus, tired from the journey, sits near Jacob's well while the others enter the village in search of food. When a woman comes alone to draw water at the well, Jesus requests a drink (4:7).[5] By speaking to her Jesus ignores prevalent cultural and religious norms. Consequently, the woman questions his request. From that moment a powerful drama unfolds.

Although the woman never responds to the two emphatic requests of Jesus, namely, for a drink of water (4:7) and to "go call your husband/man" (4:16), she actively engages in conversation with him. The range of topics moves from well water to a "spring of water gushing up to eternal life" (4:15), from the woman's personal marital history to her proclamation that Jesus is truly a prophet (4:19), from relations between Jews and Samaritans to the meaning of true worship, from the woman's final disclosure to Jesus about the arrival of the Taheb (Messiah) to Jesus' acknowledgment that he fulfills that role (4:26). As the woman opens her heart, listens, and responds to Jesus the discussion deepens and climaxes in Jesus' *egō eimi* saying, "I am he," i.e., the long-awaited Messiah. The Samaritan woman is the first person in the gospel to whom Jesus confides this reality. Earlier in 1:41 Andrew tells Simon that "we have found the Messiah," but here Jesus himself proclaims his identity to her. He demonstrates his high regard for the woman through verbal gifts, namely, his continued conversation with her as well as his offer of "living water" (4:14) and the revelation of his Messiahship. Throughout the conversation Jesus never condemns the past actions of her life. Rather, he respects and confides in her.

Through the evangelist's portrayal of the other characters in John 1–4 the gospel intimates that this woman exemplifies the ever-deepening faith and risk-taking of a true disciple. She believes in Jesus solely through his words. In this way the unnamed woman stands above all the other disciples or seekers who have preceded her in the gospel. Such discussion will change her life forever because ultimately she responds lovingly to Jesus with a transformed heart.

While Jesus shared the revelation about Messiahship with the woman, the disciples returned from the village to the well (4:27). They witnessed the two engrossed in conversation and "were astonished" because Jesus conversed with her. Both cultural and religious mores prohibited such verbal exchange. Unlike the woman, who did not hesitate to question Jesus, these male disciples seem afraid to ask him about what they were encountering (4:27). The woman's courage contrasts strongly to the timidity of the other disciples.

The returning disciples had not yet embarked on their mission to others in Jesus' name, as the Samaritan woman does. Jesus expresses this point in his parable-like remarks. He says to them, "I sent you to reap that for which you did not labor. Others have labored, and you have entered into their labor" (4:38-39). Besides Jesus, the only other laborer at that moment is the unnamed woman, who leaves her water jar at the well and returns to speak to her neighbors who have shunned her. Here Jesus encourages the disciples to appreciate her leadership and selfless fortitude. Everyone will benefit from the generous labors of this Samaritan woman.

When the story returns to the transformed woman, the evangelist presents her as one who ministers to others rather than keeping the "good news" to herself. As she returns to the village she proclaims Jesus to the others. This pronouncement illustrates the woman's spiritual strength and concern for them, even for those who may have persecuted her. She freely invites to "come and see a man who told me everything I have ever done!" (4:29). The announcement almost guarantees the movement of the villagers to the well, even out of sheer curiosity. In this way the woman chooses complete vulnerability so that the townspeople also may be transformed if they so choose. Additionally, the phrase "come and see" functions in the Fourth Gospel as a technical invitation to discipleship.[6] In this instance the woman becomes the first person in the gospel to speak for Jesus and carry out his revelatory mission to a group. The gospel verifies the woman's apostolic significance when it asserts that "many Samaritans from that city believed in him (Jesus) because of the woman's testimony" (4:39).

In the past many exegetes have concentrated only on the figure of Jesus in the narrative. As a consequence, they neglected the woman's leadership role, overlooked her deep faith, criticized the woman's marital status, or viewed her as immoral without sufficient textual evidence.[7] To counteract such inaccuracies Mary Rose D'Angelo points out that "the text imputes neither sin nor shame to the woman. She expresses no repentance and Jesus neither forgives her nor warns her against sinning again."[8]

From the outset of the story the woman risks her already suspect place in society and responds openly to Jesus. Among his disciples only the woman communicates freely with him. In contrast to other dialogues within the gospel, Jesus' conversation with the woman never reverts to a long monologue. Rather, together the two dialogue in a lively and enlightened discussion. As a result the woman benefits greatly from a profound realization of the person of Jesus.

Through her charismatic leadership and bravery the unnamed woman effects a transformed life for her townspeople. She partners with Jesus to spread the "good news" to others. As Sandra Schneiders clearly states, the Samaritan woman at the well represents the only disciple to exercise a truly apostolic role during the lifetime of Jesus.[9] She remains a model of leadership, faith, and mission for all times. The once estranged Samaritan woman now delivers the gift of eternal life to her community, which causes a re-creation in their own lives.

MARTHA LEADS AND INITIATES RE-CREATION (JOHN 11:1-44)

Background

Within John 11:1-44, the climax of Jesus' ministry and the restoration of Lazarus' life, the dramatic dialogue between Martha and Jesus in 11:21-27 remains the focal point of the entire narrative. Martha, however, appears throughout the story. For example, she, along with Mary, informs Jesus about her brother's critical illness (11:3). She converses with Jesus about the death of her brother and the significance of life. She comforts mourning neighbors and deepens their faith in Jesus. In effect, Martha models faithful discipleship of Jesus through her dialogue as well as her actions. Ultimately she inspires Jesus to bring a creative new life to Lazarus and to those who witness the sign.

Although some of the other signs throughout the gospel briefly describe a particular miracle and then proceed quickly to the discourse that interprets the sign, John 11 follows a different pattern. Here the evangelist presents three conversations that precede the miracle: (a) Jesus with Thomas and other disciples (vv. 7-16a); (b) Jesus with Martha (vv. 21-27); (c) Jesus with Mary (vv. 28-34). The conversations explore the significance of the sign before it even takes place. Within these dialogues Martha's initiative, openness, and spiritual insights cannot be missed. Her insightful conversation with Jesus represents the most important of the three exchanges and the theological center of the entire story.

From the beginning (11:1) the pericope introduces Martha, Mary, and Lazarus as a family from Bethany. It asserts that Lazarus was ill. As a consequence his sisters send a personal message to alert Jesus: "Lord, he whom you love is ill" (11:3). The text notes "though Jesus loved Martha and her sister and Lazarus . . . he stayed two days longer in the place where he was" (11:5-6). While Jesus' decision in 11:6 seems inconsiderate, it functions as a literary device. The delay provides the opportunity for Jesus to talk about life and death, both for Lazarus and for himself. It also demonstrates the divine independence of Jesus' decision from human timetables.

Before any further considerations, it is important to note that in 11:5 the evangelist identifies the family as individuals when he speaks of Jesus' love for each of them. In addition, although ancient lists begin usually with male names, here the list begins with Martha, which suggests her leadership role and/or her closeness to Jesus. Throughout the story the evangelist emphasizes the leadership initiative of Martha as she interacts with Jesus, an initiative that results in the most important sign of his earthly ministry. Moreover, her developed faith in Jesus identifies her as a role model for others.

Discipleship plays a key role in the Fourth Gospel, where it is associated with love. When Jesus discovers another person who responds openly to him, he begins to cherish that person and shares his teachings and revelation with the other. The dialogue with the Samaritan woman in John 4 exemplifies this point. In John 11:5 the fact that Jesus loves Martha indicates her special position as disciple and friend. Later Jesus defines the term "friend" in such a way that it becomes a synonym for "disciple" (15:15). The following discussion will highlight Martha as disciple, leader, and friend of Jesus.

Martha's Friendship Invites Jesus' Self-Revelation

When Jesus finally arrives in Bethany, Lazarus has already died and been entombed four days (11:17). This development reintroduces Martha into the narrative. The exchange between Martha and Jesus contains the most substantial dialogue in the entire story because of the theological realities they share with each other.[10]

As soon as Martha hears that Jesus was near Bethany, "she went and met him" (11:20). Her gracious hospitality and love lead her straight to Jesus. Nothing keeps her from him. As soon as they meet, Martha shares her inner thoughts and feelings. Initially she utters, "Lord, if you had been here, my brother would not have died" (11:21).

Martha speaks freely about the death of her brother. Her next statement expresses confidence in future possibility: "But even now I know that God will give you whatever you ask of him" (11:22). It does not matter that Lazarus has already died and that Jesus had not arrived in time. Martha's belief in Jesus cannot be shaken. Despite her grief and anguish over her brother's death, she trusts her close friend. Both her speech and actions radiate her faithful discipleship.

In typical Johannine fashion, the conversation deepens when Jesus assures Martha that her brother "will rise again" (11:23). She replies, "I know that he will rise again in the resurrection on the last day" (11:24). Here Martha acknowledges her belief in Jesus' statement and expresses her hope of resurrection in accordance with contemporary Jewish belief. Such futuristic eschatology echoes the ideas of the first-century Pharisees about resurrection from the dead.[11] Moreover, it deepens the dialogue.

Her reply prompts Jesus to trust Martha with a new and profound reality when he proclaims, "I am the resurrection and the life" (11:25). This *egō eimi* saying moves the discussion to the level of realized eschatology. The hope of resurrection shifts from the future into the present moment. What has been a traditional Jewish theology for Pharisees now leads to a profound self-revelation by Jesus to his trusted friend, Martha. He develops his point with her as he adds that "those who believe in me, even though they die, will live, and everyone who lives and believes in me will never die" (11:25-26). Jesus chooses to make this deep theological proclamation to Martha because of her warm friendship, open heart, and attentive listening skills.

Jesus' question, "Do you believe this?" (11:26) offers Martha a further opportunity to demonstrate her unwavering confidence in her friend's powerful proclamation. With deep conviction she responds: "Yes, Lord, I believe that you are the Messiah, the Son of God, the one coming into the world" (11:27). Martha's three-part theological testimony reveals her complete faith in the person of Jesus. It also anticipates the evangelist's compelling confession in John 20:31: "but these are written so that you may come to believe that Jesus is the Messiah, the Son of God, and that through believing you may have life in his name." Both pronouncements echo the heart of the gospel's message, namely that faith leads to true life. Here Martha authenticates her personal belief in the life offered by Jesus and thus serves as a model for all disciples.

The importance of Martha's insightful christological proclamation, "You are the Messiah, the Son of God," must not be overlooked. Some authors hold that it corresponds to Peter's confession at Caesarea Philippi in Matthew 16:16.[12] There Peter responds to Jesus' question, "Who do people say that the Son of Man is?" with the words, "you are the Messiah, the Son of the living God." This forceful acknowledgment leads Jesus to commission Peter to a leadership role in the future apostolic era. So, too, in John, should not the same leadership apply to Martha? Exegetes like Robert Karris suggest that "her confession of faith [is] the foundation of the Johannine community . . . the confession of faith of a woman [is] the very foundation of John's Church."[13] Sandra Schneiders remarks that "if this confession given during the life of Jesus [recorded in Matthew's Gospel] grounds the promise of the primacy of Peter, it is not less significant as foundation of community leadership when given by a woman."[14]

The parallel between the confessions of Peter and Martha in Matt 16:16 and John 11:27 suggests powerful inferences about Martha's life-giving role within the community. As Peter's confession of faith reflects his future position as leader in Matthew's gospel, so, too, Martha's leadership within the Johannine community may be documented through her response to Jesus. His self-revelation to her verifies the conclusion that Jesus regards her highly as faithful friend and leader. Finally, her words, echoing the sentiments of the final summary message of the gospel (20:31), identify Martha as "a," if not "the," well-respected leader and initiator within the Johannine circle. She conveys the message of the Fourth Gospel. In effect Martha continues as a ministerial partner with Jesus in her ability to dialogue with him, to acknowledge his extraordinary self-revelation, and to collaborate in the re-creation of new life for her brother, the neighbors, and herself.

In summary, Martha plays an integral role in John 11:1-44. As Jesus converses seriously with the Samaritan woman in John 4, here, too, he speaks freely and theologically to a woman who has the courage to articulate the truth and the fortitude to act as a leader within her own community. Martha's creative leadership generates both a divine revelation and new life for Lazarus.

CONCLUSION

Both the unnamed woman of Samaria and Martha of Bethany partner with Jesus in ministry and serve as re-creators of others within the Fourth Gospel. Both women emerge as recognized mediators, disciples, apostolic witnesses, and leaders of the early church. While the Samaritan woman may represent outcasts in society, both she and Martha serve as role models who re-create the community to new levels of belief.

Moreover, their roles as disciples and leaders equal those of their male counterparts. The powerful dialogues between Jesus and the Samaritan woman and between Jesus and Martha point to the realization that from the very inception of the Christian community, God intended to choose and depend on women to inspire and lead the Church. In the Johannine community these two women did so.

These courageous women represent role models of leadership for both the early Johannine community and the present world. Although the unnamed Samaritan woman and Martha were often neglected or invisible to exegetes throughout the centuries, these strong faithful heroines of service, nevertheless, offer hope to twenty-first-century women who lack ecclesial support and attempt to live leadership roles faithfully in the Church today.

NOTES: CHAPTER 8

[1]While traditionally the figures of Martha and Mary are rarely separated, the biblical texts in Luke and John clearly indicate that they possess individual personalities and strengths. Due to space limitations, only Martha in John 11 will be discussed, despite the fact that her role in John 12:2 as one who serves *(diekonei)* is described with a technical term for leader and one having an authorized position in church ministry (cf. Acts 6:2; Rom 16:2).

[2]Postcolonial feminist readers such as Musa Dube see the journeys of Jesus associated with privilege, a foreshadowing of domination and subjugation of foreign people in their own land (*Postcolonial Feminist Interpretation of the Bible* [St. Louis: Chalice Press, 2000] 146–53). While points of her comments come from valid personal and social history and often prove accurate, I propose that we must keep in mind the invitational aspect of this pericope in John 4. As

Jesus speaks to the Samaritan woman he invites her into his world. She keeps the dialogue moving.

[3]See Bruce Malina and Richard Rohrbaugh, *Social Science Commentary on the Gospel of John* (Minneapolis: Fortress, 1998) 99–100; Jerome Neyrey, "What's Wrong With This Picture? John 4, Cultural Stereotypes of Women, and Public and Private Space," *BTB* 24 (1994) 77–91.

[4]Judith Schubert, "A Formula for Friendship (John 4)," *TBT* 32/2 (March 1994) 89.

[5]The topic of water connects the evangelist's remarks about baptism in 4:1-2 with this narrative. The water Jesus will later offer the woman symbolizes the new life of a baptized person.

[6]Cf. John 1:39, 46.

[7]Raymond Brown, *The Gospel according to John.* AB 29 (New York: Doubleday, 1966) 1:171; Robert Kysar, *John's Story of Jesus* (Philadelphia: Fortress, 1984) 30; Francis J. Moloney, *Belief in the World* (Philadelphia: Fortress, 1993) 144; Leon Morris, *The Gospel according to John* (rev. ed. Grand Rapids: Eerdmans, 1995) 229–38.

[8]Mary Rose D'Angelo, "(Re)Presentations of Women in the Gospels," in Ross S. Kraemer and Mary Rose D'Angelo, eds., *Women and Christian Origins* (New York: Oxford University Press, 1999) 135.

[9]Sandra Schneiders, *Written That You May Believe* (New York: Crossroad, 1999) 215.

[10]*Contra* Raymond Brown, *John*, 1:434; Robert Kysar, *John's Story of Jesus*, 57; Francis Moloney, "The Faith of Martha and Mary: A Narrative Approach to John 11:17-40," *Biblica* 75/4 (1984) 471–93.

[11]Acts 23:8; Josephus, *War* 2.8.14.

[12]E.g., R. Alan Culpepper, *The Gospel and Letters of John* (Nashville: Abingdon, 1998) 188; Robert J. Karris, *Jesus and the Marginalized* (Collegeville: The Liturgical Press, 1990) 87; Sandra Schneiders, "Women in the Fourth Gospel and the Role of Women in the Contemporary Church," *BTB* 12 (1982) 40.

[13]Karris, *Jesus and the Marginalized*, 87.

[14]Schneiders, "Women in the Fourth Gospel" (1982) 41.

9

All Creation Groans in Labor: Paul's Theology of Creation in Romans 8:18-23

Sheila E. McGinn

*O*ne of the key critiques feminist theologians have leveled against traditional malestream theologians, including Paul, has concerned their theology of creation.[1] At best the creation has been viewed as subordinate to human beings. Furthermore, this subordinate role has often been expressed in such a way that creation is to be "subdued," even conquered by humans, for their benefit or pleasure. At worst nature has been denigrated and viewed in a dualistic opposition to "spiritual" reality. In such a view nature is held to be irrational, corrupt, subject to evil and decay, and a source of temptation and evil for the "spiritual man." In this dualistic view women—because of their alleged proximity to the earth due to their roles in gestation, childbirth, and lactation—have been denigrated along with nature. Woman/nature is capricious and irrational while man/Spirit is trustworthy and rational. Hence unruly woman/nature must be subdued and controlled by man/Spirit. Feminists do well to bridle at such a theology, which justifies paternalism, patriarchy, and men's abuse of women and nature.

That this is not the only way to envision a theology of creation has been made amply clear by a host of writers since the 1970s. The "creation-centered spirituality" movement associated with Matthew Fox is only one example of this re-visioning movement. Feminist theologians like Rosemary Radford Ruether, Sallie McFague, and Elizabeth Johnson have deconstructed the dualist view of nature/creation and suggested a new model in which creation and humanity are both valued, and God is in relationship with both.[2] Feminist Scripture scholars were slower to take up this task. Beverly Roberts Gaventa, in her brief essay on Romans for *The Women's Bible Commentary*,[3] mentions "the solidarity of humankind with the remainder of creation" as one of the four themes in Romans that has direct implications for women.[4] She highlights Romans 8:18-25 as a key locus for this argument, but does not develop the idea in her examination of this pericope.

This point is worth developing. Although he was not a systematic theologian and his letters were occasional pieces, Paul does adumbrate a theology of creation in Romans 8. God's primordial act of creation is assumed; it is the result of this divine act—Creation as an object—that is Paul's concern. Beginning with a description of the dichotomy between pure physicality *(sarx)* and spirit *(pneuma)* and its ramifications for the Christian life, he then moves into a description of the current state of the creation. He is interested in the nature of the creation and, in particular, its purpose and role in God's saving plan. A close examination of the view of creation in Romans 8:18-23 can make a significant contribution to developing a critical feminist theology of creation.

CREATION IN ROMANS 8:18-23

> I believe that the sufferings of this present moment are nothing in comparison to the glory [of God] about to be revealed to and among us. For the creation *(ktiseōs)* waits with eager longing for the children of God *(tōn huiōn tou theou)* to be revealed; the creation was subjected to futility—not of its own will but by the will of the one who subjected it—in hope that this very same creation will be set free from its slavery to decay for the freedom of the glory of the children of God *(tōn teknōn tou theou)*. We know that the entire creation has been agonizing and groaning together in labor pains until now; and not only this, but we who have the first fruits of the Spirit, we ourselves groan together with it while we await adoption, the liberation of our bodies *(tou sōmatos hēmōn)*. (Rom 8:18-23)[5]

Here is a view of nature as God's creature actively anticipating the glorious fulfillment of the divine plan. Creation is eager for freedom. Like humanity, creation is enslaved, but unlike humanity, creation did not cause this bondage. In the present age creation's bondage means it is unable to do what it truly is designed to do, i.e., to have meaning and purpose that is lasting. Instead, creation is subject to futility and decay, but this is through no fault of its own. Indeed, it is God who has placed that limit on the creation. This subjection is only for a time, since creation will be set free when God's glory is fully revealed.[6] Paul envisions creation as an animate being on a par with humanity, for he claims that it also will receive "the freedom of the glory of the children of God."

Elizabeth Castelli, in her essay on Romans in *Searching the Scriptures,*[7] argues that "[a] feminist commentary . . . will critically gloss the text by examining the ways in which language, ideology, and imagery underwrite certain relationships of power while rendering others impossible or unthinkable."[8] Castelli acknowledges that there is no explicit mention of the female-male opposition in the letter, in spite of the presence of other dichotomies; however, she asserts that "the influence of such dualistic discourse is ubiquitous" in Paul.[9] She uses the pericope immediately preceding this one on creation, Romans 8:1-17, as a case in point. She argues that dualism of any kind is a problem for feminism because of the way it "appears to set the world and relationships within it in stark relief and does so in a totalizing fashion."[10] Hence the flesh/spirit dualism of Romans 8:1-17, in the ancient context, implies all the other dualities (woman/man, nature/culture). Thus Romans 8:1-17 must be read as implicitly valuing man over woman, humanity over nature, and vv. 18-23 also must be read in this dualistic context.

Nonetheless, the converse is also true: Verses 18-23 provide the literary context for vv. 1-17 and must nuance our reading of this prior passage.

In Romans 8:18-23 we do find a duality, yet it seems an overstatement to label it a dualism akin to what Castelli noted in the previous pericope (8:1-17, especially vv. 15-17). Here the duality represents an eschatological tension rather than a hierarchical, metaphysical ranking. To be sure, Paul never departs from the idea that God is Creator and the rest of the cosmos is creature, which certainly implies a hierarchy of God *over* creation, including humanity. There is an interdependence, however, between nature and humanity in their shared status as creatures of God, not a superiority of humans *over* nature. In prior letters Paul challenged even this hierarchy of God over creatures when speaking of the divine condescension in the Christ-event (e.g., Phil 2:6-8). God is monarch, but not like any human one, just as Jesus is Lord, but not like any human lord.

Appearances alone are not a sure guide to understanding the truth about reality, whether this pertains to God or humans or nature. This became clear in the Christ-event. Paul makes this explicit connection in the other key passage in which he discusses creation, in 2 Corinthians:

> From now on, therefore, we regard no one from a purely physical stand-point *(kata sarka);* even though we once knew Christ from such a purely physical standpoint, we know him no longer in that way. So if anyone is in Christ *(en Christō),* there is a new creation *(kainē ktisis):* everything old has passed away; behold, everything has become new. . . . That is to say, God was in Christ reconciling the cosmos to himself . . . . (2 Cor 5:16-17, 19a)

Human beings, including Paul, misjudged the significance of Jesus because they understood him *kata sarka.* They saw only what was on the surface and understood only from the standpoint of conventional thinking, which is bound up with structures of domination. Jesus was executed as a criminal. For conventional wisdom this fact said he not only was guilty of the crime of sedition but also was accursed by God (Gal 3:13). In such a view Jesus' life and teaching dishonored God, so the cross—made "accursed"—to restore God's honor, shamed him.

When God raised Jesus from among the dead, this conventional wisdom was confounded. Jesus' shame became his glory and God's "curse" was shown to be exaltation (Phil 2:9-12). The way to wisdom now is to think and act and live "in Christ" *(en Christō),* where reversal is the rule. Weakness is strength, folly is wisdom, vulnerability is power, humiliation is honor, and curse is glory. In the Christ-event the present worldly structures of domination *(sarx)* were overturned. God's honor and justice *(dikaiosynē)* did not require the shaming of Jesus by his death on a cross. Instead, the resurrection proclaimed that divine honor and justice are bound up with reconciling the entire cosmos, restoring the creation to the freedom and purpose and meaning God intended for it from the beginning. Surely, there is a hierarchy here in the sense that God has the power to limit creation and then to restore it, but this is not a unilateral kind of power.

Creation also has integrity and power, or God would not have had to place limits on it for the sake of human beings. In Christ nature is not destroyed, but rather is released from its bondage and renewed. In Christ, God joins with nature, working with and through it to reconcile the entire cosmos. Creation itself labors in its own rebirth. Nature is an active partner with God. Like an architect without a builder, God could not accomplish the divine purpose without creation. In this sense one could just as easily say that creation has power over God.

Humanity, as an integral part of the creation, also finds liberation and power *en Christō*. Life "in Christ" or "according to Spirit" *(kata pneuma)* comprises a radically new reality in which conventional power structures are overturned so that conventional patterns of language and thought (i.e., according to *sarx*) do not work. This is a reality in which one person finds honor not at the expense of others but precisely in union with others (1 Cor 12:26). Life "according to Spirit" is not opposed to material existence or life in the body; it is opposed to life according to *sarx*, i.e., life according to the mindset of this age of domination. Since life "according to Spirit" *is* life "in Christ," one cannot be joined with Christ while living according to *sarx*. In short, to be a Christian is to live "according to Spirit." There is no other alternative.

Here is a clear example in Paul where his "language, ideology, and imagery underwrite certain relationships of power while rendering others impossible or unthinkable,"[11] and where Castelli's objection to dualism *per se* must be tested. She rightly observes that dualism sets stark contrasts between two alternatives, essentially preventing the audience from even entertaining the possibility of other alternatives, and certainly precluding the possibility of compromise.

Can one really compromise with a system of thought or a structure of power based on domination if one believes that the human project is mutual edification through shared power? Or can one really compromise with a system of thought or a structure of power based on mutuality if one believes that the only kind of power that is worthwhile is power over others? In fact, *are* there other acceptable alternatives that Paul is suppressing in his dualism between *sarx* and *pneuma*, or is it simply one way of stating the fact of the radical divergence between these two fundamental life orientations? I suggest the latter is the case. Feminists, like liberation theologians, have been dealing with this issue from the beginning. Feminist writers have offered various descriptions of what mutuality in power and equity in relationships would comprise or suggestions for how to establish such a reality. None has recommended the use of coercion to bring this about. This would not be compromise, but capitulation.

The other key objection to the *sarx/pneuma* duality is the way in which this dichotomy has been linked with and used to justify the claim of superiority of mind over matter, spirit over body, God over humanity, humanity over nature, man over woman. Woman and nature have been linked with *sarx*, while man is associated with *pneuma*. This is the fundamental grounding for patriarchy itself, and the excuse for powerful men's domination and exploitation of women and nature.

These facts are incontrovertible, yet the objection is not. The fact that the *sarx/pneuma* duality can be and has been used to justify oppression does not mean either that it is limited to that end or that Paul intended it to serve that purpose. It does not even mean that Paul assumed such a relationship of domination to be the "natural" mode of human relationship. On the contrary, this passage in Romans 8:18-23 assumes the integration of humanity with nature, and teaches that both strive together for the same freedom. It is this freedom of creation, including humanity, that finally reveals the fullness of God's glory. Not only are humanity and nature dependent on each other and on God, but even God is dependent on humanity and nature.

In this context of mutuality Romans 8:1-17 conveys an ethical dualism, not an existential one. It urges the readers to a transformation of world view "according to Spirit" *(kata pneuma)* so that human persons can actually experience being "children of God" and "heirs of God and joint heirs with Christ" to God's glory (8:16-17).

It is not a disembodied "spiritual" humanity that celebrates this freedom and glory, but an embodied humanity enlivened and transformed by the spirit of God (8:11). Adoption by God entails a physical liberation, "the redemption of our bodies" (8:23). Life "according to Spirit" is not some non-corporeal reality, but a glorious freedom *in the body*, a life in harmony with God and nature—truly a new creation.

Perhaps this is a moot point for women, since Paul's affirmation of the special relationship of Christians to God as children and heirs is based on his notion of their "adoption as sons" *(huiothesias)*, and the evidence suggests that this legal term he employs had an exclusive, not inclusive, meaning.[12] One might allege that Paul's use of *huiothesias* marginalizes women's experience, since it seems never to have been used to indicate a woman's adoption to insure inheritance rights. However, there was not a comparable term for Paul to use regarding adoption-as-daughter. According to this view, the fact that Paul does not coin a parallel term for adoption-as-daughter but uses the term *huiothesias* to indicate divine adoption implies that women must "become male" before they can become heirs to God and joint heirs with Christ.[13] However, even if Paul had used *huiothesias* to refer to male Christians' adoption-as-sons by God, and then he had coined a new term for female Christians' adoption-as-daughters, it is not at all clear that this activity would put female Christians on a par with their brothers. While it might have been a more direct way of highlighting women's experience, their common experience of inheritance was one of inequity in comparison with men's. For Paul to claim that a woman would be adopted as a daughter-heir could easily have reinforced this inequity in the minds of the Roman Christians rather than overturning it.

A daughter's inheritance rights in Jewish tradition were quite circumscribed in comparison to a son's. According to the law, daughters inherited no property unless there were no sons to inherit. If they had brothers, daughters did not receive an equal portion of the estate, but only a small living allowance. Calling someone an adopted "daughter-heir" would suggest that she would receive, at best, the same kind of limited portion designated for a natural-born daughter. For Paul to use the notion of "adoption as daughters" along with "adoption as sons" would elevate this inequity in human experience and raise it to the level of the divine. Female Christians might have their common experience reinforced, yet given the choice, it seems more likely that they would have wanted that experience overturned.

Paul's claim that a Christian woman is adopted as "son-heir" does not require her to become male, but rather affirms that her inheritance will be an equal portion with the other heirs.[14] When God saved Israel from slavery in Egypt, *all Israel* was rescued, not just the men. The reality of Israelite history remains true today. God does not evaluate a person's worth according to *sarx*, but according to *pneuma*. Male privilege is subverted and all Christians, female and male, become heirs on an equal basis. They become co-heirs, equal not only with each other but, more wondrously yet, even with Christ himself.

CONCLUSIONS

From this examination of Romans 8:18-23 we can glean an outline of a Pauline theology of creation: (1) The universe is a creature of God. (2) As a creature, it has a purpose and goal. (3) Creation is not a static entity, but a dynamic reality still in the process of fulfillment. (4) Creation works with God and humanity to attain its purpose. (5) Creation and humanity are intimately bound with each other. Creation is eager for human salvation, i.e., adoption as God's children and heirs to God's freedom and glory. (6) Human fulfillment and the fulfillment of creation are mutually contingent. (7) The fulfillment of the creation will reveal a nature organically connected to what presently exists, but also qualitatively different ("new"). (8) The fundamental feature of this difference is freedom/liberation characterized by clarity of purpose (liberation from futility) and endurance (freedom from decay).

Many features of a feminist creation-theology come to the fore in this outline of Paul's theology of creation. As Paul did, we will start with the assumption that there is a loving Deity who generated this universe (1). Feminist theologians have been concerned with the question of the role of human beings in this creation, and have developed several themes in response to this question.

Feminists insist on the connectedness of all of creation, flora and fauna, with human beings as one component of this web of life (5). The earth and its creatures have a right to exist and to endure, quite apart from the benefits human beings can gain from this (2). Indeed, the creation is a dynamic reality, growing and changing all the time (3). The role of the human animal in this matrix of life is to preserve, protect, and foster not only humanity but also all the other forms of life on earth, and indeed the earth itself (6).

Human liberation, including the liberation of women and other marginalized persons from structures of domination, is the undergirding principle and goal of feminist theology (8). This requires a model of power that is reciprocal rather than unilateral. Hence humans must live with each other—and with the earth and other creatures—rather than dominating them. Living out this reciprocity is the key way to become fully human. In this process of living with the creation, human beings may make claims on the earth and its creatures, but the earth and its creatures also make claims on humanity (7). Central among these is self-preservation.

Among the feminist critiques of traditional theologies of creation is the "species-centrism" imbedded in them. The preceding outline of a feminist theology of creation illustrates several of the ways in which this human elitism is undercut. These also are features that a feminist theology of creation shares with the Pauline view.

What is interesting about Paul's brief encomium on creation is that it goes two steps further than the feminist model outlined above. Romans 8:18-23 depicts creation as alive, active, striving for a goal it shares with humanity. Both of these points—the active role and the goal-orientation (4 and 6)—are significant features of Paul's view. Markedly different from many feminist views, Paul's theology of creation is intricately intertwined with eschatology: creation is an active being precisely because it has a goal it is eager to reach.

Feminists have shied away from eschatology, and for good reasons. Traditional eschatology often has been marked by a model of "redemptive violence" based on precisely the kind of dualism Castelli challenges. In this case the spirit-man over body-nature dualism leads to a fierce devaluation of creation. It is disdain for the material world, including the human body, and insistence that eschaton means the "end of the world," i.e., annihilation of the earth and its creatures. Feminists cannot accept disdain for the body, and even less the notion that human "salvation" could come about by cosmic holocaust.

Curiously, Paul hints at precisely this same sensitivity without giving up his eschatological vision. The eschaton will bring not holocaust but revelation of a reality already nascent in creation's present form (7). Far from being destroyed, the creation will be liberated to achieve its full potential (8). The one thing that has prevented this is a deficiency not in the creation but in humanity. Human salvation is not yet complete, and creation waits for its sibling (6, 7). When humans are adopted as God's children and become heirs to God's freedom and glory, creation likewise will find its fulfillment in the freedom and the glory of God. Without his vision of the goal of creation, Paul's claims about its active role in human salvation would make no sense.

This suggests that feminist theologians would do well to reconsider the role of eschatology in a constructive Christian theology. Deconstruction of the kind of traditional, world-negating eschatology mentioned above has been an important and necessary task. Stopping at that point, however, leaves a vacuum. Better it should be filled with a new, liberating construction rather than a recycled, dualistic one.

NOTES: CHAPTER 9

[1]The term "creation" can either refer to the divine act of creating or the result of that divine act, i.e., the creatures that are made. Throughout this essay the term "creation" refers to the creatures rather than the act. "Nature" could be a synonymous term, but it is used in a derogatory way in the dualistic systems that are the topic of discussion below. I have chosen to use "creation" rather than "nature" in the hope that the connotations of the former term are significantly more positive than those of the latter.

[2]For some examples see the following texts: Rosemary Radford Ruether, *Gaia and God: An Ecofeminist Theology of Earth Healing* (San Francisco: HarperSanFrancisco, 1992, 2nd ed. 1994) and eadem, *Women Healing Earth: Third World Women on Feminism, Religion and Ecology* (Maryknoll, N.Y.: Orbis, 1996); Sallie McFague, *Super, Natural Christians: How We Should Love Nature* (Philadelphia: Fortress, 1997) eadem, *The Body of God: An Ecological Theology* (Philadelphia: Fortress, 1993) and eadem, *Models of God: Theology for*

an Ecological, Nuclear Age (Philadelphia: Fortress, 1987) especially chs. 3–4; Elizabeth A. Johnson, *Women, Earth, and Creator Spirit.* Madeleva Lecture in Spirituality for 1993 (Mahwah, N.J.: Paulist, 1993) and eadem, *She Who Is: The Mystery of God in Feminist Theological Discourse* (New York: Crossroad, 1996) especially chs. 9 and 11.

[3]Beverly Roberts Gaventa, "Romans," in Carol A. Newsom and Sharon H. Ringe, eds., *The Women's Bible Commentary* (Louisville: Westminster John Knox, 1992) 313–20.

[4]Ibid. 316.

[5]Translations are my own unless otherwise indicated.

[6]Paul implies that the divine subjection of creation serves a purpose in the salvation of human beings, although he does not spell out what this is. Perhaps he has in mind the fact that the experience of futility and death is one of the things that causes humans to ask the "ultimate questions." In that case, the incomplete nature of the creation would be a divine goad to prod humanity to recognize the Creator—rather than divinizing the creature—and to seek God's help in dealing with the vagaries of life (cf. Rom 1:25).

[7]Elisabeth A. Castelli, "Romans," in Elisabeth Schüssler Fiorenza, ed., *Searching the Scriptures: A Feminist Commentary* (New York: Crossroad, 1994) 313–20.

[8]Ibid. 276.

[9]Ibid. 284.

[10]Ibid. 286.

[11]Ibid. 276.

[12]Ibid. 291, citing an unpublished essay by Kathleen E. Corley, "Women's Inheritance Rights in Antiquity and Paul's Metaphor of Adoption."

[13]Ibid.

[14]Such an inclusive reading of *huiothesias* is reinforced by Paul's choice of the neuter term *tekna* (children), rather than the masculine plural *huioi* (sons), to refer to those who experience this adoption by God.

10

Of New Songs and an Open Window

Mary Ann Donovan, S.C.

*L*iving theology lives from the Word. To engage the subject of creation with biblical scholars offers the possibility of richer understanding to all. For that reason I enter upon these reflections eagerly. In this essay I first comment briefly on the essays of Professors Cook and McGinn that are included in this book. Then, from within my own discipline—that of an historical theologian with a specialization in the early church—I offer some points for further reflection with the hope of advancing the discussion.

The choice of Second Isaiah as the focus for study of the biblical teaching on creation is a salutary reminder that the biblical teaching itself developed over time. We are all too familiar with the ambiguities around women present in the Genesis creation stories. The common perception, untouched by the work of scholars like Phyllis Trible, accepts at face value the New American Bible translation of Genesis 1:27: "God created man in his image; in the divine image he created him; male and female he created them."[1] So not surprisingly we have the stream of interpretation in which "man" carries the *imago Dei* and "woman," at best, carries the *imago hominis*. The first ambiguity is compounded in Genesis 2:21-24, where God, whose actions are described like those of a divine plastic surgeon, creates Eve from Adam's rib. Uncritical use of these two passages in the Genesis creation narratives reinforces the understanding that the Bible supports the subordination of women to men.

We find none of this position in Second Isaiah, although it has strong ties to Genesis. However, neither is the word "woman" spoken in Second Isaiah. Rather, the poor and needy have priority of place. (Certainly women are included in that group, and disproportionately so in this country at this time, but to develop this idea here would lead us astray.) Even a cursory review of the problems around identifying author and editor of Second Isaiah makes apparent the importance of the location of the intended recipients of the text.[2] An audience of exiles who are grieving the loss of the Temple cries out for comfort. Not surprisingly, the resultant work is what we know as the "Book of Consolation." The third passage discussed by Joan Cook, Isaiah 41:17-20, identifies the situation. The poor and needy cry out for water, and the Holy One of Israel, the Creator, promises salvation.

Cook's detailed work with the texts sets the stage for an exercise in application. She suggests that we see what happens when we read Isaiah 42:5-9 with the singular form of "you." Such an exercise asks each of us to read the text as the one to whom it is addressed. I have rewritten the text, stressing the singular "you," and placing it in the present context.

Hear the Word of the Lord. Thus says God, the LORD: I, the LORD, have called *you*. I have made *you* holy. I look on *you*, and I find *you* lovely. Your weight, your height, your skin color, your accent. *You*, poor and needy. *You*, homeless. *You*, immigrant. *You*, woman. Yes, *you*, man. *You* are acceptable to me. I take *you* by the hand. And *you*, *you* I give as a pledge to the people. *Me?* The way *I* look? Three of my grandparents were immigrants, but *I'm* native-born American. *I* have a home. *I* am not poor. *I'm* not—w e-e-ellll—yes, I *am* needy. And a pledge? What's that about?

God the Holy One speaks: I love the poor and the needy. Stay close to them. Don't trust your riches, your citizenship, your home, your hard-earned possessions. Don't even trust your degree. It is I—and none of those—who have saved you. What I have done for you I can and will do for the poor and needy—and I will do it *through you*. I call *you* to open blind eyes. Teach. Write. Speak the truth. Set people free. Shelter them. Give them sanctuary. Undo injustice wherever *you* find it.

This is what our God will use *me* for? Is this then my *glory*?

Ah, the LORD God says: My glory I give to *no other*. Too bad for the one who glories in any other! I am the LORD God, HOLY is my name. But have courage. Remember. What's done is done. Today I do new things. Before they even happen, I trust *you* with them. I give *you* as pledge to the people. *I* am to glorify the LORD my Savior! *I* am to *live* as God's pledge to the people.

The Word of the Lord.

Cook asked us to attend to what happens when such a reading is done. I note that the text gives pride of place to the oppressed without qualification, and extends salvation to all of them through the prophet. I experience the gift of salvation when I identify with the poor and needy to whom Second Isaiah is addressed. I also learn my role in the salvation of others when I stand in the place of the prophet. As a theologian I find this reading helpful because of the links it establishes between creation and universal salvation, and because of the foundation it lays for the chronologically later notion that we, the Body of Christ, are called to do the work of Christ. As a woman I find this reading affirms my self-worth and my sense of mission.

Such an understanding of the Isaian material is congruent with the interpretation Sheila McGinn gives to Romans 8:18-23. Her presentation focuses on the dualism between *pneuma* and *sarx*. In Romans 8:1-13 she understands Paul to develop the tension between *pneuma* and *sarx* as an opposition between two ways of living: in Christ *(kata pneuma)* or in the flesh ("according to the mindset of this age of domination"). McGinn suggests that Paul is setting up a choice between two mutually exclusive life orientations.[3] Life in Christ assumes "that the human project is mutual edification through shared power," which is incompatible with a situation that assumes "that the only kind of power that is worthwhile is power over others."[4] Such a position is compatible with my understanding of *pneuma* and *sarx* as two different lenses through which to view the human being rather than as two constituent parts of the human being. The latter is the view introduced into Christian anthropology by Stoic thinkers. It is indeed true that the *sarx/pneuma* duality, as McGinn writes, "has been linked with and used to justify the claim of superiority of mind over matter, spirit over body, God over humanity, humanity over nature, man over woman."[5] Paul can be read that way; that is exactly what the Stoics did. However, he need not be, and the problem can be as much with the philosophical and/or hermeneutical presuppositions of his readers as with his text.

Turning to Romans 8:18-23, McGinn reminds us that there is a basic distinction between God the Creator and all the rest of the cosmos, including both nature and humanity, which share creaturely status. Life in Christ is not life according to appearances *(kata sarka)*. In using its own integrity and power, Nature works in Christ to bring about its renewal. As she points out, the situation of humanity is exactly parallel, with one exception. Renewal here will include adoption. She treats ably the varying positions of the Roman matron, the Greek woman, and the Jewish woman. What is critical, she concludes, is: "God does not evaluate a person's worth according to *sarx*, but according to *pneuma*. Male privilege is subverted and all Christians, female and male, become heirs on an equal basis . . . not only with each other but . . . with Christ himself."[6]

In both essays we see a connection drawn between creation and salvation. Among our predecessors in the Christian tradition not a few have contributed to a positive theology of creation. One of these is Irenaeus, second-century bishop of Lyons. We can gain entry into his thought through responses to three questions: (1) What is his teaching on creation? (2) What does his doctrine of recapitulation contribute? (3) How does Eucharist open a window in time? I will suggest how his work can be used to further a feminist theology of creation. We turn to question 1: What is the Irenaean teaching on creation? Not surprisingly, it is consistent with the Jewish Scriptures: The One God creates, and does so through his Word and his Wisdom. Irenaeus' concepts of Word and Wisdom, however, have been enriched by his reflection on his Christian faith. So he writes that the one God and Father of all made all things, and among "all things" are us and our world. To those who suggest other intermediaries were needed in the creative work, Irenaeus retorts:

> As if the Father didn't have his own hands! For there were always with Him the Word and the Wisdom, the Son and the Spirit, through whom and in whom he freely and spontaneously made all things, to whom he spoke, saying: "Let us make humankind in our image and likeness."[7]

Word and Wisdom here are personified as the two hands of God who are identified with the Son and the Spirit. Irenaeus wants to insist simultaneously on the oneness of the Creator God and on the Son and Spirit who belong with God. A developed Trinitarian vocabulary, let alone Trinitarian theology, lies many years in the future. Later in this text he will speak of their distinct roles, the Son being the one who gives shape or form to creatures, and the Spirit being the one who "adorns" them. Perhaps Irenaeus thinks that creatures owe their beauty to the Spirit. The creatures of God, that is, the cosmos and all it contains, are the work of God and of no one else. As God's, the cosmos is precious. However, precisely as a work, creation had a beginning and it will end. Irenaeus agrees with all his contemporaries when he writes: "All that begins in time must necessarily end in time."[8] Yet we will shortly find that for him the Eucharist opens a window in time.

When we turn to question 2, we notice that the Irenaean teaching on recapitulation adds a further dimension to his doctrine of creation. The theme of recapitulation is a Pauline one that is notably developed in Romans 5. The parallel between Adam and Christ is such that Christ's obedience undoes the consequence of Adam's disobedience.

Irenaeus reads Romans and Genesis together, developing the parallelism so as to address specific christological concerns of his day. He argues that the first Adam was formed by the Hand of God, that is, by the Word of God, using intact or virgin earth; so the second Adam was formed by that same Word, using an intact woman, the virgin Mary.[9] In my judgment this argument is not anti-woman but pro-earth, pro-creation. The recapitulation is so important in his view that the possibility of God modeling Christ anew, as it were, from fresh mud, is excluded. The likeness or similitude between the two Adams is at two levels: both are formed by the Word of God, and both are from the original virgin earth. In the case of the first Adam it is the mud of that virgin earth that is used; in the case of the second Adam it is the flesh of a descendant of the first Adam that is used —so there is continuity, but that flesh is virginal so there is parallelism. In his words:

> Why did not God take up mud anew but work from Mary to make the modeled thing? That there would not be one modeled work made and another saved, but the same thing which is itself recapitulated, [is protected by] retaining the similitude [in the stuff from which it is modeled].[10]

If Christ is the recapitulation of the first Adam, then he is born of a virgin through the action of the Word of God. This interpretation is an argument against those who say he was the son of Joseph, born of human seed.

He further argues that if Christ did not receive flesh from Mary, one would not read in the Scriptures that he ate, was hungry after fasting, grew tired, wept, sorrowed, sweat blood, and that from his pierced side there flowed blood and water. Irenaeus comments: These are all signs of flesh which has been drawn from earth, which he has recapitulated in himself, saving the work he modeled.[11] Parenthetically, in a beautiful comment on the crucifixion highlighting the immense value of the natural world, he writes that at the invisible level creation is carried by the Father, while at the visible level it carries his Word.[12]

Finally, in a move that may startle some biblical scholars, Irenaeus refers to the genealogy from Luke 2. Why, in this context? In his view the role of the genealogy is to connect the end, the second Adam, with the beginning, the first Adam, to show that the fullness of the recapitulation would include all nations, tongues, and generations.[13] What, then, does the Irenaean doctrine of recapitulation contribute to this discussion of creation? First, it lays heavy emphasis on the unity of creation and salvation: the old Adam, formed by the Word, lost what the new Adam, formed by the same Word, restores. In treating the Second Isaiah passages Joan Cook pointed out that when they were written salvation was becoming understood as a goal of creation. Here, some centuries later, we see a bishop explain in Christian terms how salvation is in fact the goal of creation.

Second, the Irenaean work on recapitulation stresses the reality of Christ's flesh, and in so doing emphasizes the worth of flesh, and with it the dignity of the earth from which it is taken. His approach is the opposite of that taken by those who shun or despise materiality. Far from it! Rather, he stresses the value of what came from the creating Hands of God and is embraced in the Incarnation. Here we begin to pick up accents heard in Sheila McGinn's material.

Third, the Irenaean position on recapitulation highlights the notion that all generations and nations descend from Adam (and so are the work of God's creative Word), and all are included in the saving work of the new Adam. Thus the universalism of Second Isaiah is continued.

Nevertheless, we saw that Irenaeus understood that creation *as* created, and so as having a beginning in time; it therefore will end with time. This would suggest that all created things have a time-limited value.

In turning to our third question, how the Eucharist opens a window in time, we find that Irenaeus makes a fundamental distinction. He asks how people can be sure that the bread and wine are the body and blood of the Lord "if they do not recognize him as Son of the Maker of the world, that is, his Word, by which the wood bears fruit and the sources of the streams flow. . . ."[14] There is a twofold assumption underlying his question: First, the eucharistic bread and wine *are* the body and blood of Christ (in some unspecified sense; the "how" is not his question). Second, there is a connection between the identity of that bread and wine with Christ and Christ's role as Word by whom creation came to be. The Incarnate One links creation and salvation in such a way as to make possible his own saving presence in the fruits of creation.

Irenaeus' next question is much more telling in terms of the temporal limit to the value of created materiality. He asks: Again, in what way do they say flesh that has been nourished by the body and blood of the Lord will go into corruption and not have part in life?[15] The assumption underlying this question is that the Incarnate One being risen, when his risen flesh feeds human flesh, that flesh has the possibility of sharing in his risen life. This is a sound reflection of the teaching of John 6, although Irenaeus does not cite that chapter here. Rather, he states:

> For we offer to him those things which are his own, proclaiming appropriately the communication and union of flesh and spirit. For just as the bread which is from the earth, receiving the invocation of God, is now not common bread, but Eucharist, constituted from two things, earthly and heavenly: so our bodies receiving the Eucharist are no longer corruptible, having the hope of resurrection.[16]

The parallel is clear: As bread receives word to become Eucharist, so through the medium of Eucharist flesh receives spirit to enable humans to share in the risen life. The concern is not with *how* the reception occurs, but with *the fact* that it occurs. The Irenaean conception of Eucharist, while still theologically somewhat naïve, is dynamic and respectful of the diverse elements joined sacramentally. It will exert immense influence in shaping patristic sacramental theology from the second century at least through the time of Augustine.

What Irenaeus does is to use bread and wine to open a window in time. Flesh that eats the bread and drinks the wine that is Eucharist will join the risen flesh of Christ. Bread and wine carry Christ to us and will carry us in our very bodiliness to Christ, even beyond the grave. Eucharistic bread and wine open the window into the eschaton. With McGinn we might ask: "What is *their* salvation [i.e., the salvation of bread and wine]?" I would add, is it in relation to Eucharist? And what of the rest of creation? It seems to me that the open window in time that Irenaeus shows us also gives us a view of a convergence between the sacramental principle (a principle central to Catholicism) and eschatology. Further examination of this point will be key in the development of a liberating eschatology of the kind toward which Sheila McGinn's work points.

NOTES: CHAPTER 10

¹See her *Texts of Terror: Literary-Feminist Readings of Biblical Narratives* (Philadelphia: Fortress, 1984), and *God and the Rhetoric of Sexuality* (Philadelphia: Fortress, 1978).

²For a convenient introduction see Carroll Stuhlmueller, "Deutero-Isaiah and Trito-Isaiah," in Raymond E. Brown, s.s., Joseph A. Fitzmyer, s.j., and Roland E. Murphy, o. carm., eds., *New Jerome Biblical Commentary* (Englewood Cliffs, N.J.: Prentice Hall, 1990) 329–48.

³Here McGinn positions herself in contrast to Elizabeth A. Castelli, who maintains that the flesh/spirit dualism in this text implies in its context all other dualities including that of woman/man. See above, 116, 118.

⁴Ibid. 118.

⁵Ibid.

⁶See ibid.

⁷Irenaeus, *Against the Heresies* IV, 20, 1. Hereafter cited as *AH*.

⁸*AH* IV, 4, 1.

⁹*AH* III, 21, 10. Also see *AH* III, 22, 1-2, and Irenaeus' *Proof of the Apostolic Preaching* 32.

¹⁰*AH* VIII, 21, 10. See also *AH* III, 18, 7; *Proof* 33.

¹¹*AH* III, 22, 2.

¹²*AH* V, 18, 1.

¹³*AH* III, 22, 3.

¹⁴*AH* IV, 18, 4.

¹⁵*AH* IV, 18, 5.

¹⁶*AH* IV, 18, 5; see also V, 2, 3.

11

Being a New Creation (2 Corinthians 5:17) Is Being the Body of Christ: Paul and Feminist Scholars in Dialogue

Mary Margaret Pazdan, O.P.

"*I*f anyone is in Christ, there is a new creation; everything old has passed away; see, everything has become new" (2 Cor 5:17). Many exegetes identify this verse with the preceding one as significant verses "under intense scholarly scrutiny yet which are all too often examined 'without regard for their function within 2 Corinthians itself.'"[1] At issue for interpreters is the meaning of the second clause in v. 17, "everything has become new." Some who prefer strong differentiation between "the old" and "the new" stress discontinuity. Others recognize transformation and posit definite continuity.[2]

Although I consider v. 17 within the broader context of the Corinthian correspondence, my attention is on how "a new creation" and "body of Christ" function as two members of a metaphor. One interpreter describes the body of Christ as "first of all the eschatological community of the Spirit, the new creation, which exists already in the present world."[3] Another links the moral responsibilities of "living in the new creation" with the body and its actions.[4] Apparently other interpreters do not consider the terms either in tandem or as metaphors.

Creating a metaphor presupposes that literal interpretation is not the final word about language and meaning. Paul Ricoeur declares that metaphorical interpretation is a "transformation which imposes on the word a sort of 'twist.' We are forced to give a new meaning to the word. . . ."[5] He notes that the strategy of metaphor is "heuristic fiction for the sake of redescribing reality. With metaphor, we experience the metamorphosis of both language and reality."[6]

Paul uses "a new creation" *(kainē ktsis)* in one other letter, in which he addresses the community in Galatia. There the phrase is linked to a major theme "neither circumcision nor uncircumcision is anything, a new creation is everything" (Gal 6:5). Still, the phrase is "evocative and enigmatic."[7] Although interpreters offer a possibility that "a new creation" is the transformation of the cosmos and human beings through the death and resurrection of Christ,[8] I am limiting my analysis to anthropological perspectives about the Corinthian community.[9]

Becoming "a new creation" meant accepting the challenge of living as "the body of Christ" among the diverse and quarrelsome members of the community at Corinth. It was a painful process of finding an identity in a wholly new symbolic universe in which "to live and move and have their being" (Acts 17:28). According to John Pobee, becoming a new creation involves "a radical transformation of character (for which) Christ is the source."[10] It is a process that involves understanding, commitment, and perseverance. What witness of this new reality does the community at Corinth offer us? What possibilities are there for women and men in Christian community today who live as members of the Body of Christ?

The first section of the article describes dimensions of the Body of Christ as constitutive of daily living in Corinth. The second section highlights how women in community responded to being "a new creation" in "the body of Christ." The third section explores contemporary feminist theological anthropology and women's bodies.

THE BODY OF CHRIST AND THE COMMUNITY AT CORINTH

Paul is the first theologian to develop the imagery of the body of Christ *(to sōma tou Christou).*[11] He attracts the Corinthians' curiosity with a familiar political image of the body. The human body "was a microcosm— a small version of the universe at large."[12] It was a common image in Greco-Roman culture to describe political structures of households, cities, regions, countries, and empire. According to Mary Douglas, "the physical experience of the body sustains a particular view of society, while at the same time the social body constrains the way in which the physical body is perceived."[13] In particular, since Paul founded a household church at Corinth, members had some guidelines for their behavior.

What happens in a household *(oikos)*? Human beings relate to one another in very different ways than in North American culture. Paul and persons who live in the Mediterranean world are not introspective. They do not consider themselves as individuals who have a separate identity from one another. Rather, they receive their identity and honor from belonging to a household in which the male protects its honor and the female encourages virtuous living. Whenever any member of the household speaks or acts in a way contrary to its values, the whole family is shamed. Correspondingly, when any member speaks or acts virtuously, the household is honored. Members of a household are embedded in a *dyadic personality* wherein communal honor is the only value.[14]

Paul recognized the household reality when he established the church at Corinth. There he found more differences in a group of less than forty persons than in other households. Some members were single, like Crispus and Gaius (1 Cor 1:14); others represented households like Stephanas' (1:16). In 1 Corinthians 7 we hear Paul's advice to married, unmarried, widows, virgins, spouses, and spouses who were nonbelievers.[15] The community also consisted of several factions who followed Apollos and Cephas (1:12) and those about whom Chloe's people reported to Paul (1:11). A. N. Wilson offers us a cameo of the environment:

> Corinth, with its eclectic racial mixture of Greeks and Jews, Levantines, North Africans, Asians and Europeans, its sailors and its dockers, its traders in spice, leather, cloth, its artists, its carvers, its sculptors, its builders, its entrepreneurs, its spivs, its weirdos, its crackpot religionists, its fortune-tellers, its quacks, its prostitutes, was ripe for the picking.[16]

Did Paul expect individuals and families alike to become a new symbolic household by relinquishing familial relationships? Did he, like Jesus, invite others to *fictive kinship,* that is, a gathering of persons who voluntarily associate with one another rather than be bound to a specific household? Paul is not explicit in describing how a household and a community of believers are related. However, in 1 Corinthians 5–15 his exhortations about vocation, sexuality, freedom, worship, and resurrection affect both groups.

Specifically, the great diversity of members would challenge household roots and participation as a community. In Corinth how would the church provide for "a sense of communal life and individual commitment, theological pluralism, a basis for mission . . ."?[17] That the community questioned Paul's leadership in these areas is evident from his topics and powerful rhetoric in both letters.

Nonetheless, Paul adopts the body metaphor to describe the significance of the members who believe in Jesus: "Now you are the body of Christ and individually members of it" (1 Cor 12:27). Not all members receive and accept Paul's description of a new identity. Some prefer to separate themselves from others because of their spiritual gifts, such as prophecy or tongues (1 Cor 14:1-5). However, Paul exhorts them to remember that each member is essential to the body.

In the Mediterranean world of the first century a male recognizes another's honor or shame by observing the other's body. The three-zone model signifies what is important to honorable living. The "foot" and "hand" enable purposeful activity such as travel, transportation, and productivity. The "ear" facilitates listening, just as the "mouth" enables speaking. Both organs work together for genuine communication. The "eye" is an indicator of the secret emotion-fused thinking of the "heart." If any zone is nonfunctioning, the person and household are shamed. Notice that when Paul is describing the community with parts of the body, he mentions specifically "foot," "hand," "ear," and "eye" (1 Cor 12:15-17).

Paul also exhorts the community to be careful about communicating with their tongues: "If I speak in the tongues *(glōssais)* of mortals and angels, but do not have love *(agapēn),* I am a noisy gong or a clanging cymbal" (13:1). He connects the necessity of love and spiritual gifts *(ta pneumatika)* for prophecy (14:1). Here Paul contrasts speaking in tongues with prophesying. The first activity builds up individuals and needs an interpreter (vv. 2, 4, 6-11, 13-18), whereas the second builds up the assembly through encouragement and consolation (vv. 3, 5). Paul also distinguishes gifts. "Tongues, then, are a sign not for believers but for unbelievers, while prophecy is not for unbelievers but for believers (v. 22). Paul implores them that "all things should be done decently and in order" (v. 40). He wants the worship to be orderly, not chaotic.[18]

How does the body grow and flourish to bring honor to its members? Paul describes the responsibility of the body that is endowed with particular spiritual gifts *(charismata).* Just as members of the human body have different functions, so, too, members have different gifts to build up the body of Christ. The Spirit who is the source of gifts provides them for the common good. God activates a variety of gifts in each person according to an individual's capacity. No one knows what that capacity is except God "who allots to each one individually just as the Spirit chooses" (1 Cor 12:4-11).

It is at Eucharist that the Corinthian community becomes the sacramental body as an assembly and as individuals. Different social and economic status affects their behavior at the Lord's Supper. Some bring fine food and wine while others are hungry. They are not attentive to one another's needs (1 Cor 11:19-22). They do not realize what they become when they eat the bread and drink the cup: "you proclaim the death of the Lord until he comes" (v. 26; cf. 2 Cor 4:10). Paul warns them: "Examine yourselves, and only then eat of the bread and drink of the cup. For all who eat and drink without discerning the body *(mē diakrinōn to sōma)* eat and drink judgment against themselves" (1 Cor 11:28-29).

Sometimes the community believes that members do not need one another. Some think they are experiencing Christ's resurrection because they understand secret wisdom. Others believe that the body is evil and needs discipline. In his pastoral instructions Paul reminds them that each relationship is sacred and embodies the presence of Christ. He warns them about not associating with "anyone who bears the name of brother or sister who is sexually immoral or greedy, or is an idolater, reviler, drunkard, or robber. Do not even eat with such a one" (5:11b).

Being members of the body of Christ who receive gifts for the common good and share the loaf and the cup does not necessarily affect how individuals relate to their bodies. Some persons may be described as "libertine." It makes no difference what type of moral or immoral lives they live with their bodies. Neither a personal body nor another's body has any intrinsic value. Abuse of bodies makes no difference. Neither abusive activity nor attitudes toward bodies are important. Why? Bodies have no value because it is the soul and/or mind that are important. These faculties gain them access to secret wisdom (knowledge) that saves them.

Other persons may be described as extreme "ascetics." They practice excessive mortification of their bodies because they know that their bodies must be purified and abandoned before entering into the spiritual realm of salvation.

Paul has different perspectives. His wisdom is Christ crucified (1 Cor 1:18-25). Christ's suffering, dying, and being raised in his body is the source of salvation. He also exhorts the Corinthians against relationships that abuse the intrinsic value of the body because they are members of Christ's body. Later he warns them that they will appear before Christ who will judge deeds "in the body" (2 Cor 5:10).

Being the body of Christ also has an eschatological dimension. When Paul offers the community a glorious vision of the end-time he speaks about the resurrection of the body. This fundamental belief is based on God who raised Christ from the dead. All will be made alive in Christ when he hands over the kingdom to God the Father after he has destroyed all enemies, including death (1 Cor 15:15-26). Nonetheless, the Corinthians question Paul: "How are the dead raised? With what kind of body do they come?" (v. 35). Paul does not respond to the questions directly. Rather, he utilizes the imagery of a seed that is sown and becomes wheat or barley. The body will be changed because perishable, mortal bodies will become imperishable and immortal. Each member will have individual glory like the sun and moon and stars. All will participate in the cosmic creation because Christ is victorious over death (vv. 36-41, 51-55).

WOMEN AND THE BODY OF CHRIST IN THE COMMUNITY AT CORINTH

How did women listen to Paul? Can we assume that they heard what men heard? Do we look only at pericopes where they are mentioned by name, e.g., "woman" *(gynē)*? How can we reconstruct their experience? These questions are problematic because we only have one side of the conversation in the letters and we know that "Chloe's people" (1 Cor 1:11) do not provide the necessary data. Historical and cultural reconstruction is one method of responding to the questions.

Antoinette Wire utilizes another method, rhetorical criticism, to reconstruct the presence of women prophets in Corinth.[19] After outlining rhetoric patterns in 1 Corinthians she employs them in a thorough analysis of the text. Renaming each section of 1 Corinthians, e.g., "Women Having Authority as Participants of Christ: 1 Corinthians 8–11," alerts the reader to new possibilities.[20] Wire's examination of the entire text contrasts to Jouette Bassler's; the latter limits her analysis to pericopes in which women are explicitly noted.[21]

Loretta Dornisch interprets First and Second Corinthians within the broader context of the Pauline corpus when she asks how women heard Paul's teaching in the first century as well as how women in Third World countries hear him today.[22] In particular she raises the question of how women who are not mentioned may have heard Paul when he raises the question of sexual immorality in 1 Corinthians 5:

> Were they the prostitutes of the time, temple prostitutes condoned in the name of religion, or prostitutes associated with brothels such as that excavated along the marble street of Ephesus? Or were they the single women who were then ostracized for a lifetime of alienation? Or were they married women compromising their own marriages, or widows dependent on income from outside sources?[23]

I limit my analysis here to women who heard Paul when he connected the Body of Christ metaphor with specific instructions to the community. In ch. 6 Paul continues his response to reports of sexual immorality begun in 5:1. After addressing the issue of grievances brought to arbitration in civil courts (6:1-8), he returns to the body *(to sōma)*. Fornication is unacceptable because of the mutual relationship of the Lord to the body (v. 13). How can they prostitute members of Christ's body? (vv. 15b-16).

> Remember your body is the temple of the Holy Spirit *(ho naos tou hagiou pneumatos)*. You have been purchased through Christ's death; "therefore, glorify God in your body" (vv. 19-20).

It is a radical rethinking for these women who may have been abused by spouses, neighbors, and strangers to envision themselves as dwelling places of the Spirit.

Married persons listen to Paul's instruction when he introduces equality between women and men as equal sexual partners with mutual conjugal rights and authority (7:3-4). He is attentive to temporary abstinence and the situation of a partner who is a nonbeliever (vv. 10-16). Nevertheless, he prefers the celibate state and advises widows not to remarry. Paul's imminent eschatological perspective exhorts all to "remain in the condition in which you were called" (v. 20). When we remember some members' spiritual preferences for ascetic celibacy or libertine moral behavior, Paul's advice is positive and counters cultural customs.[24] Again, women could imagine themselves as equal partners and valuable persons whether married, virgins, or widows. Their bodies are holy.

Later, Paul recalls their ancestors' struggle in the desert as idol worshipers, sexually immoral persons, and complainers (10:1-11). He recognizes how that struggle continues among them: "flee from the worship of idols" (v. 14). Paul appeals to their conscience: Choose to share the cup and break the bread of the Lord as one body or choose food sacrificed to demons (vv. 15-21). It is either communion with the Lord and one another or with idols. Be sensitive to the conscience of others (vv.

25-28). Women, too, can sustain freedom of their bodies as members of the Body of Christ. It is their choice to participate in communion with the Lord and with the household of believers.

Next, Paul exhorts the community to recognize participation in the sacramental body of Christ (1 Corinthians 11–12; see above). Women appropriate their freedom to participate at this table of the Lord, unlike other tables from which they are excluded. They understand the ritual of sharing bread and cup from their experience that "proclaims the Lord's death until he comes" (11:26). They recognize the three-zone model of personality and rejoice in their bodies as well as their particular gifts *(charismata)* to build up the body of Christ (12:4-26; see above).

That women (as well as men) speak in tongues and prophesy is apparent in ch. 14, where vv. 34-35 are niggling:

> Women should be silent in the churches. For they are not permitted to speak, but should be subordinate, as the law also says. If there is anything they desire to know, let them ask their husbands at home. For it is shameful for a woman to speak in church.

In the past thirty years different interpretive solutions have been proposed. The verses either may be an interpolation from the end of the first century that shares the viewpoints of 1 Timothy, or the verses ought to follow v. 40.[25] Paul may be quoting male slogans, e.g., 6:13; 8:1, 4, and responds with his rebuttal: "Or did the word of God originate with you? Or are you the only ones it has reached?" (v. 36).[26]

Antoinette Clark Wire and Elisabeth Schüssler Fiorenza, however, accept 1 Corinthians 14:34-35 as genuine. Paul is attempting to curtail women's leadership in the church. Schüssler Fiorenza notes that Paul wants to maintain a community that is socially acceptable. He needs "to prevent the Christian community from being mistaken for one of the orgiastic, secret, oriental cults that undermined public order and decency."[27]

The three-zone personality model offers another argument. Women are shamed if they cannot communicate through prophecy since one of their zones would be nonfunctioning. Being members of the body of Christ means the utilization of each individual's gifts. If women need to ask their husbands to speak in a public ecclesial space, the limitations of the private/domestic space intrude upon their freedom. The Spirit prompts women to prophesy as baptized members of the household at Corinth.

CONTEMPORARY FEMINIST THEOLOGICAL ANTHROPOLOGY AND WOMEN'S BODIES

During the last twenty years many historians, philosophers, and theologians have focused on the role of the body. According to Susan M. Ross, "Gendered, historical, social, postmodern—all these perspectives on the human body have expanded human self-understanding in a number of ways. . . ."[28] Three distinctive interpretations identify the particular role of gender vis-à-vis the body. First, a traditional perception considers the body and mind as dualistic and oppositional to one another. The body identifies women and the mind (soul) identifies men. Second, a liberal understanding emphasizes the universal, common experience of being human and ignores the body. Third, an essentialist position explains unchanging "male" and "female" natures that are valid for all persons no matter what their social context.[29] Paula Cooey adds an American essentialism of "cultural determinism, particularly as that is manifested by language."[30]

Pluralism, too, characterizes recent feminist literature about theological anthropology. Anne E. Carr notes that "radically different interpretations of the experience of women in our culture" account for distinctive contributions to the field.[31] Although feminists are not unanimous in their thinking about gender differences and the body, they critique the current prevalent positions.

For women, dualist and essentialist perspectives are negative because they predicate oppositional, fixed categories. Specifically, essentialism neither accounts for the cultural construction of body and nature, nor does cultural determinism regard the fundamental level of existence, the human body. Both positions cannot embrace individual and social transformation.[32] A liberal perspective, too, disregards particular contexts of women's lives in their struggle for equality because the male model is normative.[33]

Susan Frank Parsons, a feminist ethicist, acknowledges the liberal position and two additional ones to account for gender differences. The naturalist position identifies sexual difference as intrinsic to one's psychological, emotional, and spiritual identity. The social-constructivist position that includes many postmodern theories argues against natural categories of "male" and "female." It attributes the categories to social conditioning that can be transcended.[34] Susan M. Ross, however, probes postmodern theories: "The postmodern take on the body, which emphasizes its endless 'play' of possibilities, its lack of stability and natural situatedness, is questionable. . . ."[35]

Susan Bordo, a feminist philosopher, agrees:

> What sort of body is it that is free to change its shape and location at will, that can become anyone and travel anywhere? If the body is a metaphor for our locatedness in space and time and thus for the finitude of human perception and knowledge, then the postmodern body is no body at all.[36]

There are numerous models of theological feminist anthropology for the body. Nonetheless, particular qualities are agreed upon as important for human flourishing, e.g., "embodiment, relationality, affectivity, and contextuality."[37] Moreover, the differences and multiplicities of women's experience and context need to be acknowledged as the root from which these qualities grow with individuality and energy.[38]

What does embodied experience mean? In 1990 Edward Schillebeeckx contributed "seven anthropological constants" for his theology of human existence that include not only sexuality but also human identity.[39] Later, Elizabeth Johnson developed them to include: "(1) corporality (inclusive of one's sexuality and ecological environment); (2) relationship to others as formative of one's individuality; (3) relationship to social, political and economic structures; (4) conditioning by time and space; (5) the dynamic of theory and praxis experienced as culture; (6) orientation to the future."[40]

Her reformulation of Schillebeeckx's "constants" accentuates difference. She comments: "Human nature is instantiated in a multiplicity of difference . . . one which allows connection . . . rather than constantly guaranteeing identity through opposition or uniformity."[41]

Susan M. Ross proposes a new understanding of the "family" model to elucidate difference. Although she is primarily focused on the "family" as a model for a feminist sacramental theology, her insights about the model are beneficial for our understanding. She notes that all human beings belong in some way to a family of origin that is multigenerational and dynamic. In the context of "family," "human beings come to know their embodiment, gender identity, as well as racial and ethnic identity. . . ."[42] Ross delineates embodiment to include biological and cultural heritages as well as "the concreteness and particularity of life and its moral obligations as well as the particular social contexts in which it is experienced."[43]

Her model is inclusive: "[A] Christian feminist understanding of the family is one that emphasizes passion, relationship, and diversity, not just within the nuclear family, but in all of one's relationships . . .

[it] builds on its basic values of affection, relationship and embodiment, and extends them to the world."[44]

Elizabeth Johnson and Susan M. Ross offer contemporary understandings of "fictive kinship" in the Mediterranean world. They are explicit about the relationships of family of origin and community(s) that Paul does not speak about in his letters. They focus on embodied experience that Paul describes in his metaphor of body for the Corinthians. They embrace qualities of diversity, the importance of individuals with their gifts and limitations, the sacramental and eschatological body.

In particular, Elizabeth Johnson creates a "kinship model" that speaks eloquently to the metaphor:

> . . . the kinship model more closely approximates reality. It sees human beings and the earth with all its creatures intrinsically related as companions in a community of life. Because we are all mutually interconnected, the flourishing or damaging of one ultimately affects all. This kinship attitude does not measure differences on a scale of higher or lower ontological dignity but appreciates them as integral elements in the robust thriving of the whole.[45]

Paul understood the metaphor of the Body of Christ as he described some of its intricacies to the community at Corinth. Women in Corinth responded variously to his letters about their identity (as members of the body) when he overturned their cultural expectations. Today feminist theological anthropologists discuss models of women's bodies that can be "a new creation" when they are in conversation with women's experience and context, a kinship conviction, the Body of Christ.

Today when we engage in discerning the body of Christ as a new creation, we are preparing and living out a communal spirituality that is necessary and formative. How we relate to one another, especially in and through our bodies, is grounded in the conviction that each person is created in the image of God *(imago Dei)*. Our minds and spirits often cooperate with our bodies to be witnesses of God's presence. It makes little difference whether our bodies are whole or impaired, because each body offers individual glory to God. We are so closely intertwined that when an individual suffers or is honored all members suffer or rejoice in the honor (1 Cor 12:26). In particular, when we are aware that our sufferings fill up what is lacking in the Body of Christ we can be motivated to accept them.

In addition, discerning the body of Christ may dispel introspection and myopia. It enables us to be joined with the great crowd of witnesses who have gone before us as well as those who will be baptized after us.

It connects us to a common eschatological future in which we and the cosmos will be glorified and brought to the fullness of creation beyond our imagination.

NOTES: CHAPTER 11

[1]Moyer V. Hubbard, *New Creation in Paul's Letters and Thought*. SNTSMS 119 (Cambridge: Cambridge University Press, 2002) 131.

[2]J. Paul Sampley, "The Second Letter to the Corinthians," *New Interpreters Bible* (Nashville: Abingdon Press, 1999) 11:94–95.

[3]Arland J. Hultgren, "The Church as the Body of Christ: Engaging an Image in the New Testament," *Word and World: Theology for Christian Ministry* 22 (Spring 2002) 127.

[4]Robin Scroggs, "Paul and the Eschatological Body," in Eugene H. Lovering, Jr., and Jerry L. Sumney, eds., *Theology and Ethics in Paul and His Interpreters: Essays in Honor of Victor Paul Furnish* (Nashville: Abingdon Press, 1996) 15.

[5]Paul Ricoeur, "Metaphor and the Problem of Hermeneutics," in C. E. Reagan and D. Stewart, eds., *The Philosophy of Paul Ricoeur: An Anthology of His Works* (Boston: Beacon, 1978) 133.

[6]Ibid.

[7]Sampley, 93.

[8]Steven J. Kraftchick, "Death in Us, Life in You: The Apostolic Medium," in David M. Hay, ed., *Pauline Theology, Volume II: 1 and 2 Corinthians* (Minneapolis, Fortress, 1993) 168. Cf. Moyer V. Hubbard, *New Creation in Paul's Letters and Thought*. SNTSMS 119 (Cambridge: Cambridge University Press, 2002) 179–80, and Hans Dieter Betz, *Galatians: A Commentary on Paul's Letter to the Churches in Galatia*. Hermeneia (Philadelphia: Fortress, 1979) 319.

[9]Jan Lambrecht (*Second Corinthians*. SP 8 [Collegeville: The Liturgical Press, 1999] 97) is convinced that the primary meaning of *kainē ktisis* in 2 Corinthians 5:17b is anthropological although the subjects in v. 17a are neuter.

[10]John S. Pobee, "Human Transformation—A Biblical View." *Mission Studies* 2 (1985) 7.

[11]For a survey of the origins of the image see Gosnell L.O.R. Yorke, *The Church as the Body of Christ in the Pauline Corpus: A Re-Examination* (Lanham, Md.: University Press of America, 1991) 2–7.

[12]Dale Martin, *The Corinthian Body* (New Haven: Yale University Press, 1995) 16.

[13]Mary Douglas, *Natural Symbols: Explorations in Cosmology*, quoted in Timothy L. Carter, "'Big Men' in Corinth," *JSNT* 66 (1997) 45.

[14]For articles about the culture of the Mediterranean world see John J. Pilch, *The Cultural Dictionary of the Bible* (Collegeville: The Liturgical Press, 1999). For applications of the cultural models for the gospels see Bruce J. Malina and Richard L. Rohrbaugh, *Social-Science Commentary on the Synoptic Gospels* (Minneapolis: Fortress, 1992), and *Social-Science Commentary on the Fourth Gospel* (Minneapolis: Fortress, 1998); for the letters of Paul see Jerome H. Neyrey and Bruce J. Malina, *Paul, in Other Words: A Cultural Reading of His Letters* (Louisville: Westminster John Knox, 1990). *The Biblical Theology Bulletin* also offers significant articles that interpret texts according to cultural models.

[15]Carolyn Osiek, "The Family in Early Christianity: 'Family Values' Revisited," *CBQ* 58 (1996) 10. Cf. Stephen C. Barton, "Living as Families in the Light of the New Testament," *Int* 52 (1998) 130–44.

[16]A. N. Wilson, *The Mind of the Apostle* (New York: Norton, 1997) 178.

[17]Osiek, "Family in Early Christianity," 14.

[18]Martin, *The Corinthian Body,* 87–103.

[19]Antoinette Clark Wire, *The Corinthian Women Prophets: A Reconstruction Through Paul's Rhetoric* (Minneapolis: Fortress, 1990).

[20]Ibid. vi.

[21]Jouette M. Bassler, "1 Corinthians," in Carol A. Newsom and Sharon H. Ringe, eds., *The Women's Bible Commentary* (Louisville: Westminster John Knox, 1992).

[22]Loretta Dornisch, *Paul and Third World Women Theologians* (Collegeville: The Liturgical Press, 1999).

[23]Ibid. 21.

[24]Mary Ann Getty, "First Corinthians," in Diane Bergant and Robert J. Karris, eds., *The Collegeville Bible Commentary* (Collegeville: The Liturgical Press, 1988) 1114. Cf. Lisa Sowle Cahill, *Women and Sexuality: 1992 Madeleva Lecture in Spirituality* (New York: Paulist, 1992) 35.

[25]William O. Walker, "Text-Critical Evidence for Interpolations in the Letters of Paul," *CBQ* 50 (1988) 622–31; Jerome Murphy-O'Connor, *Paul: A Critical Life* (Oxford: Clarendon Press, 1996) 290.

[26]Getty, "First Corinthians," 1129. Cf. Wire, "Appendix 11: 1 Corinthians 14:34-35," *The Corinthian Women Prophets,* 229–35; Robert Jewett, *Paul the Apostle to America: Cultural Trends and Pauline Scholarship* (Louisville: Westminster John Knox, 1994) 54–57.

[27]Elisabeth Schüssler Fiorenza, *In Memory of Her: A Feminist Theological Reconstruction of Christian Origins* (New York: Crossroad, 1988) 232. Cf. Neil Elliott, *Liberating Paul: The Justice of God and the Politics of the Apostle* (Maryknoll. N.Y.: Orbis, 1994) 52–54.

[28]Susan M. Ross, *Extravagant Affections: A Feminist Sacramental Theology* (New York: Continuum, 1998) 97.

[29]Ibid. 101. For a survey of classical anthropological positions and current discussion, especially about women and *imago Dei* see Rosemary Radford Ruether, "Feminist Hermeneutics, Scriptural Authority, and Religious Experience: The Case of the *Imago Dei* and Gender Equality," in Werner G. Jeanrond and Jennifer L. Rike, eds., *Radical Pluralism and Truth* (New York: Crossroad, 1991) 95–106; idem, "Christian Anthropology and Gender: A Tribute to Jürgen Moltmann," in Miroslav Volf, Carmen Krieg, and Thomas Kucharz, eds., *The Future of Theology* (Grand Rapids: Eerdmans, 1996) 241–57; Mary Catherine Hilkert, "Cry the Beloved Image: Rethinking the Image of God," in Ann O'Hara Graff, ed., *In the Embrace of God: Feminist Approaches to Theological Anthropology* (Maryknoll, N.Y.: Orbis Press, 1995) 190–205; Elisabeth Gössman, "The Image of God and the Human Being in Women's Counter-Tradition," in Deborah F. Sawyer and Diane M. Collier, eds., *Is There a Future for Feminist Theology?* (Sheffield: Sheffield Academic Press, 1999) 26–56; Sally Alsford, "Women's Nature and the Feminization of Theology," in *Is There a Future for Feminist Theology?* 126–38.

[30]Paula Cooey, "The Word Became Flesh: Woman's Body, Language and Value," in Paula M. Cooey, Sharon A. Farmer, and Mary Ellen Ross, eds., *Embodied Love: Sensuality and Relationship as Feminist Values* (New York: Harper & Row, 1988) 18.

[31]Anne E. Carr, *Transforming Grace: Christian Tradition and Women's Experience* (New York: Harper & Row, 1988) 119.

[32]Ibid.

[33]Ross, 101.

[34]Susan Parsons, *Feminism and Christian Ethics*, quoted in Ross, 126.

[35]Ross, *Extravagant Affections*, 126.

[36]Susan Bordo, *Unbearable Weight: Feminism, Western Culture, and the Body*, quoted in Ross, *Extravagant Affections*, 127.

[37]Ginger Andrews, *What We Have Seen and Heard and Touched: Embodiment of the Word in Women as Preachers* (Ann Arbor: UMI Dissertation Services, 2000) 38.

[38]Ibid. 69.

[39]Edward Schillebeeckx, *Christ: The Experience of Jesus as Lord*, quoted in Andrews, *What We Have Seen*, 37.

[40]Elizabeth Johnson, quoted in Andrews, *What We Have Seen*, 77.

[41]Elizabeth Johnson, "The Maleness of Christ," in Anne E. Carr and Elisabeth Schüssler Fiorenza, eds., *The Special Nature of Women* (Philadelphia: Trinity Press International, 1991) 111.

[42]Ross, *Extravagant Affections,* 130–31.

[43]Ibid. 181.

[44]Ibid.

[45]Elizabeth Johnson, *Women, Earth and Creator Spirit,* quoted in Andrews, *What We Have Seen,* 79.

12

Creation in the Image of God and Wisdom Christology

Mary Catherine Hilkert, O.P.

*T*he claim that human persons are created in the image and likeness of God has been foundational to Christian anthropology and spirituality since the early Christian era. Yet the symbol of *imago Dei* has not always been interpreted in a way that included all human persons equally. Early Christian and medieval texts questioned whether women were created in the image of God. Even those that did not negate that claim at times concluded that women were less in the image of God than men, most fully in the image of God when in union with a man, or in the image of God in their spiritual souls, but not in their carnal bodies. The use of the symbol of *imago Dei* to foster the notion that the subordination of women to men was "divinely intended" has been so pervasive in the Christian tradition that in the early 1980s a consultation of the World Council of Churches concluded that "[t]he doctrine of God's image *(imago Dei)* has by tradition been a source of oppression and discrimination against women."[1] In the present era gay and lesbian persons have been told that as persons they are created in the image of God, but that their sexual orientation is "fundamentally flawed in its disoriented attraction because it can never 'image' God and never contribute to the good of the person or society."[2]

Sexuality has not been the only basis for excluding persons from full human rights or questioning whether they image God as fully as others. In the sixteenth century Indians in the so-called "New World" were not viewed by their colonizers as having full human dignity and rights until prophetic voices such as Antonio de Montesinos began to question: "Are they not human beings? Have they no rational souls? Are you not obliged to love them as you love yourselves?"[3] That prophetic denunciation of the treatment of Indians in Hispaniola as if they were inferior human beings was grounded in the conviction that they were created in the image of God, as Bartholomé de Las Casas was later to argue.[4]

The shift beyond the anthropological "turn to the subject" to the cosmological "turn to the heavens and the earth" has highlighted yet another ambiguous—and at times destructive—use of the symbol of *imago Dei*.[5] Already in 1967 Lynn White identified the Christian instrumentalist view of nature rooted in the mandate in Genesis that human beings are to "fill the earth and subdue it" (Gen 1:28) as a primary source of Western arrogance toward nature that has resulted in growing ecological devastation. The question facing Christians today is whether the symbol can be interpreted in a way that promotes not only human well-being and rights, but also awareness of human limits, ecological responsibility, and the interrelatedness of all creatures in the larger community of creation. The wager of this chapter is that the symbol can function in the service of life—both human life and the life of God's entire beloved creation. Two resources that can help promote a recovery of the symbol of *imago Dei* that functions to foster respect for human dignity and the flourishing of creation are Edward Schillebeeckx's understanding of negative contrast experience and a historically grounded Wisdom christology read through the lenses provided by feminist and ecological theologians.

RETRIEVING A THREATENED SYMBOL

Before we turn to resources for a critical and creative retrieval of the symbol of *imago Dei* in our day it is important to consider whether the retrieval of a symbol with such a problematic history of interpretation is a worthwhile endeavor. One of the primary reasons for reinterpreting the symbol is precisely because it has functioned to foster anthropocentrism, the subordination of women, and the denial of full human dignity to others such as disabled persons, gay and lesbian persons, or indigenous peoples in the past. The power of religious symbols and religious naming has been recognized by many beyond the realms of theology or religious studies. In 1990 scientists appealed to religious leaders to become actively involved in preventing the impending "crimes against creation" and to become active in efforts to preserve the environment of the Earth. They explicitly noted that "religious teaching, example, and leadership are powerfully able to influence personal conduct and commitment" and that "what is regarded as sacred is more likely to be treated with care and respect. Efforts to safeguard and cherish the environment need to be infused with a vision of the sacred."[6]

Likewise, a symbol that holds the power to define human identity as sacred cannot simply be dismissed, nor can it be assumed. At a time when violence against gays and lesbians is on the rise, when homosexuality has been identified by some with a propensity toward sexual violation of children and teenagers, and when some Vatican spokespersons and Catholic bishops have stated publicly that homosexual persons should not be ordained, the importance of emphasizing that persons and their vocations are not determined by their sexuality or sexual orientation, a position clearly articulated in other Vatican statements, becomes all the more urgent.

While the affirmation that women are created equally in the image of God is explicitly affirmed in the Catholic tradition today, the ability of women to image the divine is implicitly denied not only in liturgical leadership, but also in liturgical speech. In *Mulieris Dignitatem,* for example, Pope John Paul II recognizes that biblical passages attribute to God both "masculine" and "feminine" qualities, thus providing confirmation of the truth that both man and woman were created in the divine image. He cites multiple passages from the psalms and the prophets that image God as mother as well as father. He further recalls that all religious language remains strictly analogical since God utterly transcends human experience, categories, and speech. Thus "even 'fatherhood' in God is completely divine and free of the 'masculine' bodily characteristics proper to human fatherhood."[7] Nevertheless, the pope argues that Jesus' naming of God as "Abba-Father" (Mark 14:36) provides the norm for Christian prayer in spite of biblical passages that image God as female as well as male.

The importance of reclaiming women's capacity to image the divine becomes all the more necessary at a point in the tradition when the Incarnation as well as the words and deeds of Jesus are regularly interpreted in gender-exclusive fashion. The assertion that the Incarnation of Jesus according to the male sex "is in harmony with the divine plan," coupled with claims that Jesus chose only male apostles and named God definitively as Abba-Father, effectively rules out women's capacity to image the divine in the realm of liturgy or prayer. But these are the very realms we hold to be most central in forming Christian imagination and discipleship. The insistence that only male imaging of the divine is appropriate in Christian speech and prayer functions not only to distort the imaginations and spirituality of the Christian community, and particularly of women, but also undercuts the more fundamental claims that God remains beyond gender and that all human names and images fail to adequately express the mystery of the incomprehensible God.[8]

An even more basic reason to revitalize the symbol comes from the ethical arena. The religious symbol of the human person as "created in the image of God" has traditionally functioned as a root metaphor for the Christian understanding of the human person, the religious way of grounding the inviolability of human dignity, and the basis for defending the human rights of all persons. Thus the 1979 United States Catholic bishops' pastoral letter "Brothers and Sisters to Us," for example, condemns racism precisely because it

> divides the human family, blots out the image of God among specific members of that family, and violates the fundamental human dignity of those called to be children of the same Father. . . . God's word in Genesis announces that all men and women are created in God's image; not just *some* races and racial types, but *all* bear the imprint of the Creator and are enlivened by the breath of his one Spirit.[9]

Mercy Amba Oduyoye notes the importance of the symbol for women around the world, especially in situations of violence and dehumanization:

> [M]any women have claimed the biblical affirmation of our being created "in the Image of God" both for the protection of women's self-worth and self-esteem and to protest dehumanization by others. Granted, this seems to be wearing thin, but without it the whole edifice of human relations seems to crumble and fall.[10]

While philosophical debate ensues about the precise meaning of personhood, the need for protection of human rights grows more urgent. Postmodern theorists argue that any attempt to define the human person or to universalize human experience is doomed because of the historical and cultural conditioning of all experience and the power relations that are inevitably operative when any person or group claims to speak for all. Yet ethicists repeatedly remind us that to abandon the ability to make claims about the dignity and rights of human persons only allows repressive power structures to operate without critique, which is to say, at the expense of the most vulnerable.

The postmodern challenge offers a necessary reminder that we can't know or define fully what it means to be human or to be created "in the image of God." But it does not follow that we can say nothing about human persons and their dignity. On the contrary, around the world there is a recurring call for some sort of international recognition of human rights and accountability. In search of a global ethic that can provide a basis for a vision of peoples living peacefully together, the second Parliament of the World's Religions took as the starting point for its "Initial Document Towards a Global Ethic" the fundamental demand that "every human being must be treated humanely."[11]

Feminist ethicists who recognize the need for postmodern cautions about any attempt to universalize human experience or gloss over radical differences such as class, race, sex, or sexual orientation, nevertheless argue that it is possible to identify enough commonality in human experience to condemn what is unjust and inhumane. Margaret Farley, for example, has proposed that

> [w]hatever the differences in human lives, however minimal the actuality of world community, however unique the social arrangements of diverse peoples, it is nonetheless possible for human persons to weep over commonly felt tragedies, laugh over commonly perceived incongruities, yearn for common hopes. And across time and place, it is possible to condemn recognized injustices and act for commonly desired goals.[12]

While we may not be able to identify fully what it means to be human, we are far more likely to reach agreement on what distorts that image or violates human dignity. In that vein, Edward Schillebeeckx's discussion of "negative contrast experience" provides a helpful way of retrieving the symbol of the human person as "image of God" that takes account of contemporary philosophical pluralism and the cultural conditionedness of any system of values and yet maintains the importance of the symbol for Christian ethics.

THE IMAGE OF GOD REFLECTED IN NEGATIVE CONTRAST
EXPERIENCE

Borrowing from the writings of critical theorist Theodor Adorno,
Schillebeeckx adopted the term "negative contrast experience" to describe those human experiences of negativity (on both personal and social levels) that evoke indignation and protest: "No. It can't go on like
this; we won't stand for it any longer!"[13] Granted that we may not know
or agree upon the full dimensions of human flourishing, Schillebeeckx
argues that we know what is *not* humane: the concentration camp,
genocide, racial discrimination, homelessness, abuse of children, do-
mestic violence, an economic system in which some face starvation and
utter poverty while a small minority controls the wealth and resources
of a country. In other words, the image of God that is available in the
concrete contours of a history laced with evil and suffering is first and
foremost the threatened image of God. If Jesus Christ is the one in
whom we recognize the face of God, the image of God is to be found in
the crucified peoples of today.

But just as the early disciples wrestled with the question of where
the God of life was to be found in the scandal of the crucifixion of Jesus,
so the question faces us today: where is the Creator God to be seen in
the violation of God's creatures?[14] Schillebeeckx argues that the mystery
of God's creative and sustaining presence in human life is hidden in the
creation, which remains vulnerable to the finitude and mortality of nature as well as to the possibility of the abuse of human freedom. It is
precisely the lament and protest over loss and violence—the claim that
"this should not be" and the ethical action it motivates—that signal
awareness that something of value is being sacrificed. Hidden in experiences of negativity and/or injustice is an implicit awareness of
deeply-held values that begin to emerge in various forms of protest and
resistance. The absence of "what ought to be" leads to dissatisfaction
and action for change, which leads in turn to a deeper awareness of
what was only intuitively grasped in the initial ethical response: an
awareness that human beings are indeed "created in the image of God"
and of inestimable value. In Schillebeeckx's words:

> If the fundamental symbol of God is the living human being—the image
> of God—then the place where human beings are humiliated, tortured,
> and forgotten, as individuals or as a community, by persons or violent
> structures, is at the same time, the privileged place where religious ex-
> perience . . . becomes possible . . . precisely *in and through* a human

action which seeks to give form to this symbol of God, the human being; [human action] seeks to raise people up and give them a voice. Only then do we come home to the liberating communion of our creator and thus the depths of ourselves.[15]

This trust in the ultimate meaning of human life that remains open to as-yet-unknown possibilities for human life and flourishing is nurtured and sustained by the fragmentary but real experiences of meaning, happiness, and well-being that also constitute some portion of human life.[16] Only when we have glimpsed what it means for persons to live in communion, when we have had some experience of what just and mutual relationships look like, when we have seen the triumph of the human spirit in spite of the violation or denials of others, can we recognize situations of dehumanization or the denial of human dignity as "blotting out the image of God in others." Without positive glimpses of what constitutes human dignity, happiness, and fulfillment, the negativity of evil and suffering would lead to the conclusion that life is absurd and unjust and that there is no inherent dignity in human persons. Without images and memories of what it means for human life and creation to flourish, the suffering human "other" and the devastation of the earth would witness only to the tragic nature of existence.

Viewing the *imago Dei* symbol through the lens of negative contrast experience suggests that human beings image God when we speak and act on behalf of life, whether that cry comes from the protest of the violated or the action of those who hold the power to change situations and structures that dehumanize or degrade. Here we can return to the question of the responsibility human beings hold within the evolutionary process and ecological web. If human action and voice on behalf of the violated "other" are ways that human persons image the God of life, a rethinking of the meaning of that vocation today requires human beings to see our connections with the Earth entrusted to us as a call to lament and repentance rather than a license for exploitation. At this point in evolutionary history, when the very survival of complex forms of life and beauty are threatened by human decision and action, the *imago Dei* symbol can function both to remind us of our responsibility in relation to the rest of creation and to call us to image the God who proclaimed all creation good. Human beings are those within the evolutionary process who can recognize and protest "ecological experiences of contrast" as well as forms of human suffering and see the connections between the two. That protest is evoked by at least an implicit awareness of the natural world precisely as "creation" that has its own integrity and value and its own capacity to manifest the glory of God. Likewise, the ethical protest calls for a recognition of our dependence on the rest of creation for our very survival and action on behalf of the exploited Earth.

Considered in relation to one another, negative experiences of contrast and positive experiences of meaning (both human "fragments of salvation" and what Thomas Berry has identified as "cosmological moments of grace") gradually disclose what is possible for the human community and for all of creation. Here the question of the relationship among anthropology, christology, and creation theology comes to the fore. The Christian vision of human flourishing is none other than the reign of God that Jesus preached in his liberating lifestyle as well as in his message of good news. Yet that vision of God's reign extended beyond human well-being to encompass all creatures in "a new heaven and a new earth" as reflected in the many images of nature in Jesus' preaching and parables.

Further, the post-resurrection faith of the early church culminated in the central Christian doctrine of the Incarnation, the proclamation that in Jesus, God became one not only with humanity, but also with matter. That doctrine, with its roots in the life, death, and resurrection of Jesus, has traditionally been presented in various forms of christology that focus on the *Logos*—the Word that became flesh and dwelt among us. However, early Christian communities also identified Jesus with another figure from the Jewish scriptures: *Sophia* or Wisdom, the female personification of God. If christology provides the lens for a specifically Christian anthropology, a christological reading of the human situation yields new meaning in light of contemporary disputes about gender and ecological justice when the story of Jesus is retold as the story of Wisdom incarnate.

JESUS THE WISDOM OF GOD AS *IMAGO DEI* AND THE COMMUNITY OF CREATION

Disputes at the time of Vatican II, and since, have often centered around the assertion that Colossians 1:15, which describes Christ as the firstborn of all of creation, rather than Genesis 1:28 with its emphasis on creation in the image of God, offers the appropriate starting point for a truly Christian anthropology. But using Colossians' image of Christ as "firstborn of all creation" as a lens for interpreting the anthropological claim that humankind is created in the image of God does not define the content of either claim or indicate that one of the two is the necessary starting point for theological anthropology.[17] Reading the creation and new creation texts in relation to one another can offer significant possibilities for theological anthropology in an ecological worldview. But as multiple classic readings of those texts have demonstrated in the history of the tradition, the primary focus need not be on the discontinuity between Jesus and the rest of humanity and creation, or on sin as having radically distorted or even destroyed the image of God in humanity. Likewise, a trinitarian reading of the Colossians text does not require an interpretation of Christ's obedience (and hence of the appropriate stance for the church, Christian anthropology, and particularly for women) as giving primacy to "receptivity," as some have argued.[18]

Further, those who argue for the primacy of Colossians 1 as the hermeneutical key to Christian anthropology rarely, if ever, attend to the fact that the hymn is derived from the Wisdom imagery of the late Old Testament and intertestamental literature, where *Sophia* is consistently referred to as female.[19] Neither is the language of "Father" or "Son" used in the Colossians hymn; rather Wisdom is said to be the image of "the unseen God" (Col 1:15). Further, the emphasis in this passage is on Wisdom as the firstborn of all creation, not only as an incarnate human being, much less an incarnate male. Connections between the Colossians hymn and earlier Wisdom traditions suggest that if the Colossians text is to serve as a christological lens for viewing what it means to be "created in the image of God," recent proposals for a Wisdom christology can help to focus that lens.

As we have observed, the dependence of Colossians 1:15 on the Wisdom literature of the Old Testament, specifically the books of Wisdom, Proverbs, and Sirach, has been noted by many.[20] Yet what often went unnoticed or at least unemphasized was that the figure of Wisdom (*Sophia* in Greek and *Ḥokmah* in Hebrew) in the Old Testament and intertestamental literature was female. Hence the hymn in Colossians 1:15-20, which in that context is applied to Christ, can be translated in a way that demonstrates its derivation from earlier tributes to Wisdom:

> She is the image of the unseen God (Gen 1:26-27; Wis 7:26),
> firstborn of all creation (Prov 8:22; Sir 24:9)
> in/by her was created everything
> in the heavens and on earth (Wis 7:22; 9:2-4; Prov 3:19-20; 8:22-30),
> seen and unseen:
> whether thrones or principalities, rules or authorities.

> All things were created through her and for her,
> And she is before all and the all subsists through her. . . .[21]

If this passage holds a key to a proper Christian understanding of what it means to be created in the image and likeness of God, as *Gaudium et Spes* suggested, retrieval of the symbol of *imago Dei* may indeed hold far richer possibilities for gender relations and ecological interdependence than either its interpreters or its critics have envisioned. Biblical scholars who were writing at the same time as the promulgation of *Gaudium et Spes* began to recognize that in Christian hymns such as this one, in the Pauline epistles (1 Cor 8:6) and the letter to the Hebrews (1:3), and in the gospels of Matthew and John, Jesus is portrayed as, and at times explicitly identified with, the Jewish figure of personified Wisdom.[22] But the feminist critical appropriation of Wisdom as specifically a female personification of the divine, and more recent work in ecological theology, has opened up new dimensions of meaning in that tradition.

Thanks to the creative theological work of Elisabeth Schüssler Fiorenza, Elizabeth Johnson, Denis Edwards, and others, Wisdom christology has emerged as a fully orthodox way of speaking of Jesus the Christ that fosters rather than restricts women's baptismal roles and identities, and that emphasizes the interconnectedness of all creation rather than a human commission to "dominate" the earth.[23] Retelling the story of Jesus as Sophia incarnate, Johnson recalls how Jesus enfleshes Sophia as she is portrayed in the Old Testament and the intertestamental literature in her prophetic street preaching, her public calls for justice, her befriending of the outcast, her promise to offer rest to the heavily burdened, her gathering of friends and strangers for an abundant feast, her healing ministry, and her initiation of disciples into friendship with God. Throughout his ministry and in a final and definitive way in his death, Jesus embodies Sophia's compassion for, and solidarity with, the lost and the least.

The impact of this reading of christology is to shift the scandal of particularity away from Jesus' maleness and toward the scandal of the reign of God he preaches and embodies. Yet a further scandal that emerges as we reflect on the anthropological significance of Wisdom christology is the realization that the reign of God is discovered among and entrusted to human persons and communities despite all our limits. In the person of Jesus, the image of God that marks human beings and can be traced throughout creation comes into clear focus. Elizabeth

Johnson has identified some of the anthropological and ministerial implications of reading the Incarnation through the metaphor of *Sophia* rather than the *Logos:*

> Jesus in his human, historical specificity is confessed as Sophia incarnate, revelatory of the liberating graciousness of God imaged as female; women as friends of Jesus-Sophia share equally with men in his saving mission throughout time and can fully represent Christ, being themselves, in the Spirit, other Christs. This has profound implications for reshaping ecclesial theory and practice in the direction of a community of the discipleship and ministry of equals.[24]

The cognitive dissonance caused by describing the male Jesus as incarnation of the divine Sophia traditionally imaged as female is not unlike the conversion of imagination that is required to recognize faithful female disciples throughout the centuries as "other Christs."

Further, if Wisdom is the firstborn of all creation and all was created through her and for her, not only human persons, but all creatures and all of creation are marked with the image of God. The sacredness of all creation from the beginning is confirmed and transformed in the Incarnation when Wisdom pitches her tent among us in the life, death, and resurrection of Jesus. The union of the divine not only with human nature, but with the material world, is sealed definitively in the resurrection. As Karl Rahner has remarked in his homily on "Easter: The Future of the Earth":

> [Christ] rose not to show that he was leaving the tomb of the earth once and for all, but in order to demonstrate that precisely that tomb of the dead—the body and the earth—has finally changed into the glorious, immeasurable house of the living God and of the God-filled soul of the Son. He did not go forth from the dwelling place of earth by rising from the dead. For he still possesses, of course, definitively and transfigured, his body, which is a piece of the earth, a piece which still belongs to it as a part of its reality and destiny. . . . Already from the heart of the world into which he descended in death, the new forces of a transfigured earth are at work."[25]

Denis Edwards draws a similar conclusion in his ecological reading of the Colossians hymn: "The rest of creation cannot be seen merely as the stage on which the drama of human redemption is played out. The Colossians hymn insists that the whole universe is caught up in the Christ event."[26]

Reading the creation story in light of Wisdom's delight in all creation and her role of connecting what is different and mending broken relationships returns us to the ethical issue of human responsibility for ecological justice. Taking Wisdom christology as the key for anthropology leads to a new appreciation of the wisdom required of those to whom God has entrusted the care of the earth: human creatures who have the capacity for moral choice and action. Seeking a retrieval of the *imago Dei* symbol that moves beyond a view of stewardship that falls short of respecting the interdependence of humans with the rest of creation, Anne Clifford has proposed an ecofeminist theology of solidarity. She remarks that solidarity does not erase difference, "be that the differences among peoples of different cultures, races and classes, or the differences between humans and other life forms," but seeks the common good of all—"a healthy planet on which all life forms can flourish."[27] This perspective does not deny the complexity within creation, but rather celebrates those very differences as reflections of the God who treasures diversity. From the beginning those differences have been a source of delight to Wisdom, who fashioned all things (Wis 7:22; Prov 8:30).

That same diversity of God's many beloved creatures is also reflected in differences among human creatures. Sexual difference is highlighted in both creation stories in Genesis, but the question remains: What is the revelatory significance of that difference? One aspect of that revelation is clear: embodiment and sexuality are integral to the blessing of creation. One aspect of what it means for human persons to image God that received little emphasis—or was downright denied—in traditional attempts to locate the image of God in some aspect of the human person was that mortal human bodies could be revelatory of the immortal God or that human sexual relationships could reflect the intimate love of the Trinity. If the Incarnation remains the key to interpreting anthropology, then with Irenaeus we are called to oppose any Gnostic versions of holiness or spirituality that deny the sacredness of the body or material creation and recall that we are created in the image of the *incarnate* Word, or as we have been stressing here, *incarnate Wisdom*.[28]

One can prize sexuality and sexual difference, however, without identifying human bodies as divinely inscribed for distinctly different roles and vocations. One can hold to the pope's primary anthropological emphasis—human persons are created as persons in relation, as destined for communion with one another—without identifying heterosexual marriage as the ultimate paradigm for persons in communion. If one were to turn to the Wisdom christology of John's gospel, for example, for the paradigm of mutual love and relationship, the model of friendship would emerge instead. Specifically, the kind of friendship into which Jesus invites his disciples is found in a community of disciples gathered—with all their differences—around a single table. Read through that lens, sexual difference does indeed mark human persons both as different and as radically relational. Revelatory significance is to be found not in divinely prescribed gender roles or the mandate to procreate, but rather in the human vocation to embrace the other who remains nevertheless "other," and in the call to participate in and foster Sophia's hospitality towards all of her beloved creatures.

Wisdom christology needs to remain rooted in the life and ministry of Jesus if we are to flesh out the concrete contours of Christian anthropology.[29] But a Wisdom christology "from below" leads finally to a trinitarian understanding of the God we are called to image—the mystery we describe as diverse and equal persons in a mutual communion of love. Drawn into that communion by the power of the Spirit, human persons and human communities are given an identity and a vocation. In terms of fundamental identity, the image of God stamped in diverse ways on all creatures can be violated, but never erased. The further invitation to human persons as conscious creation to embrace that identity as God's beloved and to grow in communion with God and all of creation is a vocation we are free to embrace or reject. Embracing that vocation in a world of sin will involve for us, as it did for the one in whose image we are formed, the way of the cross. Imaging the God of friendship of John's gospel will mean following Wisdom Incarnate in being willing to lay down one's life for one's friends (John 15:13).

Does the symbol of *imago Dei* have a future in a world of violence, exclusion, and ecological devastation? In the end it appears that the answer is up to us. Human beings and human communities—including ecclesial communities—hold the power to deny, and in that sense to "blot out" the image of God in those we consider to be "other." In doing so, however, we blot out our own participation in the image of the God whose love has no bounds. The sacramental vision of John's gospel suggests that an even more incredible power is entrusted to us as well. Because Wisdom has pitched her tent among us and sent her Advocate to seal us in the truth, we have the power to enflesh the communion that is our final destiny—if only in fragmentary ways.

The image of God continues to take flesh where Wisdom's children delight in creation and learn to live within limits that respect the common good of the whole community of the living. Human communities, and specifically ecclesial communities, reflect God's image when foot-washing, forgiveness, and a common table open possibilities for relationships and reconciliations beyond our power or imagining. By naming one another and fragile human and ecological communities as capable of imaging God—if only in fragments—we hold open our imaginations to how different our future could be.

NOTES: CHAPTER 12

[1]Quoted in *The Ecumenical Review* 33 (1981) 77.

[2]Andrew R. Baker, "Ordination and Same Sex Attraction," *America* 187/9 (September 30, 2002) 8.

[3]Preaching of Antonio de Montesinos as recorded by Bartholomé de Las Casas in *Historia de las Indias,* Book 3, Chapter 4; *Obras escogidas* 2:176. See Gustavo Gutierrez, *Las Casas: In Search of the Poor of Jesus Christ* (Maryknoll, N.Y.: Orbis, 1993) 29.

[4]Bartholomé de Las Casas, *The Only Way* (Mahwah, N.J.: Paulist, 1992).

[5]See Anne Clifford, "When Being Human Becomes Truly Earthly," in Ann O'Hara Graff, ed., *In the Embrace of God: Feminist Approaches to Theological Anthropology* (Maryknoll, N.Y.: Orbis, 1995) 173–189. For the cosmological turn in theology see Elizabeth A. Johnson, "Turn to the Heavens and the Earth: Retrieval of the Cosmos in Theology," *Proceedings of the Catholic Theological Society of America* 51(1996) 1–14.

[6]"Preserving and Cherishing the Earth: An Appeal for Joint Commitment in Science and Religion," in Carl Sagan, ed., *Billions and Billions* (New York: Random House, 1997) 145.

[7]John Paul II, *Mulieris Dignitatem,* Apostolic Letter "On the Dignity and Vocation of Women," *Origins* 18, No. 17 (October 6, 1988) #8, p. 267.

[8]On this point see Elizabeth A. Johnson, "The Incomprehensibility of God and the Image of God Male and Female," *TS* 45 (1984) 441–65; eadem, *She Who Is: The Mystery of God in Feminist Theological Discourse* (New York: Crossroad, 1992); and Sandra M. Schneiders, *Women and the Word* (New York: Paulist, 1986).

[9]National Conference of Catholic Bishops, "Brothers and Sisters to Us: A Pastoral Letter on Racism, November 14, 1979," in *Quest for Justice: A Compendium of Statements of the United States Catholic Bishops on the Political and Social Order 1966–1980* (Washington, D.C.: U.S. Catholic Conference, 1981) 375, 378.

[10]Mercy Amba Oduyoye, "Spirituality of Resistance and Reconstruction," in *Women Resisting Violence: Spirituality for Life* (Maryknoll, N.Y.: Orbis, 1996)

170. Oduyoye also notes there: "If one is in the image of God, then one is expected to practice the hospitality, compassion, and justice that characterize God. The Akan say, 'All human beings are the children of God.' What this calls for is mutuality in our relationships, seeking 'one earth community,' one household of the God of life."

[11]*A Global Ethic: The Declaration of the Parliament of the World's Religions,* with commentaries by Hans Küng and Karl-Josef Kuschel (New York: Continuum, 1998) 21.

[12]Margaret A. Farley, "Feminism and Universal Morality," in Gene Outka and John P. Reide, Jr., eds., *Prospects for a Common Morality* (Princeton: Princeton University Press, 1993) 178.

[13]See Edward Schillebeeckx, "Church, Sacrament of Dialogue," in *God the Future of Man,* trans. N. D. Smith (New York: Sheed & Ward, 1968) 136. For more development of the notion of negative contrast experience see Schillebeeckx, *Christ: The Experience of Jesus as Lord,* trans. John Bowden (New York: Seabury, 1980) 817–19, and 897, n. 158; idem, *Church: The Human Story of God,* trans. John Bowden (New York: Crossroad, 1990) 5–6. For another approach to the positive role of indignation giving rise to ethical activity see Beverly Wildung Harrison, "The Power of Anger in the Work of Love," *USQR* 36 (1981) 41–57.

[14]For further discussion of Schillebeeckx's interpretation of the crucifixion as negative contrast experience see Mary Catherine Hilkert, *Naming Grace: Preaching and the Sacramental Imagination* (New York: Continuum, 1997) 112–16; and Janet M. O'Meara, "Salvation: Living Communion with God," in Mary Catherine Hilkert and Robert J. Schreiter, eds., *The Praxis of the Reign of God* (New York: Fordham University Press, 2002) 111–13. In the same volume see also John Galvin, "The Story of Jesus as the Story of God," 79–95.

[15]Edward Schillebeeckx, "The Other Face of the Church," in idem, *For the Sake of the Gospel,* trans. John Bowden (New York: Crossroad, 1990) 164. See also idem, *Christ,* 837.

[16]Schillebeeckx, *Church: The Human Story of God,* 6.

[17]For concerns at the time of the Council see Joseph Ratzinger, "The Dignity of the Human Person" [Commentary on *Gaudium et Spes,* Introductory Article and Chapter I], in Herbert Vorgrimler, ed., *Commentary on the Documents of Vatican II* (New York: Herder and Herder, 1969) 5:115–63. For one version of subsequent concerns see David L. Schindler, "Christology and the *Imago Dei:* Interpreting *Gaudium et Spes,*" *Communio* 23 (1996) 156–84. Schindler criticizes the treatment of the *imago Dei* symbol in *Gaudium et Spes* as insufficiently defined in terms of christological content, a problem that has enabled, in his judgment, an unfortunate assumption of a basic harmony between (Anglo-American) liberalism and conciliar Catholicism on the matter of

"rightful human creativity and autonomy." In place of this "merely theistic" anthropology Schindler proposes a version of a "trinitarian-christological" reading of anthropology, but that reading reflects its own set of assumptions about anthropology, politics, and gender.

[18]According to Schindler, "[w]hat it means to be created in Christ, the image of the invisible God, the first-born of all creation (Col 1:15), is to be *called*, in Christ, to become "sons in the Son". . . . To be created in Christ therefore means first to be *from*, hence receptive in the face of the Other." Schindler draws on von Balthasar's version of trinitarian-christocentric anthropology in which human activity images the creativity of the Father only by way of the mediating receptivity not only of Christ, but of Mary's obedient love summed up in her *Fiat*. See Schindler, "Christology and the *Imago Dei*," 176–83.

[19]Eduard Schweizer has commented that "there is no passage in the New Testament, apart from the prologue to the Fourth Gospel and Hebrews 1:3, whose roots can be traced so clearly to Jewish Wisdom Literature as the hymn in Colossians 1:15-20. *The Letter to the Colossians: A Commentary* (Minneapolis: Augsburg, 1982) 246.

[20]See, for example, Joseph A. Grassi, "The Letter to the Colossians," in Raymond E. Brown, S.S., Joseph A. Fitzmyer, S.J., and Roland E. Murphy, O. CARM., eds., *The Jerome Biblical Commentary* (Englewood Cliffs, N.J.: Prentice Hall, 1968) 334–40, at 335–36. For a brief discussion of the debated origins of the hymn see Mary Rose D'Angelo, "Colossians," in Elisabeth Schüssler Fiorenza, ed., *Searching the Scriptures: A Feminist Commentary* (New York: Crossroad, 1994) 313–24, at 317–18.

[21]Translation by Mary Rose D'Angelo in "Colossians," *Searching the Scriptures: A Feminist Commentary,* 318.

[22]In his commentary published in 1966 Raymond E. Brown noted that in the Gospel of John "Jesus is personified Wisdom." See Raymond E. Brown, *The Gospel according to John, I–XII* (Garden City, N.Y.: Doubleday, 1966) cxxv and 521–23. Shortly after, M. Jack Suggs referred to Jesus in Matthew's gospel as "Sophia incarnate," in *Wisdom, Christology and Law in Matthew's Gospel* (Cambridge, Mass.: Harvard University Press, 1970) 58. For thorough discussion of the biblical sources for Wisdom christology see Elizabeth A. Johnson, "Jesus, the Wisdom of God: A Biblical Basis for Non-Androcentric Christology," *EThL* 61 (1985) 261–93.

[23]See Elisabeth Schüssler Fiorenza, *In Memory of Her: A Feminist Theological Reconstruction of Christian Origins* (New York: Crossroad, 1983) 130–40; eadem, *Jesus: Miriam's Child, Sophia's Prophet* (New York: Continuum, 1994) 131–62; Elizabeth A. Johnson, "Jesus, the Wisdom of God"; eadem, "Redeeming the Name of Christ," in Catherine Mowry LaCugna, ed., *Freeing Theology* (San Francisco: HarperCollins, 1993) 115–37; eadem, "Wisdom Was Made Flesh and Pitched Her Tent Among Us," in Maryanne Stevens, ed., *Reconstructing the Christ*

Symbol (New York: Paulist, 1993) 95–117; eadem, *She Who Is,* 86–100, 150–69; Denis Edwards, *Jesus, the Wisdom of God: An Ecological Theology* (Maryknoll, N.Y.: Orbis, 1995). See also Schneiders, *Women and the Word,* 50–54; and Ellen M. Leonard, "Women and Christ: Toward Inclusive Christologies," *Toronto Journal of Theology* 6 (1990) 266–85.

[24]Johnson, "Redeeming the Name of Christ," 131.

[25]Karl Rahner, "Easter: A Faith that Loves the Earth," in Albert Raffelt, ed., *The Great Church Year* (New York: Crossroad, 1993) 195.

[26]Edwards, *Jesus: The Wisdom of God,* 82.

[27]Clifford, "When Being Human Becomes Truly Earthly," 185.

[28]See Irenaeus, *Against the Heresies* V, 16, 2.

[29]On this point see Elizabeth Johnson's response to Roger Haight's critique of Wisdom christology as a Christology "from above," in Phyllis Zagano and Terrence W. Tilley, eds., *Things New and Old: Essays on the Theology of Elizabeth A. Johnson* (New York: Crossroad, 1999) 104–107.

Epilogue

Carol J. Dempsey, O.P., and Mary Margaret Pazdan, O.P.

*T*he poet Gerard Manley Hopkins once wrote:

> The world is charged with the grandeur of God.
> It will flame out, like shining from shook foil;
> It gathers to a greatness, like the ooze of oil
> Crushed. . . .
> There lives the dearest freshness deep down things. . . .[1]

A people loved by God, we have been divinely entrusted with God's great gift: creation. As biblical scholars and theologians we, together with the rest of humanity, bear the responsibility of keeping the ethical imagination and creative consciousness alive as we strive with others to articulate both a vision and a praxis that will bring about the promised new heavens and new earth already dawning in our midst.

Earth, Wind, and Fire: Biblical and Theological Perspectives on Creation is no ordinary volume. As contributors to this text, we write as critical *readers*. Certainly, there is cognizance of authorial intention and the text(s). We represent, however, the paradigm shift from author-centered to reader-centered interpretation.[2] We are also feminist and liberationist scholars who began this enterprise with critical appreciation for our particular social locations that include religious, economic, and political convictions.[3] While we do and have done individual work as demonstrated in this volume, we do not do idiosyncratic interpretation. We are connected to other professional communities of readers through conferences and meetings as well as being representatives of a living tradition who appear in print and media.

Besides representing the paradigm shift from author-centered to reader-centered interpretation, we as contributors also represent another paradigm shift—the dialogue between Bible and theology, and the exchanges among Bible, theology, and science. The articles in this volume attest to the interdisciplinary conversation already taking place in these respective academic disciplines.

The central theme and starting point for this volume has been creation. This specific focus represents yet another paradigm shift, namely from *Heilsgeschichte* in the anthropocentric sense to *Heilsgeschichte* in the cosmic sense. The work of Claus Westermann, Helmut Schmid, Rolf Knerim, and James Barr among others accepts creation and not history as the primary locus for biblical theology.

All contributors investigated the reality of creation from a wide horizon of perspectives. Although we seriously consider biblical accounts of creation, ongoing creation today is an underlying thread. We are not content with the status quo of biblical and theological tradition. Rather, each article brings insights about creation for contemporary consideration and reflection. In our feminist horizon there is no ranking of created reality. The interrelatedness of all creation is a fundamental conviction that is explicit in many articles.

Connecting creation with salvation/redemption is another common thread. Linking these theological categories with a non-dualistic framework advances broader considerations of life, death, and resurrection. In particular, the explorations of eschatology with creation offer new possibilities in constructing models of feminist eschatology. The articles with a hermeneutics of aesthetics, re-visioning the symbol of *imago Dei*, and a renewed understanding of Sabbath offer refreshing possibilities for people in our wounded, chaotic, and often empty cultures.

Finally, the collaboration and cooperation of the contributors is a symbol of what is necessary in order for creation and salvation to become apparent in our world, church, neighborhoods, and families. Reinterpreting biblical and theological perspectives on creation at the local level as well may be a catalyst to reconcile what is divisive today. The big questions for local, national, and international cooperation are: Who will be the advocates? Where will the common ground discussion take place? What venues will be utilized? When can the academy and local groups of people share honestly and freely of their wisdom? As we move forward together with these questions haunting our hearts, and as we struggle to answer these questions with our lives and collective efforts, may the vision and prayer of W. L. Wallace from Aotearoa, New Zealand, find a home within us and give us hope:

> All life is holy, all life is one.
> Awaken us, O God, that all life may be Holy Communion
> and the whole creation Eucharist.[4]

NOTES: EPILOGUE

[1]John Pick, ed., *A Hopkins Reader* (rev. and enl. ed. New York: Doubleday Image Books, 1966) 47–48.

[2]Gale A. Yee, "The Author/Text/Reader and Power: Suggestions for a Critical Framework for Biblical Studies," in Fernando F. Segovia and Mary Ann Tolbert, eds., *Reading from This Place: Social Location and Biblical Interpretation in the United States* (Minneapolis: Fortress, 1995) 1:109–18, describes the paradigm shift in the past two decades and allies it with access to power.

[3]Elisabeth Schüssler Fiorenza, *But She Said: Feminist Practices of Biblical Interpretation* (Boston: Beacon, 1992) 35, identifies feminist reader-response criticism with its focus on the complex process of reading that indicates "both how patriarchal discourse constructs the reader, and how gender, race and class affect the way we read; such an approach [underscores?] the importance of the reader's textual and sociocultural location."

[4]W. L. Wallace, "Eucharistic Benediction," *600 Blessings and Prayers from Around the World,* compiled by Geoffrey Duncan (Mystic, Conn.: Twenty-Third Publications, 2000) 64.

Bibliography

Alsford, Sally. "Women's Nature and the Feminization of Theology," in Deborah F. Sawyer and Diane M. Collier, eds., *Is There a Future for Feminist Theology?* Sheffield: Sheffield Academic Press, 1999.

"And God Rested," *Weavings: A Journal of the Christian Spiritual Life* 7/2 (1993).

Anderson, Bernard. *Understanding the Old Testament.* Abridged 4th ed. Upper Saddle River, N.J.: Prentice Hall, 1998.

Andrews, Ginger. *What We Have Seen and Heard and Touched: Embodiment of the Word in Women as Preachers.* Ann Arbor: UMI Dissertation Services, 2000.

Ayala, Francisco. "Evolution and the Uniqueness of Humankind," *Origins* 27/34 (February 12, 1998) 566–74.

Baker, Andrew R. "Ordination and Same Sex Attraction," *America* 187/9 (September 30, 2002) 7–9.

Barbour, Ian G. *Nature, Human Nature, and God.* Minneapolis: Fortress, 2002.

Barnett, Paul. *The Second Epistle to the Corinthians.* NICNT. Grand Rapids: Eerdmans, 1997.

Barton, Stephen C. "Living as Families in the Light of the New Testament," *Int* 52 (1998) 130–44.

Bassler, Jouette M. "1 Corinthians," in Carol A. Newsom and Sharon H. Ringe, eds., *The Women's Bible Commentary.* Louisville: Westminster John Knox, 1992.

Bay, Gerald, ed. "1–2 Corinthians," *Ancient Christian Commentary on Scripture.* New Testament 8. Downers Grove, IL: Intervarsity Press, 1999.

Betz, Hans-Dieter. *Galatians.* Hermeneia. Philadelphia: Fortress, 1979.

Birch, Bruce C., Walter Brueggemann, Terence Fretheim, and David L. Petersen. *A Theological Introduction to the Old Testament.* Nashville: Abingdon, 1999.

Boadt, Lawrence. *Reading the Old Testament: An Introduction.* Mahwah, N.J.: Paulist, 1984.

Boer, Martinus de. "John 4:27. Women (and Men) in the Gospel and Community of John," *Women in the Biblical Tradition* 31. Lewiston: Edwin Mellen Press, 1992.

Boers, Hendrikus. "2 Corinthians 5:14–6:2: A Fragment of Pauline Christology," *CBQ* 64 (2002) 727–47.

Borg, Marcus. *Conflict, Holiness, and Politics in the Teachings of Jesus.* Rev. ed. Harrisburg: Trinity Press International, 1998.

————. *Jesus: A New Vision.* San Francisco: HarperSanFrancisco, 1987.

Brock, Rita Nakashima, and Susan Brooks Thistlethwaite. *Casting Stones: Prostitution and Liberation in Asia and the US.* Minneapolis: Fortress, 1996.

Brodie, Thomas. *The Gospel According to John.* New York: Oxford University Press, 1993.

Brueggemann, Walter. *The Land: Place as Gift, Promise, and Challenge in Biblical Faith.* Overtures to Biblical Theology. 2nd ed. Minneapolis: Fortress, 2002.

————. *The Prophetic Imagination.* 2nd ed. Minneapolis: Fortress, 2001.

Butkus, Russell A. "Creation-in-Crisis: Biblical Creation Theology and the Disclosure of God," in Carol J. Dempsey and William P. Loewe, eds., *Theology and Sacred Scripture.* College Theology Society Annual Volume 47. Maryknoll, N.Y.: Orbis, 2002, 35–52.

Byrne, Patrick. "Economic Transformations: The Role of Conversions and Culture in the Transformation of Economics," in Timothy P. Fallon and Philip Boo Riley, eds., *Religion and Culture: Essays in Honor of Bernard Lonergan, s.j.* Albany: State University of New York Press, 1987, 327–48.

Cahill, Lisa Sowle. *Family: A Christian Social Perspective.* Minneapolis: Fortress, 2000.

————. *Women and Sexuality.* New York: Paulist, 1992.

Carroll, Denis. "Creation," in Joseph A. Komonchak, Mary Collins, and Dermot Lane, eds., *The New Dictionary of Theology.* Collegeville: The Liturgical Press, 1987, 246–58.

Carter, Timothy L. "'Big Men' in Corinth," *JSNT* 66 (1997) 45–71.

Castelli, Elizabeth A. "Romans," in Elisabeth Schüssler Fiorenza, ed., *Searching the Scriptures: A Feminist Commentary.* New York: Crossroad, 1994, 272–300.

Chardin, Pierre Teilhard de. *The Divine Milieu.* New York: Harper & Row, 1960.

Clifford, Anne M. "Creation," in Francis Schüssler Fiorenza and John P. Galvin, eds., *Systematic Theology: Roman Catholic Perspectives.* Minneapolis: Fortress, 1991, 2:193–248.

———. "When Being Human Becomes Truly Earthly," in Ann O'Hara Graff, ed., *In the Embrace of God: Feminist Approaches to Theological Anthropology.* Maryknoll, N.Y.: Orbis, 1995, 173–89.

Clifford, Richard J. *Creation Accounts in the Ancient Near East and in the Bible.* CBQMS 26. Washington, D.C.: Catholic Biblical Association of America, 1994.

———, and John J. Collins. *Creation in the Biblical Traditions.* CBQMS 24. Washington, D.C.: Catholic Biblical Association of America, 1992.

Cobb, John and David Griffin. *Process Theology: An Introductory Exposition.* Philadelphia: Westminster, 1976.

Collins, Raymond. *These Things Have Been Written: Studies on the Fourth Gospel.* Grand Rapids: Eerdmans, 1990.

Cooey, Paula. "The Word Became Flesh: Woman's Body, Language and Value," in Paula M. Cooey, Sharon A. Farmer, and Mary Ellen Ross, eds., *Embodied Love: Sensuality and Relationship as Feminist Values.* New York: Harper & Row, 1988.

Corley, Kathleen E. "Women's Inheritance Rights in Antiquity and Paul's Metaphor of Adoption." Unpublished essay cited in Elizabeth A. Castelli, "Romans," *Searching the Scriptures: A Feminist Commentary,* 272–300.

Countryman, L. William. *Dirt, Greed, and Sex: Sexual Ethics in the New Testament.* Philadelphia: Fortress, 1988.

Culpepper, R. Alan. *The Gospel and Letters of John.* Nashville: Abingdon, 1998.

Cummings, Charles. *Eco-Spirituality: Toward a Reverent Life.* New York: Paulist, 1991.

D'Angelo, Mary Rose. "Colossians," in Elisabeth Schüssler Fiorenza, ed., *Searching the Scriptures: A Feminist Commentary.* New York: Crossroad, 1994, 313–24.

Davies, Paul. *God and the New Physics.* New York: Simon & Schuster, 1983.

Davis, Ellen. "Sabbath: The Culmination of Creation," *The Living Pulpit* 7/2 (April–June 1998) 6–7.

Dempsey, Carol J. *Hope Amid the Ruins: The Ethics of Israel's Prophets.* St. Louis: Chalice, 2000.

———. *The Prophets: A Liberation Critical Reading.* Minneapolis: Fortress, 2000.

————, and Russell A. Butkus, eds. *All Creation Is Groaning: An Inter-disciplinary Vision for Life in a Sacred Universe.* Collegeville: The Liturgical Press, 1999.

Dever, William G. "Is There Any Archaeological Evidence for the Exodus?" in Ernest S. Frerichs and Leonard H. Lesko, eds., *Exodus: The Egyptian Evidence.* Winona Lake: Eisenbrauns, 1997.

Dewey, Joanna. "The Gospel of Mark," in Elisabeth Schüssler Fiorenza, ed., *Searching the Scriptures: A Feminist Commentary.* New York: Crossroad, 1994, 470–509.

Dornisch, Loretta. *Paul and Third World Women Theologians.* Collegeville: The Liturgical Press, 1999.

Dube, Musa W. *Postcolonial Feminist Interpretation of the Bible.* St. Louis: Chalice, 2000.

Edwards, Denis. *The God of Evolution: A Trinitarian Theology.* New York and Mahwah: Paulist, 1999.

————. *Jesus, the Wisdom of God: An Ecological Theology.* Maryknoll, N.Y.: Orbis, 1995.

————. ed. *Earth Revealing, Earth Healing: Ecology and Christian Theology.* Collegeville: The Liturgical Press, 2001.

Elliott, Neil. *Liberating Paul: The Justice of God and the Politics of the Apostle.* New York: Orbis, 1994.

Ellis, Peter. *The Genius of John.* Collegeville: The Liturgical Press, 1984.

Farley, Margaret A. "Feminism and Universal Morality," in Gene Outka and John P. Reide, Jr., eds., *Prospects for a Common Morality.* Princeton, N.J.: Princeton University Press, 1993, 313–24.

Ford, Josephine Massyngbaerde. *Redeemer, Friend and Mother: Salvation in Antiquity and in the Gospel of John.* Minneapolis: Fortress, 1997.

Fragomeni, Richard N., and John T. Pawlikowski, eds. *The Ecological Challenge: Ethical, Liturgical, and Spiritual Responses.* Collegeville: The Liturgical Press, 1994.

Frick, Frank S. *A Journey Through the Hebrew Scriptures.* Fort Worth: Harcourt Brace, 1995.

Galvin, John P. "Jesus Christ," in Francis Schüssler Fiorenza and John P. Galvin, eds., *Systematic Theology: Roman Catholic Perspectives.* Minneapolis: Fortress, 1991, 1:249–324.

Gaventa, Beverly Roberts. "Romans," in Carol A. Newsom and Sharon H. Ringe, eds., *The Women's Bible Commentary.* Louisville: Westminster John Knox, 1992, 313–20.

Getty, Mary Ann. "First Corinthians," in Dianne Bergant and Robert J. Karris, eds., *The Collegeville Bible Commentary.* Collegeville: The Liturgical Press, 1988.

————. "The Ministry of a Reconciled Community," *TBT* 37 (1999) 155–61.

Gilkey, Langdon. *Blue Twilight: Nature, Creationism, and American Religion.* Minneapolis: Fortress, 2001.

A Global Ethic: The Declaration of the Parliament of the World's Religions, with commentaries by Hans Küng and Karl-Josef Kuschel. New York: Continuum, 1998.

Gössman, Elisabeth. "The Image of God and the Human Being in Women's Counter-Tradition," in Deborah F. Sawyer and Diane M. Collier, eds., *Is There a Future for Feminist Theology?* Sheffield: Sheffield Academic Press, 1999.

Gottwald, Norman K. "From Tribal Existence to Empire: The Socio-Historical Content for the Rise of the Hebrew Prophets," in J. Mark Thomas and Vernon Visick, eds., *God and Capitalism: A Prophetic Critique of Market Economy.* Madison, WI: A-R Editions, 1990.

Grassi, Joseph A. "The Letter to the Colossians," in Raymond E. Brown, Joseph A. Fitzmyer, and Roland E. Murphy, eds., *The Jerome Biblical Commentary.* Englewood Cliffs, N.J.: Prentice Hall, 1968, 334–40.

Gundry-Volf, Judith. "Spirit, Mercy, and the Other," *ThTo* 51 (1995) 508–23.

Gutierrez, Gustavo. *Las Casas: In Search of the Poor of Jesus Christ.* Maryknoll, N.Y.: Orbis, 1993.

Habel, Norman, ed. *Readings From the Perspective of the Earth: The Earth Bible,* Vol. 1. Sheffield: Sheffield Academic Press, 2000.

Habel, Norman, and Shirley Wurst, eds., *The Earth Story: Genesis. The Earth Bible,* Vol. 2. Sheffield: Sheffield Academic Press, 2000.

————. *The Earth Story in the Psalms and the Prophets: The Earth Bible,* Vol. 4. Sheffield: Sheffield Academic Press, 2001.

Haight, Roger. *Jesus: Symbol of God.* Maryknoll, N.Y.: Orbis, 1999.

————. "Sin and Grace," in Francis Schüssler Fiorenza and John P. Galvin, eds., *Systematic Theology: Roman Catholic Perspectives.* Minneapolis: Fortress, 1991, 2:75–142.

Halkes, Catharina J. M. *New Creation. Christian Feminism and the Renewal of the Earth.* Louisville: Westminster John Knox, 1989.

Hallman, David G., ed. *Ecotheology: Voices From South and North.* Maryknoll, N.Y.: Orbis, 1994.

Hamm, Dennis. "The Freeing of the Bent Woman and the Restoration of Israel: Luke 13:10-17 as Narrative Theology," *JSNT* 31 (1987) 23–44.

Hanson, K. C., and Douglas E. Oakman, *Palestine in the Time of Jesus.* Minneapolis: Fortress, 1998.

Harrison, Beverly Wildung. "The Fate of the Middle 'Class' in Late Capitalism," in J. Mark Thomas and Vernon Visick, eds., *God and Capitalism: A Prophetic Critique of Market Economy.* Madison, Wisc.: A-R Editions, 1990, 53–71.

———. "The Power of Anger in the Work of Love," *USQR* 36 (1981) 41–57.

Hasel, Gerhard F. "Sabbath," in David Noel Freedman, ed., *Anchor Bible Dictionary.* 5 vols. Garden City, N.Y.: Doubleday, 1992, 849–56.

Haught, John. "Evolution's Impact on Theology," *Origins* 27/34 (February 12, 1998) 574–80.

———. *God After Darwin: A Theology of Evolution.* Boulder, Colo.: Westview Press, 2000.

———. *Responses to 101 Questions on God and Evolution.* New York and Mahwah: Paulist, 2001.

———. "Revelation," in Joseph A. Komonchak, Mary Collins, and Dermot A. Lane, eds., *The New Dictionary of Theology.* Collegeville: The Liturgical Press, 1987, 884–99.

Hawking, Stephen. *A Brief History of Time.* New York: Bantam, 1988.

Hayes, Zachary. "New Cosmology for a New Millennium," *NTR* 12/3 (1999) 29–39.

———. *The Gift of Being: A Theology of Creation.* Collegeville: The Liturgical Press, 2001.

Heschel, Abraham Joshua. *The Sabbath. Its Meaning for Modern Man.* New York: Farrar, Strauss and Giroux, 1951.

Hilkert, Mary Catherine. "Cry the Beloved Image: Rethinking the Image of God," in Ann O'Hara Graff, ed., *In the Embrace of God: Feminist Approaches to Theological Anthropology.* Maryknoll, N.Y.: Orbis, 1995.

———. *Naming Grace: Preaching and the Sacramental Imagination.* New York: Continuum, 1997.

———, and Robert J. Schreiter, eds. *The Praxis of the Reign of God: An Introduction to the Theology of Edward Schillebeeckx.* New York: Fordham University Press, 2002.

Horsley, Richard A., and Neil Asher Silberman. *The Message and the Kingdom: How Jesus and Paul Ignited a Revolution and Transformed the Ancient World.* Minneapolis: Fortress, 1997.

Hubbard, Moyer V. *New Creation in Paul's Letters and Thought.* SNTSMS 119. Cambridge: Cambridge University Press, 2002.

Hultgren, Arland J. "The Church as the Body of Christ. Engaging an Image in the New Testament," *WW* 22 (Spring 2002) 124–32.

Hurtado, Larry W. *One God, One Lord: Early Christian Devotion and Ancient Jewish Monotheism.* Philadelphia: Fortress, 1988.

Irenaeus. *Against the Heresies* 1–5. A. Roberts and James Donaldson, eds., in *Ante-Nicene Fathers* 1. Grand Rapids: Eerdmans, 1973; reprint of 1867 ed., 309–567.

———. *Proof of the Apostolic Preaching.* Joseph P. Smith, s.j., ed. Ancient Christian Writers 16. New York: Newman Press, 1952.

Jewett, Robert. *Paul the Apostle to America: Cultural Trends and Pauline Scholarship.* Louisville: Westminster John Knox, 1994.

John Paul II, "Message to Pontifical Academy of Sciences on Evolution," *Origins* 26/22 (November 14, 1996) 350–52.

———. *Mulieris Dignitatem.* Apostolic Letter "On the Dignity and Vocation of Women," *Origins* 18/17 (October 6, 1988) 262–83.

Johnson, Elizabeth A. "God's Beloved Creation," *America* (April 16, 2001) 8–12.

———. "The Incomprehensibility of God and the Image of God Male and Female," *TS* 45 (1984) 441–45.

———. "Jesus, the Wisdom of God: A Biblical Basis for Non-Androcentric Christology," *ETL* 61 (1985) 261–93.

———. "Redeeming the Name of Christ," in Catherine Mowry LaCugna, ed., *Freeing Theology: The Essentials of Theology in Feminist Perspective.* San Francisco: HarperSanFrancisco, 1993, 115–37.

———. *She Who Is: The Mystery of God in Feminist Theological Discourse.* New York: Crossroad, 1996.

———. "Wisdom Was Made Flesh and Pitched Her Tent Among Us," in Maryanne Stevens, ed., *Reconstructing the Christ Symbol.* New York: Paulist, 1993, 95–117.

———. *Women, Earth, and Creator Spirit.* Mahwah, N.J.: Paulist, 1993.

Josephus. *Jewish Antiquities.* Books IX–XI. Trans. Ralph Marcus. Cambridge, Mass.: Harvard University Press, 1987.

———. *The Jewish War.* Books I–III. Trans. Henry St. J. Thackeray. Cambridge, Mass.: Harvard University Press, 1976.

Karris, Robert J. *Jesus and the Marginalized in John's Gospel.* Collegeville: The Liturgical Press, 1990.

Kasper, Walter. *The God of Jesus Christ.* London: S.C.M., 1983.

Knight, Christopher C. *Wrestling with the Divine: Religion, Science, and Revelation.* Minneapolis: Fortress, 2001.

Kraemer, Ross Shepard, and Mary Rose D'Angelo, eds. *Women and Christian Origins.* New York: Oxford University Press, 1999.

Kraftchick, Steven J. "Death in Us, Life in You: The Apostolic Medium," in David M. Hay, ed., *Pauline Theology, Vol. II: 1 and 2 Corinthians.* Minneapolis: Fortress, 1993.

Kysar, Robert. *John's Story of Jesus.* Philadelphia: Fortress, 1984.

Lambrecht, Jan. "'Reconcile Yourselves . . .' A Reading of 2 Corinthians 5, 11-21," in Reimund Bieringer and Jan Lambrecht, eds., *Studies in 2 Corinthians.* BETL 112. Leuven: Leuven University Press, 1994.

———. *Second Corinthians.* SP 8. Collegeville: The Liturgical Press, 1999.

Las Casas, Bartholomé de. *The Only Way.* New York: Paulist, 1992.

Leonard, Ellen M. "Women and Christ: Toward Inclusive Christologies," *TJT* 6 (1990) 266–85.

Levenson, Jon. *Creation and the Persistence of Evil: The Jewish Drama of Divine Omnipotence.* San Francisco: Harper & Row, 1988.

Lips, Hilary M. "Women, Education and Economic Participation" *Work of Women.* http://www.workofwomen.org/index.htm (accessed 5/18/02).

Lonergan, Bernard. *Method in Theology.* New York: Herder and Herder, 1972.

———. *Insight: A Study of Human Understanding.* London: Darton, Longman and Todd, 1957.

Loning, Karl, and Erich Zenger. *To Begin with God Created . . . . Biblical Theologies of Creation.* Trans. Omar Kaste. Collegeville: The Liturgical Press, 2000.

Lowery, Richard H. *Sabbath and Jubilee.* St. Louis: Chalice Press, 2000.

Malina, Bruce J. "Dealing with Biblical (Mediterranean) Characters: A Guide for U.S. Consumers," *BTB* 19 (1989) 135.

———. *The New Testament World: Insights from Cultural Anthropology.* Rev. ed. Louisville: Westminster John Knox, 1993.

Malina, Bruce J., and Richard L. Rohrbaugh, *Social-Science Commentary on the Synoptic Gospels.* Minneapolis: Fortress, 1992.

Martin, Dale. *The Corinthian Body.* New Haven: Yale University Press, 1995.

Matthews, Shelley. "2 Corinthians," in Elisabeth Schüssler Fiorenza, ed., *Searching the Scriptures: A Feminist Commentary.* New York: Crossroad, 1994.

McFague, Sallie. *Super, Natural Christians: How We Should Love Nature.* Philadelphia: Fortress, 1997.

———. *The Body of God: An Ecological Theology.* Philadelphia: Fortress, 1993.

———. *Models of God: Theology for an Ecological, Nuclear Age.* Philadelphia: Fortress, 1987.

Meeks, M. Douglas. *God the Economist: The Doctrine of God and Political Economy.* Minneapolis: Fortress, 1989.

Miller, James B., and Kenneth E. McCall. *The Church and Contemporary Cosmology.* Pittsburgh: Carnegie Mellon University Press, 1987.

Moloney, Francis J. *Belief in the Word.* Minneapolis: Fortress, 1993.

—————. "The Faith of Martha and Mary: A Narrative Approach to John 11:17-40," *Bib* 75 (1994) 471–93.

—————. *The Gospel of John.* Sacra Pagina 4. Collegeville: The Liturgical Press, 1998.

Moltmann, Jürgen. "Sabbath: Finishing and Beginning," *The Living Pulpit* 7/2 (April–June 1998) 4–5.

Morris, Leon. *The Gospel according to John.* Rev. ed. Grand Rapids: Eerdmans, 1995, 229–38.

Murphy, Roland E. "Reflections on 'Actualization' of the Bible," *BTB* 26 (1966) 79–81.

Murphy-O'Connor, Jerome. *Paul: A Critical Life.* Oxford: Clarendon Press, 1996.

National Conference of Catholic Bishops. "Brothers and Sisters to Us: A Pastoral Letter on Racism," November 14, 1979. In J. Brian Benestad and Francis T. Butler, eds., *Quest for Justice: A Compendium of Statements of the United States Catholic Bishops on the Political and Social Order 1966–1980.* Washington, D.C.: U.S. Catholic Conference [1981] 373–85.

Neyrey, Jerome H. "What's Wrong With This Picture? John 4, Cultural Stereotypes of Women, and Public and Private Space," *BTB* 24 (1994) 77–91.

—————, and Bruce J. Malina. *Paul, in Other Words: A Cultural Reading of His Letters.* Louisville: Westminster John Knox, 1990.

O'Day, Gail. "John," in Carol A. Newsom and Sharon H. Ringe, eds., *The Women's Bible Commentary.* Expanded ed. Louisville: Westminster John Knox, 1998.

O'Donovan, Leo. "Evolution," in Joseph A. Komonchak, Mary Collins, and Dermont A. Lane, eds., *The New Dictionary of Theology.* Collegeville: The Liturgical Press, 1987, 363–66.

Oduyoye, Mercy Amba. "Spirituality of Resistance and Reconstruction," in Mary John Mananzan et al., eds., *Women Resisting Violence: Spirituality for Life.* Maryknoll, N.Y.: Orbis, 1996, 161–71.

O'Murchu, Diarmuid. *Quantum Theology: Spiritual Implications of the New Physics.* New York: Crossroad, 1997.

O'Neill, Mary Aquin. "The Mystery of Being Human Together—Anthropology," in Catherine Mowry LaCugna, ed., *Freeing Theology: The Essentials of Theology in a Feminist Perspective.* San Francisco: HarperSanFrancisco, 1993.

Osiek, Carolyn. "The Family in Early Christianity: 'Family Values' Revisited," *CBQ* 58 (1996) 1–24.

Patterson, Stephen. *The God of Jesus: The Historical Jesus and the Search for Meaning.* Harrisburg: Trinity Press International, 1998.

Pawlikowski, John T. "Christology, Anti-Semitism, and Christian-Jewish Bonding," in Rebecca S. Chopp and Mark Lewis Taylor, eds., *Reconstructing Christian Theology.* Minneapolis: Fortress, 1994, 245–68.

Perlitt, Lothar. *Bundestheologie im Alten Testament.* WMANT 36. Neukirchen Vluyn: Neukirchener Verlag, 1969.

Pick, John, ed. *A Hopkins Reader.* Rev. and enlarged ed. New York: Doubleday Image Books, 1966, 47–48.

Pilch, John J. *The Cultural Dictionary of the Bible.* Collegeville: The Liturgical Press, 1999.

Pobee, John S. "Human Transformation—A Biblical View," *Mission Studies* 2 (1985) 5–9.

Polkinghorne, John. *Belief in God in an Age of Science.* New Haven and London: Yale University Press, 1998.

Pontifical Biblical Commission, "Interpretation of the Bible in the Church," IV.A.2. *Origins* 6 (January 1994) 499–524.

Powell, Mark Allan. *Fortress Introduction to the Gospels.* Minneapolis: Fortress, 1998.

Rahner, Karl. "Easter: A Faith that Loves the Earth," in Albert Raffelt, ed., *The Great Church Year.* New York: Crossroad, 1993, 143–46.

Ratzinger, Joseph. "The Dignity of the Human Person," Commentary on *Gaudium et Spes,* Introductory Article and Chapter 1, in Herbert Vorgrimler, ed., *Commentary on the Documents of Vatican II.* New York: Herder and Herder, 1969, 5:115–63.

Reagan, Charles E., and David Stewart, eds. *The Philosophy of Paul Ricoeur: An Anthology of His Work.* Boston: Beacon, 1978.

Reagan, Michael. *The Hand of God: Thoughts and Images Reflecting the Spirit of the Universe.* Philadelphia and London: Templeton Foundation Press, 1999.

————. *Inside the Mind of God: Images and Words of Inner Space.* Philadelphia and London: Templeton Foundation Press, 2002.

Reid, Barbara E. *Choosing the Better Part? Women in the Gospel of Luke.* Collegeville: The Liturgical Press, 1996.

Reinhartz, Adele. "The Gospel of John," in Elisabeth Schüssler Fiorenza, ed., *Searching the Scriptures: A Feminist Commentary.* New York: Crossroad, 1994.

Ricoeur, Paul. "Biblical Hermeneutics," *Semeia* 4 (1975) 27–148.

―――. "Metaphor and the Problem of Hermeneutics," in Charles E. Reagan and David Stewart, eds. *The Philosophy of Paul Ricoeur: An Anthology of His Work.* Boston: Beacon, 1978.

Roberts, Elizabeth, and Elias Amidon, eds., *Earth Prayers.* San Francisco: HarperSanFrancisco, 1991.

Ross, Susan M. *Extravagant Affections: A Feminist Sacramental Theology.* New York: Continuum, 1998.

Ruether, Rosemary Radford. "Christian Anthropology and Gender. A Tribute to Jürgen Moltmann," in Miroslav Volf, Carmen Krieg, and Thomas Kucharz, eds., *The Future of Theology.* Grand Rapids: Eerdmans, 1996.

―――. "Feminist Hermeneutics, Scriptural Authority, and Religious Experience. The Case of the *Imago Dei* and Gender Equality," in Werner G. Jeanrond and Jennifer L. Rike, eds., *Radical Pluralism and Truth.* New York: Crossroad, 1991.

―――. *Gaia and God: An Ecofeminist Theology of Earth Healing.* San Francisco: HarperSanFrancisco, 1992, 1994.

―――. *Women Healing Earth: Third World Women on Feminism, Religion and Ecology.* Maryknoll, N.Y.: Orbis, 1996.

―――. *Women and Redemption: A Theological History.* Minneapolis: Fortress, 1998.

Sagan, Carol, ed. "Preserving and Cherishing the Earth: An Appeal for Joint Commitment in Science and Religion," in Carl Sagan, ed., *Billions and Billions.* New York: Random House, 1997, 143–46.

Sampley, J. Paul. "The Second Letter to the Corinthians," *New International Bible* 11. Nashville: Abingdon, 1999.

Sanders, E. P. *Jesus and Judaism.* Philadelphia: Fortress, 1985.

Santmire, H. Paul. *The Travail of Nature: The Ambiguous Ecological Promise of Christian Theology.* Philadelphia: Fortress, 1985.

Scharper, Stephen B. *Redeeming the Time: A Political Theology of the Environment.* New York: Continuum, 1997.

Schillebeeckx, Edward. *Christ: The Experience of Jesus as Lord.* Trans. John Bowden. New York: Seabury, 1980.

―――. *Church: The Human Story of God.* Trans. John Bowden. New York: Crossroad, 1990.

―――. "Church, Sacrament of Dialogue," in idem, *God the Future of Man.* Trans. N. D. Smith. New York: Sheed & Ward, 1968.

―――. "The Other Face of the Church," in idem, *For the Sake of the Gospel.* Trans. John Bowden. New York: Crossroad, 1990.

Schindler, David L. "Christology and the *Imago Dei:* Interpreting *Gaudium et Spes," Communio* 23 (1996) 156–84.

Schneiders, Sandra M. "Death in the Community of Eternal Life," *Int* 41 (1987) 44–46.

———. *The Revelatory Text.* 2nd ed. Collegeville: The Liturgical Press, 1999.

———. *Women and the Word.* New York: Paulist, 1986.

———. "Women in the Fourth Gospel and the Role of Women in the Contemporary Church," *BTB* 12/2 (1982) 35–45.

———. *Written That You May Believe: Encountering Jesus in the Fourth Gospel.* New York: Crossroad, 1999.

Schubert, Judith. "A Formula for Friendship (John 4)." *TBT* (March 1994) 84–89.

Schüssler Fiorenza, Elisabeth. *But She Said: Feminist Practices of Biblical Interpretation.* Boston: Beacon, 1992.

———. *In Memory of Her: A Feminist Theological Reconstruction of Christian Origins.* New York: Crossroad, 1984.

———. *Jesus: Miriam's Child, Sophia's Prophet: Critical Issues in Feminist Christology.* New York: Continuum, 1995.

Schüssler Fiorenza, Francis. "Redemption," in Joseph A. Komonchak, Mary Collins, and Dermot A. Lane, eds., *The New Dictionary of Theology.* Collegeville: The Liturgical Press, 1987, 836–51.

Schweizer, Eduard. *The Letter to the Colossians: A Commentary.* Minneapolis: Augsburg, 1982.

Scroggs, Robin. "Paul and the Eschatological Body," in Eugene H. Lovering, Jr. and Jerry L. Sumney, eds., *Theology and Ethics in Paul and His Interpreters: Essays in Honor of Victor Paul Furnish.* Nashville: Abingdon Press, 1996.

Simkins, Ronald A. *Creator and Creation: Nature in the Worldview of Ancient Israel.* Peabody, Mass.: Hendrickson, 1994.

Sloyan, Gerard S. *The Crucifixion of Jesus: History, Myth, Faith.* Minneapolis: Fortress, 1995.

Sölle, Dorothee. "God's Economy and Ours: The Year of Jubilee," in J. Mark Thomas and Vernon Visick, eds., *God and Capitalism: A Prophetic Critique of Market Economy.* Madison, Wisc.: A-R Editions, 1990, 87–103.

Stegemann, Ekkehard W. and Wolfgang Stegemann. *The Jesus Movement: A Social History of Its First Century.* Trans. O. C. Dean, Jr. Minneapolis: Fortress, 1999.

Stibbe, Mark. "A Tomb With a View: John 11:1-44 in Narrative-Critical Perspective," *NTS* 40 (1994) 38–54.

Stuhlmueller, Carroll. "Deutero-Isaiah and Trito-Isaiah," in Raymond E. Brown, Joseph A. Fitzmyer, and Roland E. Murphy, eds., *The New Jerome Biblical Commentary*. Englewood Cliffs, N.J.: Prentice Hall, 1990.

Suggs, M. Jack. *Wisdom, Christology and Law in Matthew's Gospel*. Cambridge, Mass.: Harvard University Press, 1970.

Swimme, Brian. *The Hidden Heart of the Cosmos: Humanity and the New Story*. Maryknoll, N.Y.: Orbis, 1996.

Talbert, Charles. *Reading John*. New York: Crossroad, 1994.

Theissen, Gerd, and Annette Merz. *The Historical Jesus: A Comprehensive Guide*. Minneapolis: Fortress, 1998.

Toolan, David. *At Home in the Cosmos*. Maryknoll, N.Y.: Orbis, 2001.

Trible, Phyllis. *God and the Rhetoric of Sexuality*. Philadelphia: Fortress, 1978.

———. *Texts of Terror: Literary-Feminist Readings of Biblical Narratives*. Philadelphia: Fortress, 1984.

van Drimmeien, Rob. *Faith in a Global Economy: A Primer for Christians*. Geneva: WCC Publications, 1998.

Walker, William O. "Text-Critical Evidence for Interpolations in the Letters of Paul," *CBQ* 50 (1988) 622–31.

Wallace, W. L. "Eucharistic Benediction," in *600 Blessings and Prayers from around the World*. Compiled by Geoffrey Duncan. Mystic, Conn.: Twenty-Third Publications, 2000, 64.

Wheatley, Margaret J. *Leadership and the New Science. Learning About Organization from an Orderly Universe*. San Francisco: Berrett-Koehler, 1992.

Whitehead, Alfred North. *Process and Reality,* corrected ed. David Ray Griffin and Donald W. Sherburne, eds. New York: Free Press, 1978.

Wilkinson, John. "The Case of the Bent Woman in Lk 13:10-17," *EvQ* 49 (1977) 195–205.

Wilson, A. N. *The Mind of the Apostle*. New York: Norton, 1997.

Wink, Walter. *Engaging the Powers: Discernment and Resistance in a World of Domination*. Minneapolis: Fortress, 1992.

Work of Women. http://www.workofwomen.org/index.htm, accessed 5/18/02.

Wuellner, Wilhelm. "Putting Life Back Into the Lazarus Story and Its Reading: The Narrative Rhetoric of John 11 as the Narration of Faith," *Semeia* 53 (1991) 113–32.

Yee, Gale A. "The Author/Text/Reader and Power: Suggestions for a Critical Framework for Biblical Studies," in Fernando F. Segovia and Mary Ann Tolbert, eds., *Reading from This Place: Social Location and Biblical Interpretation in the United States.* Minneapolis: Fortress, 1995, 1:109–18.

Yorke, Gosnell L. *The Church as the Body of Christ in the Pauline Corpus: A Re-Examination.* Lanham, Md.: University Press of America, 1991.

Zagano, Phyllis, and Terrence W. Tilley, eds. *Things New and Old: Essays on the Theology of Elizabeth A. Johnson.* New York: Crossroad, 1999.

List of Contributors

Barbara E. Bowe, R.C.S.J. received her Th.D. in New Testament and Christian Origins from Harvard University in 1986. After three years teaching in a graduate school of theology in the Philippines she came to the Catholic Theological Union in 1990. At CTU she teaches courses in New Testament, early Christianity, and Biblical Spirituality and serves as the Director of CTU's Biblical Spirituality Certificate Program. She has a special interest in Johannine and Pauline studies as well as issues of early Christian ecclesiology. In addition to articles in *The Bible Today,* on whose editorial board she serves, *U.S. Catholic, Theological Education,* and the *Journal of Early Christian Studies,* her publications include *A Church in Crisis,* a study of the ecclesiology of *1 Clement.* She is also a co-editor of *Silent Voices, Sacred Lives,* an anthology of women's readings for the liturgical year, and associate editor and contributor for *Prayer from Alexander to Constantine,* a critical anthology of prayer texts from the ancient world. Among her most recent publications is "A Response to Peter J. Tomson," in *Reinterpreting Revelation and Tradition: Jews and Christians in Conversation,* edited with an Introduction by John T. Pawlikowski, O.S.M. and Hayim Goren Perelmuter Franklin (Sheed & Ward, 2000).

Joan E. Cook, S.C. is Associate Professor of Sacred Scripture at Washington Theological Union in Washington, D.C. Her studies of biblical women have appeared in her book *Hannah's Desire, God's Design: Early Interpretations of the Story of Hannah* (Sheffield: Sheffield Academic Press, 1999), as well as in other works including "Four Marginalized Foils—Tamar, Judah, Joseph, and Potiphar's Wife: A Literary Study of Genesis 38–39," in *EGLBS Proceedings,* 2001; "Women in Ezra and Nehemiah," *The Bible Today* 37/4 (July–August 1999); "Hannah's Later Songs: A Study in Comparative Methods of Interpretation," in Craig A. Evans and James A. Sanders, eds., *Early Christian Interpretation of the Scriptures of Israel: Investigations and Proposals* (Sheffield: Sheffield Academic Press, 1998).

Carol J. Dempsey, O.P., Associate Professor of Biblical Studies and Theology at the University of Portland, Ore., received her Ph.D. in Biblical Studies from The Catholic University of America in Washington, D.C., in 1994. Carol is the author of two books, *The Prophets: A Liberation Critical Reading* (Fortress, 2000), and *Hope Amid the Ruins: The Ethics of Israel's Prophets* (Chalice, 2000), and editor of three others: *The Spirituality of the Psalms* (The Liturgical Press, 2002); *Theology and Sacred Scripture* (Orbis, 2002), and *All Creation Is Groaning: An Interdisciplinary Vision for Life in a Sacred Universe* (The Liturgical Press, 1999). Her forthcoming works include *Justice: A Biblical Perspective* (Chalice); *Jeremiah: Preacher of Grace, Poet of Truth* (Liturgical Press); *Micah, Hosea, Amos, Zephaniah, Habakkuk, and Nahum* for *The New Collegeville Bible Commentary,* and *Isaiah 1–39* in the series *Berit Olam: Studies in Hebrew Narrative and Poetry* (The Liturgical Press). A Caldwell Dominican, Carol was a biblical consultant on *Columbia River Pastoral,* is an Associate Editor for *The Catholic Biblical Quarterly,* has written many articles in the areas of biblical ethics, prophets, biblical theology and ecology, and is co-editor of this book with Mary Margaret Pazdan.

Mary Ann Donovan, S.C., Ph.D. is a Sister of Charity of Cincinnati who has taught at the Jesuit School of Theology in the Graduate Theological Union for twenty-five years, and recently served a year as Acting Academic Dean. A member of both the doctoral and the Masters of Divinity faculties, she is Professor of Historical Theology and Spirituality. She is a lecturer and author who has published several books and many articles in her fields, including *One Right Reading? A Guide to Irenaeus* (The Liturgical Press, 1997), which won the College Theology Society book award, and has served as president of the Catholic Theological Society of America.

Mary Catherine Hilkert, O.P. is Professor of Theology at the University of Notre Dame, Ind. A systematic theologian, Mary Catherine is author of *Speaking with Authority: Catherine of Siena and the Voices of Women Today* (Paulist, 2001); *Naming Grace: Preaching and the Sacramental Imagination* (Continuum, 1997); co-editor of *The Praxis of the Reign of God: An Introduction to the Theology of Edward Schillebeeckx* (Fordham University Press, 2002); and has published numerous articles on contemporary theology, spirituality, and preaching. A member of the Sisters of St. Dominic of Akron, OH (Order of Preachers), she has lectured in Catholic and ecumenical contexts in the United States, Canada, Ireland, Australia, and South Africa. Mary Catherine is the current president-elect of the Catholic Theological Society of America.

Elizabeth A. Johnson, C.S.J. is Distinguished Professor of Theology at Fordham University. She earned her Ph.D. from The Catholic University of America in 1981. Her many publications include *Consider Jesus: Waves of Renewal in Christology* (Crossroad, 1991), *She Who Is: The Mystery of God in Feminist Theological Discourse* (Crossroad, 1992), *Friends of God and Prophets: A Feminist Theological Reading of the Communion of Saints* (Continuum, 1998), and *Truly Our Sister: A Theology of Mary in the Communion of Saints* (Continuum, 2003). She has served as president of the Catholic Theological Society of America.

Alice L. Laffey is Associate Professor in the Department of Religious Studies at the College of the Holy Cross in Worcester, MA. Her primary scholarly focus has been on the interpretation of the Old Testament from historical, liberationist, and comparative perspectives. Included among her works are "The Influence of Feminism on Christianity," in Yvonne Haddad and John Esposito, eds., *Daughters of Abraham* (Gainesville, Fla.: University Press of Florida, 2001) and "The Interpretation of Scripture," in Maureen Fieldler, ed., *Rome Has Spoken* (Crossroad, 1998).

Sheila E. McGinn received her Ph.D. from Northwestern University and is Associate Professor of Religious Studies at John Carroll University, where she specializes in Biblical Studies and Early Christianity. She teaches courses on a wide variety of New Testament topics and has presented frequent academic papers on the New Testament Gospels, the Pauline Letters, and the New Prophecy or "Montanist" movement. Recent publications include studies of the Montanist Oracles; 1 Cor 11:10 and the Ecclesial Authority of Women; the women in Matthew's Passion-Resurrection story; *The Acts of Thecla;* and "Galatians 3:26-29 and the Politics of the Spirit." She has authored a commentary on the Gospel of Matthew, a bibliography of twentieth-century research into the book of Revelation, and currently is developing a history of Christianity's first hundred years.

Kathleen M. O'Connor is Professor of Old Testament Language, Literature, and Exegesis at Columbia Theological Seminary in Decatur, Ga. Her most recent book is *Lamentations and the Tears of the World* (Orbis, 2002). She is also the author of *The Wisdom Literature* (The Liturgical Press, 1988), *The Confessions of Jeremiah* (Scholars Press, 1988), and co-editor of *Troubling Jeremiah* (Sheffield Academic Press, 1999). An active member in the Society of Biblical Literature and the Catholic Biblical Association, she has written many articles on Jeremiah, cross-cultural interpretation, and women and the Bible. Currently she is working on the book of Job. She lives in Decatur, GA with her husband Jim Griesmer.

Mary Margaret Pazdan, O.P. is Professor of Biblical Studies at Aquinas Institute of Theology, St. Louis, MO, where she is engaged in teaching Master's courses and seminars as well as Biblical Hermeneutics and Preaching for the Doctor of Ministry in Preaching. Professor Pazdan specializes in courses, conferences, books, and articles that engage readers in post-modern biblical hermeneutics as well as how hermeneutics can shape course conversations and preaching. Her publications include articles in *The Collegeville Bible Commentary, The Lectionary Commentary: Theological Exegesis for Sunday's Texts, Lectionary Homiletics, The Anchor Bible Dictionary, The Bible Today, Perspectives in Religious Studies, Theological Education, Spirituality Today, Ecumenism,* and *Biblical Theology Bulletin.* A Sinsinawa Dominican, she is co-chair with Carol Dempsey, O.P., of the Feminist Biblical Hermeneutics Task Force of the Catholic Biblical Association and co-editor of this book.

Barbara E. Reid, O.P. is a Grand Rapids Dominican. She holds a Ph.D. in Biblical Studies from The Catholic University of America in Washington, D.C., and is Professor of New Testament at Catholic Theological Union in Chicago. She is the author of six books, the most recent of which are *Parables for Preachers* (3 vols.; Liturgical Press, 1999, 2000, 2001). She has published various articles on New Testament topics in journals such as: *Biblical Research, The Bible Today, Chicago Studies, Currents in Theology and Mission, Interpretation,* and *New Theology Review.* She frequently leads CTU's Israel Study Programs and Retreats.

Judith Schubert, R.S.M., Ph.D., is Professor of Religious Studies at Georgian Court College in Lakewood, N.J. A member of the Sisters of Mercy of the Americas, Judith teaches both graduate and undergraduate students, and directs the College's Master of Arts Program in Theology as well as the Institute for Lay Ecclesial Ministry for the Diocese of Trenton. She has published articles in *The Bible Today* and *Homily Review.* Having expertise in New Testament, she lectures widely on biblical topics to both general and scholarly audiences.

Tatha Wiley, a systematic theologian, earned her Ph.D. from Boston College. She has taught in the fields of Theology and Biblical Studies at St. Olaf College, St. John's University, St. Thomas University, United Theological Seminary, and Metropolitan State University. Tatha's latest book is *Original Sin: Origins, Developments, Contemporary Meanings* (Paulist, 2002). The author of many articles, she is currently the editor of a christology textbook for Continuum Publishers. She lives in Minnesota with her husband, Michael West of Fortress Press, and their two children, Rachel and Nathan.

Biblical Index

Subject and Author Index